Long Melford

Lavenham

SUFFOLK

Sudbury

Ilphamstone

Flatford Mill

East Bergholt

Mount Bures

Wormingford

Dedham

R.Stour

ne Engaine

Mistley

Harwich
Dovercourt

Earls Colne
White Colne
Wakes Colne
West Bergholt
Gt.Tey
Copford
A120 (Stane Street)
Marks Tey
Bradwell

Ardleigh

Colchester
Stanway
Lexden

Beaumont
cum Moze

Hamford Water

A12

Layer

Wivenhoe
Arlesford

Walton-on-the-Naze

rne

Abberton
Gt.Wigborough
Lt.Wigborough

Frinton

vedon

Fingringhoe

B'tlingsea

St Osyth

Clacton

Tiptree

Gt.Braxted
Little Braxted

Tolleshunt Knights

Mersea
Island

Jaywick

Gt.Totham
Peverel

Tolleshunt D'Arcy

Tolleshunt Major
Elms
Farm
Goldhanger
Heybridge

Tollesbury

aldon
am
er
urleigh

Blackwater
estuary

Bradwell

Steeple
Tillingham

Asheldham

Latchingdon

Ferrers

Southminster

Burnham-on-Crouch

Canewdon

Wallasea
Island

Foulness
Island

Hockley

Paglesham

Rochford

Barling
Lt.Wakering
Gt.Wakering
Southchurch
Shoebury

ath

Southend

N

0   5   10   15   20 miles

0   20km

The Essex Landscape
A study of its form and history

The Essex Landscape

A study of its form and history
by John Hunter

ESSEX RECORD OFFICE
PUBLICATIONS

CHELMSFORD
1999

To the memory of three good friends who were champions
of the historic landscape of Essex:

Gerald Curtis, Chairman of the County Planning Committee 1971-77

John Tabor, of Bovingdon Hall, the Demonstration Farm for the Boulder Clays

Colin Ranson, the Nature Conservancy Council's
officer for Essex 1967-1984

Published by
ESSEX RECORD OFFICE
County Hall, Chelmsford CM1 1LX

A catalogue reference of this book
is available from the British Library

ISBN 1 898529 15 9

Essex Record Office Publication No. 140

Designed and produced by Keith Mirams MCSD

Printed in England by
Lavenham Press Limited

Frontispiece: Hornbeam wood-pasture at Bush End, Hatfield Forest.

Contents

List of illustrations

Acknowledgements

LOOKING BACK, THE gathering of the material that forms this book began in 1972 when Essex County Council's Planning Committee resolved, in the wake of Dutch Elm disease, to play an active role in furthering a future landscape where an awareness of amenity would play a part together with productivity and other demands on the countryside. As landscape specialists a small group of us were required to give practical advice, and to do this we needed an historical awareness of how and why the landscape had evolved as well as a practical knowledge of the needs of the present. We were fortunate in our mentors, kindly and generous men : Ken Newton, County Archivist, who had studied the great manors of Writtle and Thaxted, and AC "Gus" Edwards with his exceptional knowledge of all aspects of Essex history; and both had the evidence contained in the Walker maps (seedbeds of landscape history) at their fingertips.

In the landscape itself, history was becoming a part of natural history. Hedges were now known to have a long pedigree, and were no longer just a bi-product of late enclosure, and George Peterkin and Oliver Rackham were demonstrating the antiquity of many woodlands and certain wood-pastures. Colin Ranson, The Nature Conservancy's officer for Essex, taught us the value of many familiar features that were all too often, and wrongly, taken for granted. "Conservation" in those days tended to be associated with historic buildings and settlements, the countryside had yet to catch up.

From 1979 until my retirement in 1996 I was responsible for the running of the Environmental Services Branch (ESB) of the Planning Department, a specialist unit which encompassed historic buildings, archaeology, design, landscape and latterly, recreational land management. With Gareth Gunning, Steve Westover and Martin Wakelin, I continued to discover the history lurking in the Essex landscape while devising planning policies to protect it and seeing off threats at public enquiries from developers and certain mineral companies. Realising that the information generally available on the geology of the county was now erroneous, I was assisted through the recent specialist literature (which is somewhat daunting to the layman) by Martin Bates, a geologist in the Minerals Section, to write the paper which has subsequently formed the basis for the first chapter of this book.

I am deeply grateful to John Hedges and Dave Buckley, his successor as County Archaeologist, from whom I have learned some of the rudiments of their fascinating science. Their achievement has been the most rewarding period in Essex archaeology, with the county's prehistory brought into the light and at least three millennia now illumined where formerly dark forests of oak were thought to exclude human activity - and the work of discovery continues. To Nigel Brown I am indebted for the clarity of his thinking, bringing order and synthesis to our understanding of those distant times. Without the achievements of archaeologists in recent years this book would be a shallow exercise. For the centuries spanning between the Norman Conquest and the arrival of the Georges, my thanks to David Andrews for his careful, sometimes critical, but always constructive scrutiny of my text and our discussions arising from it.

I have space here to thank only a few of my many friends and former colleagues in ESB for their insights, fruitful discourse and the intellectual stimulus their company provided, but many of their names appear in the Bibliography and chapter notes, and I hope that they will feel that the book is a product of the work of the Branch as a whole to which we all made our contributions. So too the members and chairmen of the subcommittee we served, who were always supportive and showed a real and continuing interest in the work.

Another group I feel privileged to have belonged to over the years is the Essex Farming and Wildlife Advisory Group, and the knowledge I have gained from their open days, discussions and farm walks has been an important factor in writing this book. I hope that my FWAG friends, if they read it, will approve. Through FWAG I had the good fortune to meet Mark Thomasin-Foster and to learn from his shrewd judgement and wide knowledge of the contemporary countryside in our many discussions.

In addition to those mentioned above, I would thank others for their helpful comments on sections of the text: Philip Crummy, Paul Moxey, Clare Thoma, Eric Robinson and John Wymer.

Acknowledgements

The last hundred years, on which little has been written, saw the farming depressions, the break up of the landed estates, and the migration of farming families from other parts of Britain who were prepared to work the land now abandoned by despairing Essex tenants. For family traditions, documents and individual research, my thanks to Sue Forsyth, Bruce Munro, Elizabeth Sellars and Tim Trembath, and to Sir John Ruggles-Brise for information on his father, Col (later Sir Edward) Ruggles-Brise's achievement in securing the passing of the Wheat Act 1932 which saved the livelihoods of perhaps 500 East Anglian farmers.

For the events of the 1970s and '80s I am grateful to Philip Shaw, former secretary of the Essex Farmers Union and a good friend to all who sought a balanced and integrated landscape, who confirmed that my memory of those times is generally correct. For the trends in farming today, my thanks to Peter Chillingworth and Richard Tattershall, and for general discussion on all aspects of the contemporary landscape Charles Webster and Mark Thomasin-Foster. For information on the achievement of Raymond Erith I wish to thank George Curtis, and for their advice on the fine and useful arts, Nigel Weaver, Fiona Cowell and Marion Swetenham.

I was delighted when Ken Hall, the County Archivist, suggested that the Essex Record Office should publish this book, as the relationship between ESB and the Record Office was always close and highly productive. My own researches into landscape history would have been still-born without this storehouse of information and its helpful staff. My particular thanks go to my editor, Janet Smith, to the book designer, Keith Mirams, to Susan Harte for bringing my typescript into a presentable form, to June Beardsley for her help in locating material and to Beryl Board for compiling the index.

The captions to the illustrations generally carry appropriate acknowledgements, but I would wish to add my particular debt to Roger Massey-Ryan of the Archaeology Section for his great help in preparing those on pages 2, 5, 16, 19, 72, 73, 77, 128, 162 and the endpapers. Copyright rests with the County Council, as also with those on pages 44, 47, 50, 61, and 133. Otherwise copyright rests with the source acknowledged in the captions.

I have, I hope, acknowledged in the notes and bibliography my debt to others who have researched and published their work on the Essex landscape. My own conclusions, which are many, will be tested in the course of time and should some be found to be erroneous the responsibility is mine alone.

Preface

ESSEX HAS BEEN a unit of government ever since the first kings of Essex are recorded in about the year 600. Apart from the creation of the new London Boroughs in 1965, its boundaries have been largely unchanged for at least 1,000 years and its name is at least 1,300 years old. As a unit it has been monarchy and shire and it has proved sufficiently strong as a geographical unit of administration to embrace everything from kingdom through feudalism to democracy. A unit that is so flexible and long-standing has a unique identity and allegiance built up over 1,300 years. It is, after all, considerably older than Parliament, the English Crown and the Kingdom of England itself.

From the submission of Essex County Council to the Local Government Commission for England in April 1994.

In the introduction to the Essex volume in his Buildings of England series (published in 1954), Nikolaus Pevsner wondered why Essex was not as popular a touring and sight-seeing county as it deserved to be. Perhaps it was Liverpool Street Station, then as awful a place as it is now splendid. More palpably, Essex was just too big and varied to be taken in as one, and this militated against a just appreciation of it. 'With its 978,000 acres it is the eighth in England, ranking behind Yorkshire, Lincolnshire, Devon, Norfolk, Northumberland, Lancashire and Somerset. In variety of character it must be given precedence over most of them'. A fair judgement, I would say, and hope that my chapter on the regions and subregions of Essex will bear this out.

Landscape history, as a mature discipline, appeared on the scene in 1955 with W G Hoskins' great work *The Making of the English Landscape*. A county series followed under the editorship of Hoskins, and volumes on our neighbours appeared in the 1960s and '70s. Essex missed out, and probably just as well for it would have been somewhat thin. Since then, a wealth of information, unimaginable in 1970, has come from the work of archaeologists. Oliver Rackham has transformed our perceptions of woodlands, wood-pastures and royal forests, and geologists have reached a new, and very different, understanding of how the land was formed. The time seems right to review what we know of how the Essex landscape was made.

Essex as a unit of government began as the Kingdom of the East Saxons, and well before 1066 had become a shire with the boundaries which remained until 1965, when 'Metropolitan' Essex was transferred into Greater London. This book is concerned with the county as it was bounded from 1965 until 1998, when Thurrock and Southend seceded, an area of 907,798 acres. The population in 1995 was 1,577,500, the largest shire county in terms of numbers. It is interesting to note that the census of 1995 gave the population of the six counties of Northern Ireland as 1,578,000, an area once again to have a degree of self-governance - a sad contrast to the English shire counties, reduced in recent years to little more than instruments of central government.

I hope this book will be of interest to those seeking an introduction to the landscape around them, and may perhaps spur some to do their own research - there are some excellent parish histories appearing. Many will approach the countryside through natural history, and I hope this book will complement David Corke's excellent study of wildlife and habitat *The Nature of Essex*. Particularly, I hope it will be welcome to farmers and landowners, whom I have frequently found to have a deep interest in the archaeology and history of their land.

John Constable, Sketch of Dedham Vale (V&A Picture Library)

CHAPTER ONE
Geology and landform

COMPARED WITH THE ancient rocks of our western shores, displayed for example in the cliff formations of Pembrokeshire and Cornwall, the geology of Essex
may seem unexciting and, in terms of geological time, very recent. But in this lies
its interest. For the study of processes at work, of the accumulation of layers, the
effects of ice, erosion and changing sea levels, Essex has much to offer; at some distant time tectonic forces will change our familiar clays, sands, gravels and silts
into forms of rock, but for now we have the intricate and highly complex geology
of the Quaternary, which has only recently come to be understood, and its buried
sequences unravelled.

Ancient rock formations underlie Essex, but far out of sight and unknown until
the 1950s when drilling took place on Canvey Island in a programme of exploration
for coal. The borehole found Devonian rocks at a depth of 400m and below these,
formations of the Silurian and Devonian periods, laid down in the Lower Palaeozoic era, some five hundred million years ago. These rocks comprise the Essex Basement, a part of the London Platform which extends into the Midlands and into
northern France and Belgium. The London Platform remained elevated above sea
level through the Upper Palaeozoic and much of the Mesozoic eras, and as a consequence no later rocks have been found beneath Essex until the Cretaceous period.

The chalk

Essex makes up the eastern sector of the London Basin, a bowl formed by the great
bed of chalk laid down in the Cretaceous, which ended some 65 million years BP
(Before Present). In a borehole at Harwich, the thickness of the bed was measured
as 890 feet (270m).[1] The Chalk comes to the surface in the north-west corner of
Essex, creating a downland landscape which links south-west to the Chiltern Hills
and northwards to the Gog Magogs. Southwards the Chalk dips and disappears
beneath younger rocks, sinking to a depth of 360 feet (110m) beneath Chelmsford,
then to surface again briefly at Purfleet and Grays Thurrock, before rising to
become the North Downs - the southern rim of the basin.

Chalk is an exceptionally pure fine-grained micro-porous limestone, formed
from coccoliths accumulated in a sea free of land detritus. Flints, mainly derived
from sponges, are abundant in the Upper Chalk, as are fossils, commonly fish,
ammonoids, gastropods, echinoids and crinoids.

The tertiary

Palaeocene levels

The end of the Cretaceous saw a marked increase in tectonic activity, the beginning of the Alpine Orogeny that elevated the most recent, and consequently highest mountain ranges in Europe, and also coincided with the extinction of the

dinosaurs. This time was marked by the opening of the North Atlantic and the separation of the European and American continents by the growth and spreading of the mid-Atlantic ridge. The chalk strata gently tilted to a new configuration, depressed to form the Thames Basin and elevated over Kent and Sussex. The advancing seas of the early Tertiary period covered much of Essex.

The drilling of key boreholes in recent years has given a virtually complete recovery of the lowermost Tertiary rocks, the Palaeocene successions, and a formal framework has been established. The completer picture has led to the definition of some new sedimentary formations, and inevitably the re-classification of older, familiar ones.

In Essex, and over much of the London Basin, the Cretaceous Chalk is overlain by the *Thanet Sand Formation*, consisting of sands and silts above a flint nodule so-called 'Bullhead Bed', resting directly on the Chalk. Seams of fine-grained sand have been used for moulding (which may have determined the site of the Woolwich Arsenal) and in places for building and glass.[2] The formation is over 30m thick in north Kent, diminishing northwards to less than 2m in the Ipswich area.

The Thanet Sand Formation is overlain by the *Lambeth Group*, a new term, coined following clarification from boreholes, to replace the Woolwich and Reading Beds of former years.[3] It now consists of the Upner, Woolwich and Reading Formations. The *Upnor Formation*, named from a village near Rochester, occurs in boreholes at Aveley, Bradwell-juxta-Mare and Wormingford, and at the Orsett Cock quarry. It consists of sands and well-rounded black flint pebbles, and as oyster shells occur, it can be judged to have been marine. The thickness is about 7.5m in the Upnor area, diminishing northwards to 2m at Bradwell-juxta-Coggeshall.

The *Woolwich Formation* consists of fine-grained sands, silts and clays. Plant debris is common and shelly beds which formed in brackish water. A thickness of 11-12m in north-west Kent thins to the north and west as it passes into the Reading Formation. It is 3.5m thick at Aveley but absent in central and north Essex. In the succeeding *Reading Formation* mottled clay dominates with sand beds, produced in a humid environment. It supersedes the Woolwich in central Essex, resting directly on the Upnor in boreholes at Wormingford and Bradwell, but is absent at Aveley.

Marine fossils occur in the Woolwich Formation, but in the Reading formation they are rare, although impressions of leaves sometimes occur.

Eocene levels

A package of sediments underlying the London Clay and overlying the Woolwich and Reading Beds was first defined in the mid nineteenth century as the 'Basement bed of the London Clay', but is now termed the *Harwich Formation*[4]. It occurs throughout the Hampshire and London Basins and consists of sandy clays and silts, while volcanic ash is common in its upper levels. A thickness of 8m is general in Essex.

The *London Clay*, a stiff, dark or bluish-grey clay which weathers to brown on exposure, and shrinks and cracks in dry weather, is the major deposit of the

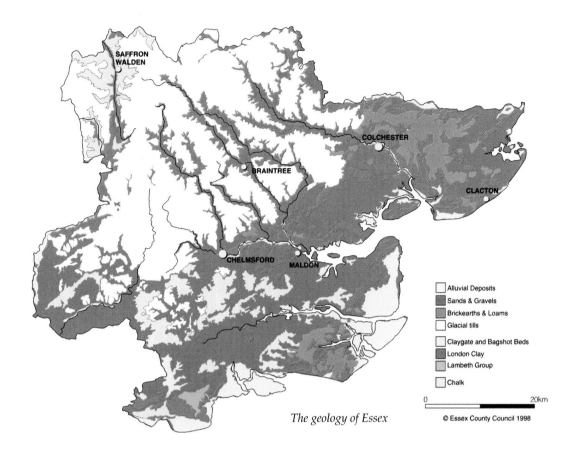

The geology of Essex

☐	Alluvial Deposits
■	Sands & Gravels
■	Brickearths & Loams
☐	Glacial tills
☐	Claygate and Bagshot Beds
■	London Clay
☐	Lambeth Group
☐	Chalk

0   20km

© Essex County Council 1998

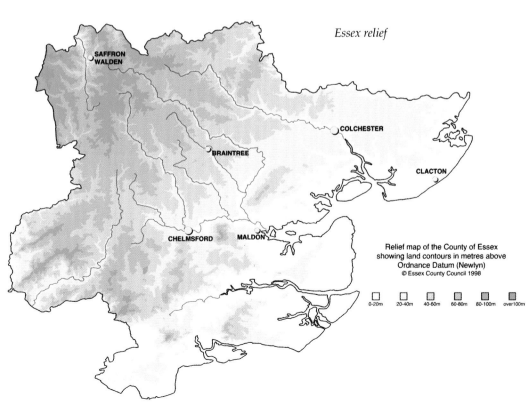

Essex relief

Relief map of the County of Essex
showing land contours in metres above
Ordnance Datum (Newlyn)
© Essex County Council 1998

0-20m   20-40m   40-60m   60-80m   80-100m   over100m

Eocene. At Brentwood it reaches its maximum thickness of about 430 feet (130m). The clay was formed in a shallow sea on a marine shelf with no hard rocks exposed to make high ground. Where fossils occur, and they are not abundant, they include mammals, birds, fish, reptiles, molluscs and crustacea; plants include palms, spurges, mimosas and acacias. The evidence from this fossil fauna and flora shows the climate as tropical; a fossil palm resembles the Nipa palm which occurs today at the mouth of the Ganges, and fossil fruits and seeds are similar to the detritus of the Ambernoh River in New Guinea.[5]

In north-east Essex, *septarian nodules* or cementstone occur, an argillaceous (clayey) limestone. The *septa* are contraction cracks filled with mineral calc-spar or pyrites; it can be used as a building stone, valuable in a county lacking hard lime or sandstone. Septaria was used in the construction of the Roman walls of Colchester and the Norman keep, and in many church walls in north-east Essex. Vast quantities are said to have been dredged up off Harwich and ground up to make stucco for Regency London, to the extent that coastal erosion of the soft clay cliffs was provoked.

London Clay can be baked into fine red bricks and tiles, and was extensively dug for this purpose, particularly in the loamy beds occurring at the junction with the Bagshot Beds at Loughton, Epping Plain and Brentwood. Of particular interest are the products of the Bulmer Brick and Tile Company, situated at the northern rim of the London Clay, which supplies bricks, tiles, paviors and 'specials' for restoration and works requiring materials of the highest quality.

The *Claygate Beds* form a sandy transition at the top of the London Clay, consisting of alternate layers of sand and clay. The formation is up to 15m thick and has been used for brick-making. Fossils are rare and confined to a few moulds of shells. The Claygates gradually change upwards into the *Bagshot Beds*, composed of fine sands with occasional seams of pipe-clay and local beds of flint pebble gravel. The full thickness does not exceed 36m. Fossils are few and limited to plant fragments and marine casts.

The quaternary

The Chalk and Tertiary levels form the solid surface geology of Essex. The Quaternary (Pleistocene and Holocene) consists mainly of fluvial and glacial drifts which have only recently been understood for what they are.[6] The era opens with the *Red Crag*, approximately 3.2 million years BP, for which the best locality is Walton-on-the-Naze, although relicts are found elsewhere in quarry sites and borings through the drifts. The richly fossiliferous deposits of the Waltonian Red Crag are marine and formed near a shoreline in a warm temperate climate. This is indicated by cross-bedding caused by strong current flows. Shells are abundant, particularly bivalve molluscs. In some places the Red Crag has been shown to be overlain by the Chillesford Sand Member of the Norwich Crag Formation of approximately two million years BP.

The principal geological and climatic processes of the Quaternary which had the most effect in forming the present landform and landscape in Essex are, first, the migration of the rivers Thames and Medway, secondly, the Anglian ice sheet with the subsequent deposition of the Lowestoft Till and formation of the present river drainage system and, thirdly, the relatively recent rise in sea level.

The Pleistocene Thames and Medway

It was established in the late 1970s that the extensive deposits of sands and gravels which lie above the earlier solid geology of Essex derive from former courses of the Thames and Medway. Previously they had been interpreted as glacio-fluvial. The proto-Thames appears to have migrated progressively south-eastwards through northern Essex, settling into the Mid-Essex Depression through Chelmsford and Colchester before final diversion by the Anglian ice sheet into its modern valley through London. This took place about 450,000 BP. The terraces which resulted from this southward migration have survived for two reasons, 'over most of the area, the river shifted uniclinally during each stage of its development. It did not rework its own deposits, so that its wide floodplains have been extensively preserved. These surfaces were then largely buried mainly by glacial deposits which protected them'.[7]

The eight pre-diversion Thames terraces are now known as the *Kesgrave Sands and Gravels*, divided into upper and lower levels. The upper, older, deposits are the Sudbury Formation, comprizing the Blushett Farm, Stebbing, Bures and Moreton deposits. The lower, and younger Colchester Formation comprizes the Waldring-field, Ardleigh, Wivenhoe and Lower St Osyth deposits. Most of this area was buried beneath the Lowestoft Till and subsequent post-Anglian erosion by the new rivers Stour, Colne, Blackwater and Chelmer has exposed the fluvial deposits on their valley sides.

At much the same time as the deposition by the Thames of the Kesgrave Sands and Gravels, the Medway laid down the *High-level East Essex Gravels*. These survive as degraded gravels at Dawes Heath, Ashingdon, and at St Lawrence on the Dengie peninsula.

Following its diversion, the Thames combined with the Medway in the late stage of the Anglian to carve a channel through from Southend through Asheldham and Cudmore Grove, East Mersea, to Clacton. This filled with depositions during the Hoxnian and the channel moved eastwards progressively, leaving beds of gravel at Southchurch, Rochford, Shoeburyness, Barling and across the Dengie. These deposits are known as the *Low-level East Essex Gravels*. Subsequent eastern levels lie submerged under the North Sea.

A fourth group of deposits are those of the *Lower Thames Terraces* following the diversion of the river. These occur at Little Thurrock, Orsett Heath and Mucking. The course of the river after diversion did not always follow exactly its present line. Evidence of abandoned meanders exists, for example the Mar Dyke valley.

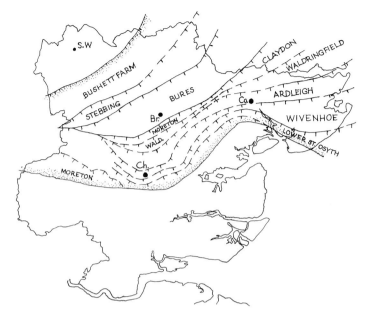

The Kesgrave Sands and Gravels

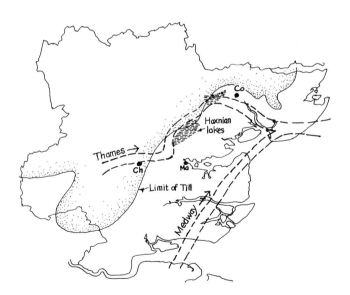

The route of the River Thames before diversion by the ice sheet during the Anglian cold phase

Climatic change

The climate of the Middle and Upper Pleistocene is termed the 'Ice Age', but while consisting of long cold phases, these alternated with warmer interglacials when temperate vegetation recolonized. Seven cold stages have been clearly identified, but there were many more.[8] The Pleistocene is a fascinating period with much unclear and, as with recent Essex geology, understanding and dating of climatic change, accepted only a few years ago, is now seen as flawed. It is a field of study which is developing continually, and knowledge and understanding steadily increase.

The Pleistocene may best be viewed as a series of cyclic, but uneven, climatic oscillations. Long cold phases of dry, treeless steppe-tundra, with grasses, sedges and abundant herbs, were interrupted by short periods of 'polar desert', while inter-stadials brought brief intervals of warmer conditions. During interglacials trees recolonized by stages: sallow and birch giving way to pine, and then to temperate broadleaved woodland. In cold phases, with heavy precipitation as well as low temperatures, vast volumes of water were locked into ice sheets, lowering ocean levels; a 50m drop in sea level connected Britain to Europe and 100m connected Ireland to south-west Scotland.

The phases affecting the surface geology and consequent topology of Essex are considered below. They are the Anglian, Wolstonian and Devensian cold stages, the Hoxnian and Ipswichian interglacials, and the final Flandrian warm phase bringing us to the present time.

The ANGLIAN glacial stage (472,000-428,000 BP) was the most severe, and it was only at this stage that an ice sheet reached Essex and covered much of the land surface. At the approach of the ice the climate changed from arctic tundra to polar desert, causing aeolian deposits of loess and cover sands on the surfaces of river terraces. Prior to the Anglian, the River Thames had reached the penultimate stage in its south-eastern migration, following a course through the Vale of St Albans, the Mid-Essex Depression and Colchester. With the arrival of the ice sheet, its course was blocked and the river diverted, cutting through soft Tertiary formations onto roughly its present line to form the Thames Valley and associated series of terraces. At its furthest extent the ice sheet reached the line of hills formed of Bagshot and Claygate Beds, penetrating at points to leave deposits of till and glacial outwash. As the ice sheet melted it deposited a thick crust of till over most of the county north of the present A12.

This crust of boulder clay, known as the Lowestoft Till, consists of clays, silts and sands with many erratics. The chalk content, leading to the term Chalky Boulder Clay, makes it highly fertile for crop growing, and the abundant flints brought from the Upper Chalk have proved a valuable building resource for paving and walling.

The melting of the ice left a plateau to be slowly dissected as new rivers formed and cut their valleys through the Till and the Kesgrave levels below, sometimes exposing the solid geology of the London Clay. The drainage network of tributary brooks and rills have subsequently moulded the plateau surface into a gentle topography, itself sometimes modified by solifluction processes (see below), and in recent millennia by the action of ploughing, causing downslope drift and the formation of lynchets. On the higher land along the watersheds areas of ancient woodland sometimes occur, often overlying drifts of glacial sands or gravels, or loess. In certain woods a mosaic of plant communities suggests that the land has never been ploughed and that the post-glacial land surface survives beneath the sylvan cover.

The HOXNIAN interglacial which followed the Anglian cold phase has particular relevance to Essex. The name is taken from Hoxne (pronounced Hoxen) in Suffolk where John Wymer directed excavations from 1974-1978 through gravels and silts overlying a lake formed from melt-waters. Flint artefacts were found similar to a wealth of material found at Clacton (from which the term *Clactonian* derives), and at Swanscombe in Kent. Clacton was a centre of flint working, sited beside the Thames-Medway, which was then flowing along a course which is termed the Clacton Channel. 'It is reasonable to picture a wide river with minor abandoned channels flowing over a wide floodplain. The landscape was one of mixed deciduous woodland and open country with a climate much like that of the present day'.[9] Besides the mass of information that has been gathered on human activity at Clacton, there is evidence for other denizens of the landscape; faunal remains were found of straight-tusked elephant, rhinoceros, lion, horse, pig, deer, bison, giant beaver and numerous small mammals. To the south, along the Clacton Channel at Cudmore Grove, East Mersea, recent erosion of the cliff face has revealed a huge range of fossil plants and animals of the Hoxnian age; the fauna of small vertebrates being the richest ever found in Britain.[10]

During the Hoxnian the new rivers, Stour, Colne, Blackwater, Chelmer and Crouch, at higher levels than today, formed their own drainage patterns and began the shaping of their valleys. Melt-water lakes in the area of Rivenhall, Marks Tey and Copford slowly silted up; the conditions being very similar to those at Hoxne, it is here that another major site may one day be discovered.

In the course of the DEVENSIAN, the final major cold stage, periglacial conditions caused the characteristic *brickearth* of south-east Essex, formed by the deposition of loess in semi-aquatic conditions. The formation of head deposits also occurred at this time, caused by solifluction - the downslope movement of soils by freeze-thaw action. Conventionally the dividing line between the Devensian (and the Pleistocene) and the FLANDRIAN, our own age, is set at 10,000 BP. But this is for convenience; the process of warming had begun well before and the tundra had given way to a woodland cover of sallow, birch and pine.

About 9,500 BP an expansion of pine replaced most of the birch, followed in order by hazel, elm, oak, alder and lime.[11] The evidence of pollen cores from organic muds and peat relate the sequence to Essex. At Enfield Lock in the Lea Valley, pollen analysis showed an open environment around 9,546 BP, dominated by sedges with some dwarf birch and shrub willow. Above this birch-pine woodland developed, and then pine-hazel-elm woods with oak and alder as later colonists by about 8,500 to 7,000 BP. By around 6,670 BP at Bradwell-on-Sea, there were lime dominated deciduous woodlands. In the Mar Dyke, pollens showed woodland of oak, lime, hazel and alder around 5,740 BP.[12]

The Flandrian saw the final development of the drainage pattern and landform familiar to us today. The rise in sea levels formed the estuaries, or drowned river valleys, as well as the southern North Sea. At first this was rapid. Around 9,500 to 9,000 BP the sea level was about 45m below that of today; between 8,500 and 7,000 it rose from 25.5m to 8.9m below. By about 1,750 BP the estuaries had taken up roughly their modern form, but on the open coast the Roman coastline could differ markedly from that of today, stretching out considerably further into the sea, with extensive salt-marshes and mud-flats.[13]

Erratics and building stones

The geological resources of Essex contain no fine-grained stones suitable for carving and dressing, and as a result these materials have always been imported. This lack stimulated the development of brickearth products as a substitute. Many Saxon and early medieval churches display Roman brick and tile in their structure (and the presence of a Roman site in the vicinity to quarry). By about 1200, brick and tile making yards had been established by the monks of Coggeshall Abbey - the earliest known in post-Roman Britain. The industry only became fully accepted in the fifteenth century when its popularity grew rapidly, to the extent that Essex is the county in which to study the brickwork of the fifteenth and sixteenth centuries. High quality products continue to be made, as has been noted above.

But if Essex lacks freestone, it is rich in erratics carried and left by the ice sheet, and along former courses of the Thames and Medway. Boulders can be found in all parts of the county, but are particularly numerous in the north on the Boulder Clay. They can be seen used as road markers, footings for buildings, bollards and mounting-blocks. A well known example is the Leper Stone, a sandstone megalith which stands in the verge just to the north of Newport. A large erratic of Jurassic limestone is to be seen near the entrance to the Saffron Walden Museum. It was found when digging foundations for Acrow's Works (now Ridgeons) on the Ashdon road where the Boulder Clay overlies the Chalk. Looking rather like a giant cheeseburger, it measures some two metres in diameter and weighs two tons. Early in this century there was considerable interest in erratic rocks and A E Salter compiled an inventory of boulders he had found while studying drift deposits.[14] In pits near the railway at Audley End he noted 'a great variety of small boulders have been observed. They include sandstones (various), quartz, basalt, fine grained pink granite, rhyolites, pebbly-greywether, porphyry, Carboniferous sandstone, purple quartzite etc'. At Bean Hill, Sewards End, he recorded that the

East end of Rayleigh Church. Masonry containing knapped flint, Kentish ragstone and Roman tile. Early sixteenth century (photo Paul Skeet)

South-east wall of chancel, Little Hallingbury Church. Masonry containing 'field' flints, Roman tile and a Bunter quartzite boulder. Thirteenth century (photo Paul Skeet)

largest boulders ranged up to three feet, but the average was from eighteen to twenty inches. They consisted of 'large flints, rounded lumps of chalk, Carboniferous limestone, some being of a purple colour, Jurassic limestone, Red Chalk (with belemnites), Kimeridge clay, Jurassic septaria, Jurassic fossils, jasper, rhyolite (the only igneous rock seen)'. Clearly there is a wealth of erratic rocks to be found, but it is not a subject which seems to awake much interest today.

Oddly, Salter missed the scatter of fine sarsens around Alphamstone Church. Sarsens are a *silcrete* which formed on the surface of the Chalk under tropical desert conditions, when quartz sand dissolved and bound sands and gravels into a new hard surface. Subsequently, under arctic conditions such sheets fragmented into blocks. On the Wiltshire Downs, prehistoric builders used them for construction, notably at Avebury and Stonehenge, and in much later times sarsens were cut up for building stone. While many Essex sarsens were brought by the ice sheet, and those found in south-east Essex by a former course of the Medway from the North Downs, the number and location of the Alphamstone examples suggest human agency.

Impressive displays of erratics may be seen in the external face of the rubble walls of many medieval churches. The materials were collected locally from the fields and river beds, set in lime mortar between shutters in annual work stages, and finally plastered over when complete. Although it was not the intention of the builders that the stones should be seen, the work is not haphazard; good stones with flat faces, if available, were placed against the shutters, and the builders may well have felt a sense of satisfaction viewing their work before the plasterer hid it from view. Plaster was often replaced by harder renders in later centuries. In the later nineteenth century, an aesthetic appreciation of natural and local materials led to the removal of the covering skins, adding considerably to the interest of these buildings and their visual quality. In addition to flints, a wide range of far older stones and salvage from Roman buildings, an attractive non-erratic material is *ferricrete*, sometimes termed ironstone, which is formed where gravels, sands and marls have been permeated by iron oxides in ground water, acting as a cement similar to lime or silica.[15] Medieval builders would have sought this useful material from local sources.

The variety and often distant provenance of the stones displayed in church walls is impressive. These walls may perhaps be seen as a substitute for the cliff faces of western counties. They are a record of what lies in the soils of a locality, and what has been brought from elsewhere by the action of extreme climatic forces; above all, they are a reminder that Essex is a county shaped in the Quaternary, and that the processes at work 10,000 years ago still continue.

CHAPTER TWO

The regions and subregions of Essex

IT HAS LONG been recognized that the landscapes of lowland England belong to two broad types: 'woodland' (or 'bocage') where enclosed fields were the rule, and 'champion' ('champagne') where open-field farming prevailed. Writing in the reign of the first Elizabeth, William Harrison, rector of Radwinter, described it thus:

> 'It is so that, our soil being divided into champaign ground and woodland, the houses of the first lie uniformly built in every town, together with streets and lanes, whereas in the woodland countries (except here and there in great market towns) they stand scattered abroad, each one dwelling in the midst of his own occupying'.[1]

Except for an area in the north-west of the county, the Essex of Harrison's day lay firmly in the woodland category. With the Enclosure Acts of the eighteenth and early nineteenth centuries, leading to the conversion of open-fields and commons into hedged fields, the distinction between the two types of landscape became, superficially, less distinct. Today, a better terminology would seem to be Oliver

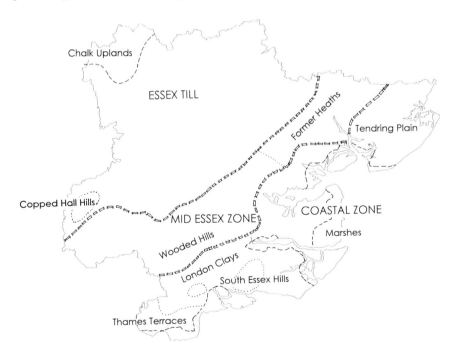

The landscape regions of Essex

Rackham's 'ancient' and 'planned' countryside;[2] 'ancient', the product of evolution and change over a long period of time; 'planned', the landscapes of surveyors, rapidly devised and implemented at the behest of the parliamentary commissioners.

In the landscapes where open-field farming was the rule, one finds nucleated villages with the older farmsteads generally lying within the village. In 'woodland' areas, scattered settlement in hamlets was usual; settlements in Essex which look like villages, are usually former towns. The field systems of 'ancient' countryside evolved in many different ways, and include common-fields, small in scale and mostly divided up into closes long before parliamentary enclosure; former deer parks and demesne fields which were being divided and hedged in late medieval and Tudor times, and the areas of ancient planned countryside which predate Domesday Book and whose origin still remains in the realm of speculation.

The variety in character of the Essex landscape, even between adjacent parishes, can be bewildering. But three broad regions are apparent, arising from surface geology and topography, and the influence these factors have had on settlement, farming and communications. Two other major factors are proximity to the North Sea and the Thames Estuary and, in recent centuries, the growth of London. The three regions are:

1 Coastal or maritime Essex. This region consists of the estuaries and their immediate hinterlands, mostly on the heavy London Clays, and the productive marshlands formed of marine and fluvial silts. Distinct subregions are the Thames Terraces, the South Essex Hills, and the Tendring Plain

2 The Mid-Essex Zone. The southern area, termed the Wooded Hills, lies on the acid soils deriving from the Bagshot and Claygate Beds, glacial outwash, and London Clays exposed in the valleys. The northern area, the Former Heathlands, lies mostly on Kesgrave Formations and glacial outwash.

3 The Essex Till. This region was directly affected by the Anglian cold phase, when an ice sheet covered the area, bringing a thick deposit of boulder clays made fertile by their chalk content. Two subregions are the Chalk Uplands and the Copped Hall Hills.

The coastal zone

Coastal Essex relates to the North Sea and the Thames Estuary. Until relatively recently its people and goods travelled mainly by water, and it is difficult now to imagine how active maritime traffic was as late as the earlier half of this century. The estuaries and creeks were welcoming to early migrants, but also to Danish raiders and, later on, to those seeking to evade the excise men. Links to the Low Countries have a long history, and probably prehistory; the huge flocks of marshland sheep recorded in Domesday Book supplied the wool for the cloth industries

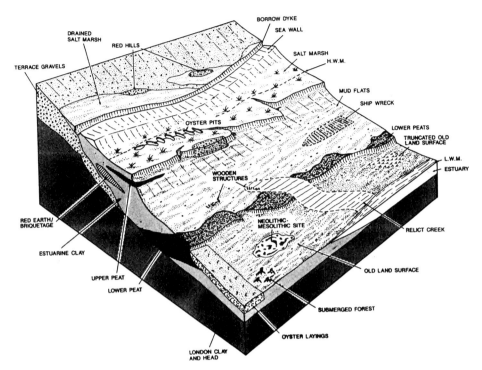

A typical section of the Essex coast, showing the different types of environment and the archaeology found there (after Wilkinson and Murphy, 1995)

of Flemish towns, and the early development of brickwork in Essex resulted from these connections. From the later Middle Ages onwards there was a symbiosis with London, which received the produce of farmland, marshland pastures, fisheries, decoy ponds and oyster beds, while the returning barges brought mountains of manure to fertilise the fields. Pleasure steamers bringing Londoners to Southend pier for a day out and the diaspora of Londoners settling along the railway lines from Fenchurch Street are only a recent phase in a long relationship.

While the seascape has been impoverished by the virtual disappearance of coastal craft, and the fleets of sailing barges are now a memory for a few, the inland landscapes have been stricken by the loss of standing trees. Over the London Clays which cover much of the area elm was the dominant hedgerow tree, amounting to a virtual monoculture. There is no factual explanation as to why this was so, but it might be reasonable to suppose that they were planted when these ancient planned field systems were laid out. The elms are of the suckering type which are usually thought to be an early importation, as opposed to some woodland species considered native - useful trees, constantly producing new poles from the rootstock which could develop into timber trees. In the early 1970s, a newly imported strain of Dutch Elm disease spread rapidly from Tilbury, killing all standing trees in its path. Areas such as the Dengie, once bosky and beautiful with elms arching over the roads, now became bleak in landscape terms. Much of the root systems remains alive but subsequent growth is reinfected when the stems become woody, so for the time being there seems no prospect of promoting new trees from the roots. However, elms have been smitten by disease before, and one hopes for a future mutation which can cope with this strain of the disease.

The coastal marshes

The traditional grazing marshes are now mostly arable, with saltmarsh, mudflats and shingle banks beyond the seawalls. They have always been valued as a productive resource and in recent years recognized as an internationally important area for overwintering birds. Despite the artificiality of the sea defences and arable crops, the marshes convey a sense of wildness and the power of natural forces. The walls have been raised since the disastrous floods of 1953, but new problems have arisen: the loss of saltmarsh that helped to protect the seawalls from the force of the waves, and the possibility that the slow rise in sea level will accelerate. These are particular problems for Essex which has a coastline of nearly 400 miles in length.

At the end of the cold phase (Devensian) around 10,000 years BP, much of the coastline was far out in the North Sea. From then, rising sea levels and the sinking of the Southern North Sea Basin have caused the progressive submergence of low-lying land. Mesolithic coastal sites are now inaccessible, but later submerged sites are visible at low tide. The process was not slow and gradual but formed a

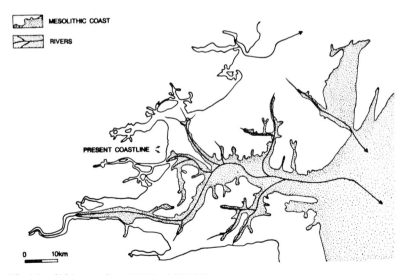

The Mesolithic coastline, 7,000 - 6,500 BC

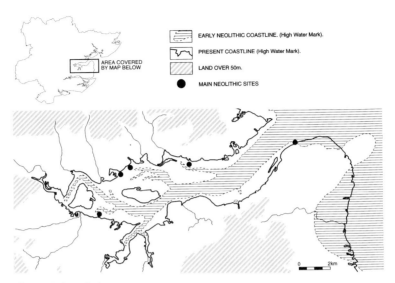

EARLY NEOLITHIC COASTLINE. (High Water Mark).

PRESENT COASTLINE (High Water Mark).

AREA COVERED BY MAP BELOW

LAND OVER 50m.

MAIN NEOLITHIC SITES

The Neolithic Blackwater, 3,500 - 2,500 BC

sequence of transgressions, when the sea advanced inland, and regressions, when it retreated, allowing the development of freshwater peat. The rise in sea levels known as the Thames III transgression, from around 4000 BP, submerged sites which are now known to have been extensively occupied in the Neolithic and Early Bronze Age, and sealed the former land surfaces under sediments of peat, mud and clay.[3]

The product of this protection is the preservation of archaeological and environmental evidence of the lives of the early peoples who inhabited these sites - their activities, diet, industries, and the landscapes in which they worked, cultivated, hunted, gathered and fished. The Stumble site on the Blackwater estuary has been sampled in detail and structural features, pits, hearths and large quantities of flints and potsherds recorded. Charred remains of crops and fruits were abundant: cereals, flax, fruitstones, nuts and tubers, indicating that there was no sudden switch from a Mesolithic foraging to a Neolithic farming economy. At that time the two economies were merged. Pollen analysis suggests a predominantly wooded landscape of oak, lime and hazel.[4]

Further south at this early stage, the coastal landscape around Burnham and the archipelago of Wallasea, Havengore, Potten and Foulness islands was radically different from today's. The whole area formed a complex of tidal flats and beach ridges of sands, gravels and shells with intervening estuaries and watercourses, features which still occur, especially off Foulness with the largest examples of such ridges in Britain. The tidal limit here appears to have been further inland than today.[5]

Generally along the coast, the pollen record suggests that the dryland slopes above the water's edge were well wooded with lime and oak dominant. Copperas Wood on the Stour estuary is now a lone example of this landscape type.

In the Middle and Late Bronze Age (c1500-800 BC), following the Thames III transgression, the Essex coastline approached its present form. The archaeological evidence shows that there was considerable activity along the estuary foreshores and the landscape was now less wooded with tracts of land cleared for pasture. The earliest known site for salt production in Essex has been identified at Fenn Creek near South Woodham Ferrers, and by the Late Bronze Age there were others, notably at Mucking. Wooden platforms and possible landing stages have been found, and a paddle, two metres long and radiocarbon dated to around 900 BC, was preserved in estuarine mud near Canewdon. One can envisage the traffic of boats in the estuaries and creeks, linking both local and distant communities, and contacts across the southern North Sea. Recent boat finds from the Humber estuary and Dover suggest the potential of the Essex coast for similar discoveries as sections are eroded.[6]

The importance of water and wetland in the Bronze and Iron Ages for ritual depositions is well established from the Thames, Fenland sites and elsewhere. There is some evidence for such activity in Essex with ritual offerings in the Blackwater and, at Fenn Creek, two human skulls were found deliberately placed on a wooden platform (dated by radiocarbon to between 927 and 823 BC).[7]

The Iron Age and Roman period may have seen a phase of marine regression since areas of former land surface showing evidence of Roman activity are submerged in the Thames estuary. There is also a lack of wooden structures compared with the Bronze Age. The distinctive sites of the period are the red hills, of which hundreds are known and others continually discovered. They are the relics of an extensive salt producing industry, the bricketage left from the containers in which brine was heated accumulating with burnt earth to form small hills. The work may have been seasonal in the late summer and early autumn, and it has been suggested that the smoke from the numerous fires could have produced an effect in the coastal zone not unlike that of the straw and stubble burning fires of recent memory.[8] In later times the hills served as refuges for stock if the marshes were flooded and as hillocks on which sheep were milked, according to William Camden writing of Canvey in 1607.

The vulnerability of the Essex coast to attack by North Sea raiders led to the building of a Saxon Shore fort at Bradwell, which lay on a promontory between two creeks and survived as a coastal settlement well into the Saxon period. The only surviving structure is Cedd's church, dedicated to St Peter and now a place of pilgrimage. The site of the fort has mostly been lost to the sea at an unknown date, whereas the marshland to north and south, which was probably saltmarsh in Roman times, is now prime arable land safeguarded by sea walls.

Domesday Book records the flocks of sheep grazing the marshes in the late eleventh century, a use, the archaeological evidence suggests, that was already well established in the Roman centuries. The grazing rights (or stocking rights if the marshes were intercommoned at an early date, as seems likely) were held by inland manors, mostly abutting the marshlands.

By the 13th century sea levels were again rising and flood defences became essential. In 1210 a 'law of the marsh' in Essex required that each man must contribute to the upkeep of the defences from which he benefited, in proportion to his land and rights,[9] and 1280 saw the first commission in Essex to enforce the upkeep of defences. Disasters occurred and were recorded: Matthew Paris wrote of the floods of 1296, caused by a combination of wind and sea, and Holinshed, the sixteenth century chronicler, found a reference to high tide flooding in 1251; in the second half of the fourteenth century there were a series of calamitous breaks, and a disastrous storm in the winter of 1376-7.[10] In 1375 and 1380 Barking Abbey was able to impress men for reconstruction and repair work on the sea walls and to set the rate of wages, which were probably well below those of the market. The Abbey, together with St Osyth's Priory, was granted generous tax concessions by reason of the damage they had suffered, which lay folk were not. Fobbing was a manor of Barking, and when the Poll Tax Commissioners arrived in May 1381 to enforce payment, it is not surprising that resentment exploded and the Peasants' Revolt had begun.[11]

Although there was some ploughing up of marshes as early as the Middle Ages, and by 1700 about a third of Foulness was arable, sheep grazing was still general on the marshes in the 17th century. Although this was a century in which there were no general catastrophes, the building of sea defences continued apace. Canvey was walled by Dutch engineers in the 1620s. Earlier defences were sometimes rationalized and improved. On Foulness each marsh had been individually protected; after perimetal walling of the whole island, the old embankments remained as relics known as 'counter-walls'.[12] Such features on the Dengie marshes record the successful endeavours of successive owners to win more land from the sea.

With the development of the flat-bottomed barges, proximity to the sea was a major asset for sales of grain as road transport was costly and often difficult in the winter months. Reclamation, or 'inning', continued through the eighteenth century, gathering added momentum as corn prices soared. The Rev Henry Bate Dudley, rector of Bradwell, enlarged his glebe by enclosing 300 acres (121ha) and a further 100 acres at Tillingham. In 1795 he reported to Vancouver's survey that 1500 acres (607 ha), about half of the marshland in his parish, was under the plough.[13] In the nineteenth century a manic proposal to reclaim 30,420 acres (17,000 ha) in the Blackwater estuary and off Mersea Island fortunately came to nothing, although approved by act of parliament in 1852. Less ambitious schemes succeeded at Foulness, Canvey, Walton and the Dengie marshes. Chapman and André's map of 1777 shows 266 miles of embankments; in 1930 this had grown to 321.[14]

Archaeological evidence for fishing and gathering of shellfish is found on the earliest sites and extensive fish traps in the Blackwater estuary date from Anglo-Saxon times. Wildfowling must be almost as ancient as fishing, but archaeological evidence only survives for the decoy ponds, usually shaped like starfish in plan, that abounded on the Blackwater and Dengie marshes in the 18th and 19th centuries. Most have been ploughed out but show up from the air as cropmarks. Daniel Defoe (an Essex lad, born at Tilbury) described Londoners venturing into the marshes on wildfowling expeditions and returning very well laden with game. Unfortunately for them they 'often return with an Essex ague on their backs, which they find a heavier load than the fowls they have shot'.[15] By 1807 Arthur Young could report that draining and cultivation had abated the notorious marshland agues (probably a form of malaria).[16]

The Bradwell shore fort was the Roman first of many such structures built in subsequent centuries to protect the vulnerable Essex coastline. Colchester Castle was a response, rapidly erected, to meet the Danish threat. Hadleigh Castle followed to meet the threat of the French and, backed by its deer park, scanned the estuary over the Hadleigh and Canvey marshes. Henry VIII built forts (now invisible) on Mersea Island and at Tilbury, where later followed the great fortress embellished by a gateway designed in Wren's office. The real threat of Napoleon

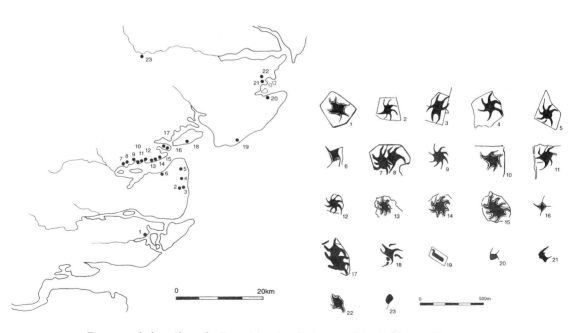

Decoy pond plans (from the Essex Mapping Project, see EAH Vol 28, 1997)

caused the building of Martello Towers and the Harwich Redoubt; and the later paper threat of his nephew led to the building of Coalhouse Fort. Beacon Hill Fort superseded the Redoubt in the late nineteenth century and, with Coalhouse, formed a useful platform in the Second World War for an anti-aircraft battery. The massive shore and beach defences of that war were rapidly and thankfully removed after the ending of hostilities, but some relic structures remain which are now venerable and important monuments to a time of peril.

In 1872 the Thames Conservancy as harbour authority forbade vessels to carry petroleum barrels upstream of Thames Haven, but in 1876 the Petroleum Storage Company established itself on the Corringham marshes, served by a jetty previously used by cattle.[17] This beginning developed into the great refineries at Shellhaven and Coryton, displaying the intriguing forms of petro-chemical engineering, appropriate in the great expanse of the Thames estuary, but inappropriate when mimicked by jackdaw architects elsewhere.

The Essex marshes as landscapes evoke emotional responses ranging from revulsion at endless tracts of marsh, mud and seeming dereliction, to a sense of the numinous and timelessness. William Morris (an Essex man) wrote of the Thameside Marshes, where much has now changed, in *News from Nowhere*. But writing of a remoter area, the description by Sabine Baring-Gould seems as apt today as it was in 1880:

Between the mouths of the Blackwater and the Colne, on the east coast of Essex, lies an extensive marshy tract veined and freckled in every part with water. At high tides the appearance is that of a vast surface of Sargasso weed floating on the sea, with rents and patches of shining water traversing and dappling it in all directions. The creeks, some of considerable length and breadth, extend many miles inland, and are arteries whence branches out a fibrous tissue of smaller channels, flushed with water twice in twenty-four hours. At noontides, and especially at the equinoxes, the sea asserts its royalty over this vast region.[18]

The South Essex Hills

These eminences, composed mainly of Bagshot and Claygate beds over London Clay, comprise two groups of hills: the larger based on Rayleigh, Hockley and Hadleigh, and the smaller, some distance to the west, forming the Langdon Hills. With their extensive tree cover and bosky skylines, both groups form a pleasing contrast to the adjacent plain, particularly since the loss of the elm hedgerows on the latter. The eastern group contains 47 woods. They have been studied by Oliver Rackham who knows of no group of rural woods that has suffered as little deterioration in the last 40 years as these; 'in particular, they have entirely escaped the replanting that ruined a third of the ancient woodland of England in the 1950s and 1960s'.[19]

Unusually for south Essex, fieldwalking revealed the presence of a large Roman site at Dawes Heath, interpreted as a villa.[20] One is tempted to speculate whether it may have been a hunting lodge for someone of high status, such as the governor or a visiting emperor. It is clear from the many placenames ending in leah (clearing) that some clearance of woodland took place in the middle Saxon period, as in Epping Forest, at first to create heathland pasture, and later enclosed into small fields, although areas of heath and common survived to be mapped by Chapman and André in 1777. In Iron Age and Roman times the woodland would have been a valuable source of firewood for the salt producers of the coastal red hills. Domesday Book shows that many of the woods were then enclaves belonging to manors on the plain which otherwise lacked woodland resources.

The eastern group are divided east-west by the enchanting valley of the upper Roach, the Hockley Woods to the north and Rayleigh to the south. Rayleigh Park, mentioned in Domesday Book, lay over much of the valley.

Urbanization came in the late nineteenth century with the development of Southend, and the plotland phenomenon early in the twentieth. Paradoxically this may have helped to preserve the woods; they are valued by the inhabitants and the larger woods are in local authority ownership. Plotland, mainly sited on former farmland, has tended to increase the wooded area.

The Thames Terraces

These form the eastern tip of the great series of terraces cut by the Thames following its diversion by the Anglian ice sheet. Since the boundary change of 1965, only a relatively small area remained in the county, and that has now gone. The soils are free draining and have always been attractive to farmers, and also to quarriers of sands and gravels who have left many scars. Settlements lie along the edge of the lowest terrace overlooking the marshes: the Thurrocks and Tilburys, Mucking and Fobbing. Inland lies the Mar Dyke valley, a relic of the early wanderings of the Thames, a wooded combe with mixed, mainly ancient woodland on its slopes and a grazed floor - an extraordinary survival that can be glimpsed from the M25, saved by early purchase by the County Council in a programme to preserve the Green Belt.

South of the Mar Dyke an outcrop of chalk has long been quarried, leaving an awesome landscape of deep pits with towering white walls. No more; commercial development has smothered the quarries, and urbanization and road construction has consumed huge tracts of the surrounding landscape. On what is left, elm disease has destroyed the former cover of standing trees.

Despite the lack now of visible history, the area is rich in archaeology, particularly evident at Mucking where intensive excavation has revealed successive settlement from the Neolithic to the Anglo-Saxons.

A development with far reaching effects took place in the Grays chalk pits in the 1860s. Flooding was impeding the work of the quarrymen, and after an eminent chemist had reported favourably on the quality of the water it seemed better to use it for supply to East London than run it to waste. The railways brought population growth in south Essex and by 1891 56,000 people were supplied. This was the origin of the Essex Water Company (now Essex and Suffolk) which went on to

21

construct the Abberton and Hanningfield reservoirs and supply most of the population of Essex.

The London Clays

London Clay is heavy but fertile, and the soils were traditionally described as 'three horse land', whereas the Boulder Clays were 'two horse land', and the light gravel soils could be ploughed with just one horse. The light soils and brickearths show a continuous record of settlement from the Neolithic onwards, but the London Clay only appears to have been occupied in the late Iron Age, and was abandoned at the end, or towards the end, of the Roman period - although rough grazing may have continued - to be reoccupied in the middle or late Saxon period. In the agricultural depression at the end of the 19th century, London Clay was the first land to be abandoned.

The South Essex Plain, with its distinctive rectilinear field patterns, lies mainly on London Clay, although it extends southwards from Orsett over the terrace and in the east, over the brickearths and gravels of Rochford, the Wakerings, Stambridge and Shoebury, to the edge of the marshes. At first sight the field patterns resemble the parliamentary enclosures of the eighteenth and early nineteenth centuries, but this is ancient countryside (albeit planned) with scattered settlement and villages little more than hamlets in size. Despite the general regularity over the whole area and the presence of principal boundary lines that may extend over several miles, it lacks overall uniformity. On closer analysis the area consists of distinct blocks with their own varying orientation. It is not a grand plan carried out at one time by someone with the authority to achieve it. Nor could it be the work of individual communities who would lack the necessary cohesion. Certainly it must predate the fragmentation of tenure in 1066 recorded by Domesday Book, and the most likely conclusion would seem that it was the work of a powerful elite.[21]

The most likely times when these landscapes were formed would seem to be in the late Iron Age and early Roman period, or the middle or late Saxon. Cropmarks on the light soils to the south of Orsett show small scale field systems on the same alignment as the later systems and, where archaeological evidence is available, it confirms a Roman date. There is, however, a lack of evidence to show that the rectilinear pattern extended over the plain as a whole. But if it once did, and subsequently shrank towards the end of Roman rule when the London Clays were abandoned, field boundaries would survive as earthworks to be reused for a similar pattern of farming when the land came to be reclaimed. Moreover, tracks crossing the plain were likely to remain in use. These, and principal field boundaries, could have served to define territories at a time when rough grazing was the main land use.

A middle to late Saxon date for the reclamation seems likely - a massive undertaking. This may have occurred during the reigns of Athelstan and Edgar, when England had been united into one kingdom, the economy was growing and the renewal of Danish invasions lay in the future. On the other hand, a case can be made that in the middle Saxon period, south Essex was divided between many large estates, each occupying the areas of several later parishes and having access to wood-pastures on the hills and grazing on the marshes. This would explain the pattern of enclaving which survived the subsequent fragmentation of landholdings. At Shoebury, a radial arrangement of roads has been shown to be post-Roman, as it overlies a Roman field system on a different orientation, and it predated the insertion of an eleventh century manorial enclosure.[22] South of Wickford, however, a Roman date does seem likely for the field system which would have served the large walled settlement known to have existed there.

The Dengie peninsula has very similar field systems to those of the South Essex Plain and, although gently undulating, a similar geology. This is predominantly of London Clay, overlain to the east by fluvial deposits left by former courses of the Thames and Medway, and then descending to the extensive marshes. It seems likely that settlement and landuse evolved along much the same lines as on the land south of the Crouch, with continuing occupation on the light soils around Southminster, Asheldham, Tillingham and Bradwell, which in the Roman period would have related to the salt industry along the marshland edge and to Othona, the 'Saxon shore' fort. Abandonment, with later reclamation, of the London Clay may have followed a similar sequence as that on the South Essex Plain. But while likely, this must remain hypothetical, because as yet archaeological evidence is sparse.

To the north, between Maldon and Colchester, the London Clays emerge from beneath Kesgrave layers, and with some scattered Thames/Medway deposits, slope down to the north shore of the Blackwater estuary and Mersea Island, the marshes and the many small creeks and inlets described by Baring-Gould. It is interesting undulating topography, sparsely settled and, sadly, deprived of much of its tree cover by elm disease. The field patterns of this area do not display the planned rectilinearity of the London Clays to the south.

The Tendring Plain

The Kesgrave levels once extended over the plain but have eroded, leaving loams that are light and fertile. Thames/Medway deposits brush the southern area around Brightlingsea and Clacton. The inland landscape is flat, open and somewhat bleak; a contrast to a coastline that is full of interest, often unexpected. There are the creeks of Alresford, Brightlingsea and St Osyth; Hamford Water, the setting for Arthur Ransome's *Secret Water*; and the sweeping scale of the Stour estuary with its sandy cliffs, and Copperas Wood, an echo of the wooded shorelines of the Neolithic. Along the North Sea coast lie sandy beaches, a scarce asset in Essex, that have given rise to the mettlesome resort of Clacton, with sedate Frinton to the north, and jolly plotland Jaywick to the south. A very different landscape to that of the Hoxnian interglacial when Clacton was the centre of a flint working industry, sited beside the wide floodplain of the Thames-Medway.

The present smooth coastline belies its relatively recent turbulent history when it has been subject to massive erosion and change. Walton in Domesday Book lay in the east of the huge manor of Adulfesness (27 hides) which stretched as a promontory, or 'ness', far into the North Sea. Morant relates that Walton 'extended considerably further east than it does now, and hath been devoured by the sea. Some hath confirmed that ruins of buildings have been discovered under water at a considerable distance. About five miles from this shore lyes a whole shole of rocks, called West rocks, which on a great ebb are sometimes dry. A spot amongst them is called the Town'.[23] The West Rocks remains an area of very shallow water, dangerous to shipping. This it seems was the original vill of Walton where there was a harbour in the late eleventh century. Dramatic change seems to have come in the late 16th century when the ness was swept away and the Town submerged. The mainland village of Walton has also suffered, with its seaward end and church submerged around 1800, and the ruins still visible in the mid 19th century.[24] All of which strikes a sombre note in the current alarm at a possible rise in sea levels.

The mid-Essex zone

The wooded hills

This area contains some of the most attractive and interesting countryside in Essex. Over much of it fields have remained relatively small, there are many small woods, and the mixed content of hedgerows has averted the disaster of elm disease. During the Anglian cold phase, a ridge of Bagshot and Claygate Beds partially withstood the assault of the ice sheet, which broke through in places depositing a stony outwash and turning the ridge into a series of hills. Subsequent erosion formed the valleys, with the rivers and brooks sometimes cutting down to the London Clay. The varied topography and acid soils were traditionally conducive to woodland and pasture farming, and there are indications that the area was once subject to extensive systems of intercommoning. Many commons have survived, but many more were lost when parliamentary enclosure was fashionable. Childerditch Common was preserved by incorporation into Thorndon Great Park and now forms part of Thorndon Country Park. Its great pollard oaks indicate its long history as wood-pasture, but with the lack of pasturing animals it is a struggle to prevent it tumbling down to scrub and secondary woodland as may be seen at Great Warley Common, Galleywood, Norton Heath, and indeed most commons in lowland England. At Danbury Common the National Trust have introduced Hebridean sheep to maintain the turf swards they have opened up, and appear to be winning.

Danbury Common retains its medieval boundaries and the enclosed pockets within are later encroachments, mainly pre-1560. Rights of common extended to the tenants and inhabitants of the bordering manors of Woodham Walter, Woodham Mortimer, Little Baddow and Sandon.[25] It would seem likely that Danbury

Hornbeam pollards in Epping Forest at the high density of the nineteenth century

was once linked to Lingwood and Woodham Walter Commons, forming a part in an extensive network, and the boundaries were defined as pressures increased on resources in the early Middle Ages. At much the same time woodland management became more intensive, and woods such as Blake's were enclosed and embanked as coppices.

The greatest Essex common to survive is Epping Forest; that welcome wooded ridge one espies after travelling eastwards on the M25 through the horror of south Hertfordshire, and knows one will soon reach true open countryside. Epping and its northern extremity, Wintry Forest, were parts of Waltham Forest, a great tract of land in south-west Essex that remained under forest law when most of Essex was disafforested (in legal terms) in 1327. Medieval forests will be discussed later on, but it should be noted here that the term 'forest' did not imply that all the land was covered with trees - far from it - but that special laws applied to protect the king's deer. Epping and Wintry are true survivors, their boundaries remaining much as they were in the Middle Ages, but the other two great wooded areas were less fortunate; most of Enfield Chase was destroyed in 1777 and all but six per cent of Hainault Forest was lost in 1851. The rumpus caused by the latter destruction

25

was a factor leading to the epic struggle to save Epping from enclosing landlords, with the unlikely alliance of QCs and city aldermen with humble commoners who had rights, most importantly for the legal outcome, of intercommon in all the manors of the forest.

These were the years when the movement came into being to preserve surviving commons and open spaces, battles were fought to preserve Hampstead Heath, Berkhamsted Common and many others, and the National Trust was founded. Across the Atlantic a parallel movement sought to preserve the wilderness areas, and in 1872 the first National Park was established at Yellowstone. This was the wider context within which the good guys eventually prevailed, and under the Epping Forest Act of 1878 some 5,500 acres (2,225 ha) were vested in the ownership of the Corporation of the City of London 'for the enjoyment in perpetuity by the citizens of London', and principles of management set out.[26] Fortunately, the guiding figure was Edward North Buxton who insisted on the primacy of the 'natural aspect' in which formal and municipal features, and organised sport would have no place. Buxton wrote the first guidebook to the Forest (1884), which ran to many editions and remains a classic. The last act of this great conservationist, be it ever remembered, was to purchase Hatfield Forest and give it to the National Trust.

Epping Forest lies on a long ridge composed of a mixture of gravels and Bagshot Beds overlying Claygates, which in turn overlie London Clay. Beech is dominant on the top of the ridge, giving way to hornbeam on the slopes where the heavier soils emerge. In 1878 virtually all the trees were pollards, cut by the commoners on a short rotation (generally 15 years) and often growing at a dense spacing, which had been made possible by regular cropping. By this time pollarding was in decline over much of the Forest, as also was grazing. It is likely that the density was a response to the demand for faggots from London's bakers and maltsters in recent centuries, and that in earlier times the forest was more open. Chapman and André's map of 1777 shows wide areas of open grassland, or plains, which were necessary to sustain the commoners' livestock, particularly given the density of the wood-pasture. The only serious damage suffered by the forest prior to 1878 was the construction of a turnpike road in 1830-4, which has subsequently brought the menace of motor traffic through its length. Fortunately the Conservators (the body responsible for the Forest) were able to ensure that when the M25 was built, it passed beneath the forest in a cut and cover tunnel.

Examination of pollen and radiocarbon dating of sediments preserved in a shallow valley bog have yielded valuable evidence of the Forest's composition and evolution over the last 4,000 years. From the Neolithic to the early Saxon period it comprised lime-dominated woodland, and despite the presence of two hill forts on the Forest ridge, Ambresbury Banks and Loughton Camp, the woodland cover

Epping Forest as depicted on Chapman and André's map of 1777. Note the wide areas of open grassland

High Beach
Green

Beak Hill

Lipped Hill

Sewardstone
Green

Silver Street

New Lodge

Mutton Row

Sewardston Bury

H A M

Loughton Street

High Standing

The New Deer

Fairmaid Bottom

Chingford
Fairmaid Bottom

Tan Hills

Bucket Green

Queen Elizabeth
Lodge

The Roe Buck

Chingford Green

Bucket Hill

110M

R E D

The Lodge
Kings Place

Pimps Hall

White Hall

The Bald Stag

Friday Hill

Monkham

Chingford Hatch

Lane Farm

Lixbord

Woodford

Wells

110M

Roger

Prospect House

Chigwell

Taver

Rawl House

Woodford Row

Higham
Hill

The Leas

Jam Wright Hill

Woodf

Green

Woodf

persisted through the Iron Age and Roman period. During the middle Saxon period, 600-850 AD, there was selective forest clearance and a dramatic decline in lime, which became extinct in the Forest. It appears that this period saw the establishment of a wood-pasture system, with the ridge an area of intercommoning and a source of timber and underwood. The manors were sited along the main lines of communication in the valleys, with their boundaries stretching up to the poorer soils of the ridge. The familiar beech-birch and oak-hornbeam associations, familiar today, date only after this phase.[27]

In his guidebook, faced with the decline of the traditional Forest management practices - lopping and grazing - Buxton recounts the situation to be faced and describes the reasoning for the principles set out and the management decisions that followed. He disliked tidiness, and in a passage reminiscent of today's conservation priorities, he argued for the retention of dead, decaying and fallen trees, 'fallen giants, gorgeous with moss and lichen, and telling the story of mighty hurricanes and snowstorms that we should miss if they were removed'. But with pollards, he had a problem, for to him and his contemporaries they were essentially artificial, and the remaining areas of intensive lopping may well have appeared as over-intensive, semi-industrial landscapes.

Buxton quotes an observer writing in 1864. 'They are not, strictly speaking, trees at all, but strange, fantastic vegetable abortions. Their trunks, seldom more than a foot or eighteen inches in diameter, are gnarled, writhed, and contorted, and at about six feet from the ground, just within reach of the axe, they spread into huge overhanging crowns, from which spring branches which are cut every other year or so, and never long escape the despoiler......It is no more nature's notion of primeval woodland than are closely-cropped hair and shaven lip and chin her intention for the real expression of the human face.' This was the view that prevailed and it was decided that drastic thinning was needed to allow the lateral growth of the branches (lopping had by then ceased), and to permit light to reach the floor to stimulate undergrowth and seedlings. As a consequence thousands of pollards were removed to allow the remainder to grow up to form 'high forest'. But Buxton seems to have had some doubts, referring elsewhere to 'old oak pollards and the venerable air their ancient boles give to this wood', and he expressed his admiration for the great hornbeam pollards in Hatfield Forest.

In recent years we have come to see pollards very differently and view anthropomorphic attitudes to trees with suspicion; after all, humans do not benefit from lopping, but it appears that many broadleaved trees find it invigorating. The biological properties and qualities were not known in 1884. A new view suggests that 'pollards are often of great age and archaeological interest as survivors of an ancient form of tree management. With other very old trees, their bizarre shapes and enormous girth are part of the romantic delight of the countryside. They are an important habitat for hole-nesting birds and certain insects and lichens; their dry hollow interiors are particularly important as bat roosts because other sites are fast being lost to bats. Fascinating plant communities - including other trees - often

Pollard management. The upper branches were lopped by the commoners for sale as faggots, the lower ones gave cover and browsing for the king's deer, and the bole (trunk) belonged to the lord of the manor. Where pollards occured in hedges on farmland, the branches customarily were cropped for fuel by the tenant, while the bole belonged to the landowner

grow in their crowns. Ancient trees should be treated with the respect due to historical monuments. Most pollards, though hollow, are stable and have a long future life'.[28]

This discussion of pollards, and acknowledgement of their importance as landscape features, is relevant to Essex as a whole. They often occur in hedgerows on farmland where the local custom allowed the tenant to coppice or trim the hedge for firewood while the standard timber trees remained the property of the landowner. Pollards were a compromise whereby the bole belonged to the landlord while the tenant cropped the branches. Pollards are rare in the landscapes of late enclosure which predominate in the midland counties.

Returning to Epping Forest, the management adopted following the thinning of the pollards was generally laissez-faire. In the century following the canopies have grown up to meet and shade out the ground flora. In many cases the trees have thrown buttresses to support the weight of the 'groves' of upward-growing branches springing from their overloaded crowns. They are a most romantic sight - in some glades one feels surrounded by an Ent army straight from the pages of Tolkien - but it is a magnificent landscape in its final stage; the trees are even aged and vulnerable to windthrow, and the succession could be to the plebeian secondary woodland familiar on many commons, and indeed on the plains, where the decline of grazing has had just this effect.

The Conservators and their staff are fully aware of these problems, and also that the sheer size of the Forest means that for them a problem will be at least tenfold that which may be encountered by managers of other commons. Undaunted, they have embarked on extensive experiments in re-pollarding, a skill that has had to be relearnt and is far from simple, and creating new pollards from young trees; tracts of scrub have been cleared and in 1995 at Long Running fencing allowed the

introduction of Longhorn cattle with the result that grazing is successfully check-
ing the bracken and purple moor grass and so allowing the heather and associated
heath plants to re-establish. These works would seem very much in the spirit with
which Buxton approached the Forest, and all who care about the historic landscape will wish the Conservators well.

A long ridge marks the southern limit of the Wooded Hills, below which lies the
South Essex Plain. The juncture has been emphasized by the construction of the
London to Southend railway which opened in 1886, and in the 1930s by the
Southend Arterial Road. These features obscure the traditional pattern of land
tenure and management which consisted of a series of narrow, parallel parishes
on a north-south axis which formed a part of the land allotment systems which
have been discussed earlier. Similar parallel dispositions occur in other parts of
England, where at some distant time, an overall authority existed able to allot a
share of the different resources - woodland, pasture and arable - in roughly equal
quantities to each community. The parish of Childerditch is typical, with the terrain dropping from 100m in the north to 6m in the south. The hall and church are
sited where the slope of the ridge is dissected by small valleys and the natural
drainage would be conducive to arable farming, while to the north lies
Childerditch Common, an area of wood-pasture covering the high ground. To the
south, the parish extends across the heavy clays to an area of former wetland,

Beech pollards near High Beach recall an Ent army from the pages of Tolkien

Childerditch Fen. In 1086 the Childerditch manors held detached areas of sheep pasture on the coastal marshes.[29]

Others in the sequence of parishes, Great and Little Warley to the east of Childerditch, and the Horndons to the west, follow a distinctly similar form and although less distinct, similarities can be seen in the parishes lying north of the Crouch from the Bursteads to Woodham Ferrers. The organization of parishes dates from the Middle Ages, but in these cases it appears that they follow the boundaries of the original estates established in the land allotment. By 1066 Childerditch had already been subdivided into three holdings, which suggests it had been in existence for some time. This seems to point to the middle Saxon period, although this may not preclude yet earlier origins.

In the area known as High Wood, on the northern edge of the Wooded Hills, lies the former royal forest of Writtle. Of a similar size to Hatfield, it is small in comparison to Epping. The soils are very poor, consisting of glacial outwash over Bagshot Beds, formerly covered with lightly wooded heathland and lying over the least productive land of the huge royal manor of Writtle. Wood-pasture, exclusive to the king or his tenant, was established in the park, whose boundaries can still be seen, and an assart was made to support a hermitage. But otherwise the land

A field maple at Downham; with a girth of fourteen feet six inches (4.42m), it is registered as the champion for Britain

remained a common, and when the woodlands were embanked to form the horn-beam springs and alder slades, the commoners retained rights of grazing. A stretch of Roman road, Mapletree Lane, survives as a bridleway and there are relict greens. It seems very remote, a mysterious and beautiful tract of country.

The parish of Downham lies to the north of the Crouch and the church stands on the crest of the ridge overlooking south Essex. A few years ago, a fine seventeenth century dovecot was moved to a site adjoining the church and, while exploring the field behind, I found a giant pollard field maple growing on the churchyard boundary. Being hollow, its age is unknown but must be considerable, and with a girth of 14 feet 6 inches (4.42m) it is now registered as the champion for Britain.[30] Its rival, a foot less in girth, grows in Hatfield Forest, and it seems fitting that a tree so characteristic of Essex hedgerows should have its champions here.

The former heathlands

Northwards, the Wooded Hills merge into an area of low relief with light, often sandy, soils which stretches around Colchester to reach the edge of the Stour Valley. It is the region of Essex where the landscape has most changed, and much of it would be unrecognizable to an inhabitant of the eighteenth century were he to be transported to it today. The extensive heaths are depicted on Chapman and André's map of 1777, with farms and smallholdings abutting the edges, much as they do elsewhere along the margins of greens and common land. A great ramified network, Tiptree Heath, which stretched northwards from Heybridge to Messing and eastwards to the Tolleshunts and Wigboroughs, was intercommoned by the inhabitants of fourteen parishes, whose rights extended to estovers of trees and underwood. The village of Tiptree, famous for its jams, did not exist in 1777.

Heaths ringed Colchester like a necklace. To the west lay Stanway and Lexden, and to the north, Bergholt, Mile End, Boxted and Dedham. To the east were Ardleigh, Crockleford, Whitmore, Wivenhoe, Elmstead and Alresford, with Old Heath Common lying on the west side of the Colne. To the south were Layer and Donyland. All succumbed to the mania for enclosing heaths and commons at the turn of the 18th to 19th centuries, doubtless to grow corn of indifferent quality.

The heaths of 1777 generally followed the boundaries that had been established by 1300, although some internal enclosures, particularly on Tiptree, may have taken place subsequently. At an earlier time the heaths may well have been more extensive, for the fourteenth century was a time of pressure to bring land into cultivation. One may wonder whether, at a much earlier time still, there was an overlay of better soils which degraded under farming, as happened on some Surrey heaths, and whether Cunobelin might have looked out from the ramparts of Camulodunum onto the heathland landscape that still survived at Lexden in 1777. It would have been ideal ground for chariot deployment. At present there is a lack of the environmental evidence that might give answers.

In between the former heaths one finds winding lanes and relicts of the medieval landscape which once linked the tracts of open land. Over the areas once covered by the heaths, however, we now see the boring landscape of late enclosure, with straight roads and lanes and straight, species-poor hedges. Of their former appearance, no pictorial evidence survives, as it does in Norfolk in the works of the Norwich School. John Constable went to Hampstead to depict a heath, for those in Essex had already gone. For some idea of these lost landscapes, we should perhaps turn to the great Dutch painters of the seventeenth century, Jacob van Ruisdael and Meindert Hobbema, who depicted their similar heathlands with studied accuracy.

Landscape after Hobbema (Essex County Council)

Hornbeam pollards in Hatfield Forest

The Essex Till

This region comprises at least one third of Essex and consists of a thick till of chalky boulder clays deposited by the Anglian ice sheet over the series of terraces (Kesgrave Sands and Gravels) left by earlier courses of the River Thames. The melting occurred around 430,000 BP and gave rise to the drainage system of rills and watercourses we see today. Initially the rivers flowed 20-30m above their present levels, gradually cutting through the Kesgraves, sometimes to reveal the underlying London Clay, to form the familiar valleys and alluvial floodplains. The topography between the valleys is one of dissected plateaux, with occasional deposits of glacial sands and gravels and loess lying on the watersheds, sometimes clothed by ancient woodland. Although the soils are highly variable, the chalk content renders them naturally fertile, their fecundity reflected by an ear of barley depicted on late Iron Age coins, and the large number of villa sites attest to its prosperity in Roman times. Due to a slight southward tilt downward, the valleys to the north are more deeply cut and topographically interesting, and those to the south broad and stately.

From the Neolithic to the Bronze Age the Till appears to have remained a vast wooded game preserve where Mesolithic practices continued on a seasonal basis. Environmental evidence from a palaeochannel at Stebbingford showed high frequencies of charcoal, which may result from deliberate woodland burning to stim-

34

Oak wood-pasture in Hatfield Forest

ulate regrowth.[31] In the late Bronze Age the fringes of the Till were being colonized by farmers, and by the Roman period the heavy but fertile soils were tamed.

The subsequent settlement pattern is scattered and diverse although not sparse, and the forms taken will be considered later. Rivers are frequently the boundaries of parishes, which then stretch upwards onto the plateau to reach a boundary along the watershed. Manorial centres with their churches tend to be sited on a terrace beside a river crossing or on a springline above, with cultivation extending over the plateau when the population was high, and receding when it fell, the further land becoming 'waste' - rough pasture and woodland. While this model applies to many riparian parishes, others on the broader stretches of plateau follow different forms, and the variety evident in adaption to geography is also to be seen in the variation with which the pattern of settlement developed within each parish.

Landscape features relate closely to topography and soil type, and suggest evolution and slow change over a long period of time. Roads and lanes are rarely straight, and have variable verges: wide on flat land, where in the days before roads were metalled, wheeled traffic sought to avoid the muddy centre, and narrow and banked on the slope. Sunken lanes, sometimes spectacular, are to be found on the steeper valley sides, formed through the process of slow erosion by frost, hoof and wheel, with the spoil washed down and away by storm water. Often the depth is enhanced by lynchets, the banks formed by the downslope shift of soil loosened by ploughing.

The maintenance of roads was a somewhat haphazard business until the early 19th century, when metalling techniques advocated by J L McAdam (d.1836) came to be adopted, which involved successive rolled layers of broken stone or gravel of even size. It was decided at that time that certain lanes were little used and could be left as they were. These are the grass roads or green lanes, now generally graded as byways, which are often striking features of the landscape, forming green tunnels through the countryside. There is even the occasional 'blue' lane where the ancient road is also the course of a brook.

Hedges tend to be species-rich as the alkaline soils favour a wide range. The rule of thumb, by which the number of species in an average 30 yard length of a given hedge are indicative of its age in centuries, seems to work well. A survey over the Tabor estate (mostly in Bocking) covering 1,971 acres (798ha), analysed all the hedges with the following result:[32]

	km	miles
Saxon and early medieval (pre 1350)	11.99	7.19
Late medieval and Tudor (1350-1600)	17.12	10.64
Later or undateable	10.74	6.68
Total	**39.85**	**24.51**

The older hedges often follow manorial and farm boundaries, trackways and changes in soil type, tend to be sinuous and are never dead straight. Field maple is ubiquitous, and oak and hazel frequent. Pollards occur in many areas, depending on local custom. Some hedges can be identified as former woodland boundaries, retained when the land beyond was cleared, and here one may find hornbeam, the woodland thorn, and occasionally lime.

In the years following the Agriculture Act 1950, the Till changed from a region of mixed farming to one predominantly arable. Fields were enlarged and this required the removal of many hedges. There was no awareness then of the age and interest of many hedges, and their removal was urged by the ministry advisers, armed with substantial grants. Modernisation and monoculture were the flavour of the time and in retrospect, the role of government in pursuing policies for the countryside in which no factor other than production was considered can be seen as disgraceful. Fortunately, although some farmers did as they were urged, others were more circumspect and it is due to them that much of the Till remained a landscape of high quality. It must be remembered, particularly at the time of writing, that traditional field sports were an important factor. No cover means no game birds, and the foxes would flee to the towns.

The 1950s and 1960s were particularly destructive decades, but in a historical perspective, the density of hedgerow cover can be seen to ebb and flow. Huge fields existed on the demesne farms of the early Middle Ages, which were then subdivided and narrow belts of woodland along field boundaries became fashionable. By the late eighteenth century these springs and shaws were out of vogue and, together with many other small woods and roadside greens, were grubbed up to grow corn. Common fields based on hamlets became divided up into the tiny closes depicted on the tithe maps, and in due course these were found to be uneconomic and the pendulum swung back to favour large fields.

At its best the Till is a fascinating and mysterious landscape with the subtle quality that is found in ancient countryside. Oxlip woods, winding lanes, rich hedgerows that may once have bounded deer parks or woodlands, pollards, lost hamlets and moated sites, mill dams hidden in woods and mill mounds, are all a part of its fabric. The species-rich hedgerows are a particular delight, with hazel catkins in January, bullace and cherry plum flowering in March, the floral sequence continues to privet and elder in June. In the autumn come hips and spindleberries, and the rich colouring of field maple and oak. Sometimes the single trees, hedgerows and woodlands coalesce in the distance to form a wooded skyline, suggesting one is still in an area of ancient forest clearance.

An example of the historic interest to be found is Brickles Wood, the largest of a group of ancient woods lying across the parish boundary between Little Laver and Abbess Roding. Brickles (or Brick kiln) adjoins Rookwoodhall Wood which belonged to the large moated manor of that name, sited half a mile to the east. Across the parish boundary, Brickles abuts the former deer park belonging to the manor of Little Laver, part of whose boundary survives with a depression indicating an internal ditch. No record of a royal licence to impark exists so it may be that the owner took a risk, trusting in the park's remoteness to escape detection. A later owner, probably in Tudor times, abandoned the old hall near the church and built a new hall in the park, itself rebuilt in the last century. In the field pattern depicted on the first edition OS six inch map (surveyed 1874), one can discern former woodland boundaries and the 'z' kinks indicative of earlier strip farming. In the second world war, the construction of Matching Airfield erased the landscape to the north and a small outlying wood, but a series of bomb storage bays hidden in the woods have added a further layer of historic interest.

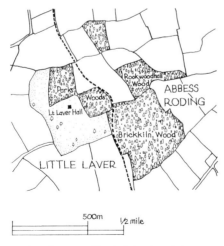

Brickles Wood; a group of ancient woodlands lying in Little Laver and Abbess Roding

Hatfield Forest: a group of hornbeams which have responded well to re-pollarding after after a gap of about 50 years

The decision to develop Stansted as London's third airport was followed by a full archaeological investigation of 1,500 acres (600 ha) of land, and has resulted in a better understanding of the settlement and landscape history of the Till. The whole area was field walked, and the number of known sites increased from five to twenty five. It was established that woodland clearance and settlement was taking place on the edge of the plateau in the late Bronze Age, and a complete Iron Age village was excavated, sited well into the plateau; by the Roman period the area was extensively settled and farmed.[33]

Epping and Writtle Forests have been described briefly above. Hatfield Forest is even more remarkable; its historian, Oliver Rackham, has written 'Hatfield is of supreme importance in that all the elements of a medieval Forest survive: deer, cattle, coppice woods, pollards, scrub, timber trees, grassland and fen, plus a seventeenth-century lodge and rabbit warren. As such it is almost certainly unique in England and possibly in the world........ Hatfield is the only place where one can step back into the Middle Ages to see, with only a small effort of the imagination, what a Forest looked like in use'.[34] These words are even truer today than when they were when written in 1976, for the National Trust has revived pollarding and extended traditional management practices throughout the Forest.

It was not always so. Until Dr Rackham researched the Forest, its value as an historic landscape was not understood and the Trust had no solid base on which to reach decisions which were sometimes, it can be seen with hindsight, wrong. It is to its great credit that it responded to new knowledge so promptly. It may be recalled that at that time the concept of historic landscapes, other than parks and gardens by known designers, was new and often resisted. The Forestry Commission, for example, was very reluctant to accept the protection of ancient woodlands. But the concept that positive traditional management was the right way to conserve historic features was gaining ground, and laissez-faire was becoming discredited.

There is much that is traditional but new to be seen at Hatfield: the conversion of areas of self-sown trees and scrub to wood-pasture, the de-canalization of the Shermore Brook; but it is the huge hornbeam and oak pollards of Bush End Plain, admired by Buxton, that never cease to amaze. The skills required to manage these living monuments have had to be rediscovered, and in the early days there were some failures, but we now see many with twenty years of regrowth, and it seems that, with this regenerative treatment, these ancients will have many further years of life. To ensure a more distant future, many young trees have also been pollarded.

Hatfield Forest: an ancient hornbeam, its life prolonged by successful re-pollarding

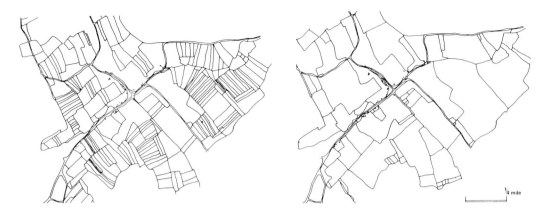

Maps of Langley in the Essex Record Office show both enclosure and pre-enclosure in 1851. The latter shows areas of strips surviving and also many that have been consolidated into fields, and were then retained in the post-enclosure landscape

The chalk uplands

In the extreme north-west of the county, the underlying chalk emerges in the valley of the Cam and its lateral rills, and on the escarpment along the boundary with Cambridgeshire. Large common-fields developed here, and were enclosed late, in the eighteenth and nineteenth centuries. The commissioners' awards may be studied in the Essex Record Office. But while this landscape was traditionally more open than the Till countryside, a skim of clays on the higher land developed features that are more characteristic of Essex than of neighbouring south Cambridgeshire, where the landscape of late enclosure dominates. Winding lanes survive unstraightened, there are dispersed hamlets and greens, and ancient woodlands. Enclosure award maps show the landscape as it would be after implementation, but an exception is Langley, for which a pre-enclosure map also survives.[35] Dating from 1851, it shows the extensive survival of strips, but also many consolidated holdings which were retained in the post-enclosure landscape. The pattern of fields has similarities to many areas of the Till where early enclosure took place by agreement.

Only one parish, Great Chesterford, is truly on the 'Midland' model, being fully open-field until enclosure in 1804, with a nucleated village and no hamlets and greens. Appropriately, it lies on the county boundary at the head of the Cam valley, where 'woodland' Essex meets 'champion' south Cambridgeshire - a boundary between two worlds.[36] The Romans saw the site as a key position and built two successive walled towns, over whose remains the later villagers farmed their

Borough Field. In 1719 Stukeley saw the husbandmen walking to their strips along the dry causeway formed by the foundations of the town walls - the Borough Bank.[37] From the valley floor, the well-drained chalk slopes rose to the clay plateau, on which were the woodlands, common and park (licensed 1303).

The importance of the Stansted Project to the understanding of early settlement and landscapes on the Till has been referred to. A very substantial area (28 square kilometres), mostly to the west of the Cam, was fieldwalked by Tom Williamson between 1979 and 1982 in a project to elucidate the development of settlement. His conclusions were illuminating. He found 34 probable Iron Age settlements, which he thought probably an underestimate. They tended to cluster near the junction of the heavy plateau soils with the freely draining clay and chalk soils on the valley sides - a pattern which continued. On the plateau he found evidence for fairly evenly dispersed settlement and concluded that by the end of the Iron Age the area was already extensively deforested, even on the level interfluvial areas.[38]

Evidence for settlement and landuse became much clearer for the Roman period owing to the large quantity of pottery in use, and the fact that settlement sites are marked by concentrations of rubble as well as sherd scatters. Some 35 probable sites were found, although not necessarily all occupied at the same time. Allowing for other known sites, such as the villa at Wendens Ambo, and other possible sites lying under non-arable land, this suggests a density of 1.2 sites per square kilometre in the mid first century rising to 1.3 by the end of the fourth. As in the Iron Age, settlements were most numerous on the margins, and these sites were larger, longer-lived, and probably of higher status than those more evenly and sparsely scattered over the heavier clays of the plateau. Williamson considered that the evidence strongly suggested that the Roman landscape of north-west Essex was very extensively cleared; it may have carried less woodland than in the eighteenth and nineteenth centuries, and even the heaviest clays were at least sporadically under arable cultivation.[39]

Evidence for Saxon settlement is much sparser, and while allowing for the difficulties in identifying Saxon sherds and the possibility of aceramic phases, it appears that population levels fell and settlement retreated. Domesday Book shows the area rather less intensively farmed and settled, and certainly less extensively cleared, than it had been in the Roman period. While little woodland is recorded for manors lying mainly on the lighter valley soils, abundant reserves are recorded for those on the heavy soils of the plateau, much of this growing over abandoned Roman farmland and settlements.

In the twelfth and thirteenth centuries the population rose and land was reclaimed, leading to a dense and varied settlement pattern. Williamson found evidence for sites abandoned in the fourteenth and fifteenth centuries, when the population had fallen due to the Black Death, but although settlement contracted, the landscape remained farmed.

Two factors may have combined to make the area somewhat atypical in the Roman period. The presence of Great Chesterford, and its position on the road

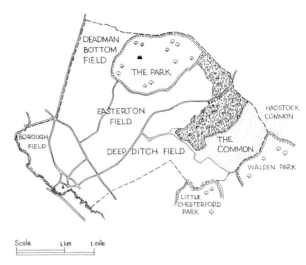

Great Chesterford parish circa 1600

network, may have influenced the extent of clearance for arable farming. Secondly, the deep dissection of the plateau by the Cam and its tributaries ensured numerous areas of chalk and well-drained clays, and limited the extent of more level and ill-drained soils. Nevertheless, the essential features - extensive Iron Age and Roman clearance, subsequent contraction of agricultural landuse, post-Roman continuity of settlement on the margins of the lighter soils, with discontinuity and mobility on the heavier clays - have a direct relevance to other areas of the Till. This should be borne in mind when, in a later chapter, we consider the development and expansion of settlements in the early Middle Ages. The clearance of woodland and waste at that time could sometimes, perhaps often, have been reclamation.

The Copped Hall Hills

This small area of attractive, rolling country is not strictly Till as it lies on London Clay, but situated between the River Lee and the Epping Forest Ridge it seems more a part of the dissected plateau than the Wooded Hills. For the westbound traveller on the M25 it is dominated by the noble shell of Copped Hall, whose former estate (but not the ruin) has been acquired by the Corporation of the City of London. This is most welcome as, together with the Warleys and Woodredon estate (inherited from the GLC), the Corporation now has a substantial purlieu of well managed countryside beside the Forest and its outlying greens and grass lanes. The character of the estates is that of late enclosure, the landscape of the eighteenth and nineteenth century, with spinneys and large fields, well fitted to the topography. But to the north of the village of Upshire, an area survives of small farms and irregular hedges, indicative of an earlier landscape that was once probably more general.

CHAPTER THREE

Emerging landscapes

AS WE HAVE seen earlier, it was only in the 1970s that the geology of the Quaternary in Essex came to be understood, mainly due to the attention given by geologists to sections revealed by boreholes and mineral extraction. Much the same
can be said of the prehistory of the county, which as late as 1970 was thought to
begin effectively in the late Iron Age with the dykes and tumuli at Lexden and a
few hillforts elsewhere although the great quantity of Bronze Age objects in
museum collections told a different story and the important remains of submerged landscapes on foreshores from Clacton to Dovercourt had been studied in
the 1930s. From the late 1950s Felix Erith and the Colchester Archaeological Group
were carefully excavating and recording the great Bronze Age cemetery at
Ardleigh, and work was in progress on the multi-period site at Mucking which
had been revealed by aerial photography, but nevertheless the general perception
was still of a region covered by dense woodland and marsh, with little or no settlement; immigrants, if they came, headed westwards along the river valleys in
search of a friendlier landscape. For the record of early peoples who had cleared,
settled and built monuments, one looked to the west, for it was there that their
sites had been studied; and understandably so, given the quantity of visible evidence and the spectacular nature of some of the monuments.

We now know that Essex is rich in the archaeology of these early cultures, and
the lack of visible monuments is due to a long history of cereal growing and a lack
of local stone to build megalithic structures that would daunt later ploughmen
and improvers. This change in our knowledge and perception of the prehistory of
Essex (and of much of eastern England) has come about for several reasons. First,
the development of aerial survey and photography in the service of archaeology
revealed the extensive cropmark evidence for settlements, field systems and monuments that hitherto had lain unknown and unexpected. The spectacular photograph of Mucking, taken in 1957, had pointed the way.[1] Secondly, the appointment
of a county archaeological officer and the establishment of an archaeological unit
by Essex County Council to co-ordinate work across the county, to establish a central Sites and Monuments Record, and to carry out excavation and recording
ahead of development.[2] Thirdly, close co-operation with environmental archaeologists, providing the analysis of faunal and botanical remains that is essential to
an understanding of past landscapes, and the interaction of humans with the natural environment.[3] Fourthly, the financial support given by agencies in both the
public and private sectors.[4] All of this has enabled the systematic excavation and
recording of sites under threat, some of which, Springfield Lyons and Elms farm,
Heybridge, for example, have proved to be of national importance. Most importantly, these sites have been studied in the context of their surrounding landscapes.

A problem for the interested follower of archaeological progress, and indeed for
archaeologists themselves, is making sense of the volume of information that has

A reconstruction of how the causewayed enclosure at Orsett may have looked around 3,400 BC, based on excavations by Essex County Council and the analysis of aerial photographs by the Royal Commission on the Historical Monuments of England. Watercolour by Frank Gardiner

become available since the early 1970s, particularly considering the blank that the Neolithic and Bronze Age formerly presented in Essex. This was addressed by the publication of a comprehensive series of papers delivered at the Clacton Conference in 1978, and at Writtle in 1993, which summarized the state of archaeological knowledge of the county at those dates.[5] In addition to the wealth of information gained from sites under threat, there have been opportunities for research, notably the study of the Essex coast - a massive achievement embracing present and past coastlines and foreshores, and spanning the period from the early Flandrian to the Middle Ages.[6]

So Essex is no longer the prehistoric lacuna it once was. Landscapes are emerging, many still foggy but others with a surprising clarity, particularly along the coast and on well-drained inland sites which were attractive to early farmers. Certain landscapes where monuments were erected seem to have been regarded as special places, and remained respected by later generations and cultures. The earliest monuments, causewayed enclosures, of which there are examples at Springfield and Orsett, were erected around 3,000 BC and continued in use for a further millennium. At Orsett, early Saxon burials were deliberately placed in the enclosure, indicating that the earthworks were still visible and respected - after a timespan of some 3,500 years. At Springfield Lyons a Bronze Age ring monument was constructed beside the causewayed enclosure, and unusually it had six points of entry, perhaps reflecting the discontinuous geometry of the earlier monument. In the Iron Age and Roman periods there were ritual depositions and an early Saxon cemetery followed where the distribution of graves and cremations again suggest that the earthworks were visible and that this was a venerated site. At Ardleigh, the Bronze Age cemetery was in use from 1,500 to 1,000 BC - a maze of tightly packed barrows. Farmers of the Roman period ignored it and placed their own dead well away, but early Saxons placed their burials within the cemetery, perhaps bestowing legitimacy to a new social order by reference to an ancient past. At Brightlingsea, another Bronze Age cemetery was sited 500 metres from a Neolithic ring ditch monument, erected 1,000 to 1,500 years earlier.

These examples show a continuity and respect for the monuments of former times, their possible power and the legitimacy they might confer. But it seems to have ended with conversion to Christianity and the establishment of new centres to address the numinous - the old monuments were redundant and no longer safe from ploughmen and levellers. On the other hand, Bede relates that Gregory the Great instructed his missionaries to Kent to convert pagan shrines where possible to Christian use, and the Northumbrian mission who converted the royal house of the East Saxons, themselves deriving from the Irish church, would have been familiar with this practice. Consequently one may wonder whether some Essex churches have an earlier provenance as sacred sites. There are the hilltop churches of south Essex where the manor was perhaps sited beside the church rather than vice versa as elsewhere. There are the sarsen stones which lie around and beneath Alphamstone church, and the circular graveyards of Great Waltham and Chipping Hill, Witham, which has been suggested as a Springfield type ring monument.[7] It is a subject that remains open and interesting

The Neolithic and Bronze Age

With the retreat of the last cold phase, tundra gave way to successive stages of colonization as plant species migrated into Britain as they had done previously in interglacials when the climate warmed. Eventually a climax cover of temperate deciduous woodland became established, with lime dominant, followed by oak and hazel, with alder on the damper soils. In the course of the fourth millennium BC gaps began to appear in the woodland cover, the work of early farmers, selecting sites on well-drained land to clear for crops and pasture. A cluster of these farms has been excavated on the gravel terraces that lie to the north of Heybridge, above the Blackwater estuary, and it is evident that the inhabitants pursued a hunter-gathering economy as well as farming - the Mesolithic and Neolithic economies had merged. The implication is of cultural assimilation rather than the displacement of existing people by incomers. Numerous spreads of charcoal around the Essex coast suggest deliberate burning, a 'Mesolithic' practice designed to open up the woodland floor to the light, so promoting fresh growth and a wide range of plants and animals.[8]

Around 3,000 BC these people were building monuments. At Orsett and Springfield, causewayed enclosures have been excavated; their purpose remains mysterious, although excavations elsewhere have suggested that they were locations for seasonal feasting, and this would fit with a ceremonial function - the nature of their geometry precludes a defensive purpose - and ceremonies to ensure fertility, supplies of game, and celebration of the harvest seem likely. It also seems probable that they defined territories, and may have been centres for the exchange of stock, seed-corn and the more durable goods, a vital role within a community or between neighbouring communities.[9]

The Springfield enclosure lies on a gravel spur, bounded by two streams, overlooking the Chelmer valley at a point where the River Chelmer turns sharply away from the northerly course it has been following after merging with the Can, to flow eastwards through a gap in the hills. The monument would thus be a focal point in the landscape for people travelling upriver from the Blackwater estuary. Due south of the enclosure lay another monument that was either a long barrow or a long mortuary enclosure. It is only known as a cropmark on an early air photograph and unfortunately it was destroyed before its existence was detected. Directly aligned on the barrow lay a cursus, 670m long by 40m wide, and together the two monuments cut off the neck of a spur within a broad loop of the Chelmer.[10] The spur is a gravel terrace, lying just above the floodplain. The river still floods despite canalization and drainage works, and in the Neolithic, winter floods may have been even more extensive, with the spur surrounded by flood water on three sides. The view south from the Springfield enclosure at midwinter, with the rising sun reflected in frozen floodwater around the monuments, must have been spectacular.[11]

Fortunately there was the opportunity to carry out excavations on the cursus ahead of development for housing. Ceramic fragments suggest that it was constructed in the later half of the third millennium BC, and although this was later than the Springfield causewayed enclosure, there appears to have been a considerable overlap in the period of time in which each was in active use. Traditionally, cursus monuments are thought to have been used for processional ceremonies, and at Springfield there is strong circumstantial evidence for an association with the disposal of the dead. Besides the mortuary enclosure (or long barrow), there is a burial within a segmental ring-ditch, partly cut into the southern cursus ditch, and in the Bronze Age the site became a focus for the construction of round barrows. The Springfield cursus is the only confirmed monument of this type in Essex, but another is sited just over the Suffolk border, at Bures St Mary beside the River Stour.

The Springfield monuments comprise a complex ritual landscape, a focal point for hunting parties from the Blackwater estuary and its farmed hinterlands, travelling to the game rich woodlands of the Boulder Clays. Springfield lies near the

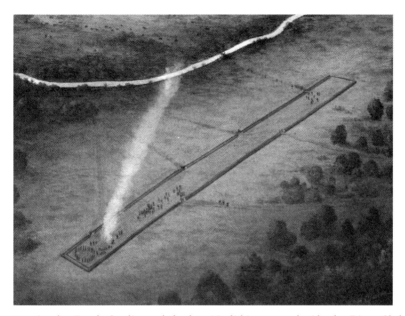

A reconstruction by Frank Gardiner of the late Neolithic cursus beside the River Chelmer at Springfield, based on excavations by Essex County Council

edge of the plateau, strategically close to the confluence of the Chelmer and Can, rivers that would have provided routeways into the wooded interior. While there is no evidence for settlement on the plateau in this period, finds of worked flints are widespread and indicate activity that is most likely to be that of roving seasonal groups.

The causewayed enclosure at Orsett occupied a similar focal point, with the wooded London Clays and Orsett Fen to the north and west, and the gravel and brickearth terraces of the Thames to the south and east. Another ritual landscape, simpler than Springfield, has emerged at Rivenhall where a mortuary enclosure (or long barrow) on an east-west alignment lay at the centre of an arc formed by a gravel spur above a bend in the River Blackwater. Altogether, thirteen long mortuary enclosures have now been identified in Essex by aerial photography.[12]

In the wider landscape, evidence for settlement in the Middle and Late Bronze Age (c1,500-700 BC) is extensive, particularly on the light, well-drained soils in the southern half of the county, which were the first choice for farming. The woodland edge was retreating to the London Clays. The fringes of the Boulder Clay plateau were also coming under pressure. At Stansted Airport, on the edge of the Stort valley, an interesting site was excavated, yielding evidence for a settlement and a drove road and preserved pollen levels which showed a reduction in tree pollen around 1,350 BC, particularly lime. The implication is for clearance of tree cover on the plateau fringes for arable and stock farming where streams provided a varied topography. It was a trend which would continue.

47

Systems of ditched rectangular fields have been identified at North Shoebury and also at Mucking, where the fields predate the later Bronze Age circular enclosures.[13] A different landscape, stretching south-east from Cressing to Rivenhall and Witham, has been revealed by cartographical analysis and may date from this time. In the early Middle Ages this was an extensive area of waste, intercommoned by tenants of the adjacent manors, except for the northern part which was reclaimed in the thirteenth century by the Knights Templar for their demesne farm based on Cressing Temple.[14] Long boundary ditches survived under rough grazing and wood pasture with related trackways, and it appears that these formed the framework for the Templars' huge fields. The remaining common was reclaimed and enclosed piecemeal in later centuries, but still with regard for these features.

The light soils of north-east Essex saw the development of a remarkable group of cremation cemeteries, or urnfields - a better descriptive term - which flourished during the Middle Bronze Age (c 1,500-1,000 BC), of which those at Ardleigh and Brightlingsea survived most complete and have been excavated. They were shown to consist of maze-like concentrations of ring-ditches, with the urns carefully placed in the labyrinthine paths between. The Brightlingsea urnfield lies on a hilltop high above the Colne estuary, and some 500 metres from a large early Neolithic ring-ditch monument; it is a site with resonances which brings to mind Sutton Hoo, of very different date, but a place where the dead were remembered and with similar incongruous shelter-belts, planted about a century ago to mitigate the force of gales off the North Sea.[15]

The Late Bronze Age (1,000-700 BC) saw the construction of ditched circular enclosures, some of which have been excavated and many more provisionally identified from aerial photographs. These are now known as Springfield Type monuments after the Springfield Lyons site which was totally excavated in the 1980s.[16]. This was enclosed by a substantial ditch and internal bank, revetted with posts to form a raised rampart. A substantial gatehouse structure marked the principal entrance, from which one approached the porch of a large central roundhouse. Springfield differs from others of the type by having, most unusually, a discontinuous ditch which is crossed by six causeways. Given the robust defensive form of the rampart, it seems surprising that the monument should be weakened by the provision of six entrances, and while there is evidence for metal working, weaving and crop processing, it seems likely that it also had a ritual function and that its form intentionally echoed the long disused causewayed enclosure that it adjoined. This could account for the deliberate placing in the ditch of two huge assemblages of clay metal working moulds (one weighed 12 cwt), the largest found in the country.

An enclosure of similar date lies directly to the south, nearly three kilometres away at Baddow on the other side of the Chelmer and also overlooking the valley. Lacking a rampart it was not as grand as Springfield, but the pairing of the two enclosures is a feature found also at Mucking, in Thurrock cropmark sites and further north in East Anglia. The inhabitants of these sites were deeply involved in farming and other forms of production, but the monuments clearly had a ceremonial or symbolic function as well. When first detected on aerial photographs several were thought to be henges, ritual monuments of earlier date, and it is possible that an archaic form was consciously adopted as in the case of Springfield. These enclosures are merely the most conspicuous of a range of settlements now known to have existed over large areas of Essex at this time.[17]

The Iron Age

The pattern of an expanding population and the clearance of woodland to feed it continues on from the transition of the age of bronze to that of iron, around 700 BC, to create a landscape dominated by farming, both pastoral and tilled. As opportunities occur for excavation on more and more sites, the evidence confirms that of aerial photography which shows a widespread scatter of farmsteads, hamlets and villages, now extending onto the heavier soils of the Till.[18] Although for convenience the Iron Age and prehistory is taken to end with the successful conquest of southern Britain by the emperor Claudius in 43 AD, history had begun in Britain with Julius Caesar, who wrote accounts of his forays in 55 and 54 BC which include some interesting comments on the terrain and its features. His operations took him through Kent, Middlesex and Hertfordshire - which we may assume were not dissimilar to much of western and central Essex - where he concluded that the population was exceedingly large, the ground thickly studded with homesteads, closely resembling those of the Gauls, and the cattle were very numerous.[19]

Caesar describes the guerrilla tactics adopted by Cassivellaunus, the leader of the Britons who, abandoning the prospect of a pitched battle, retained a force of chariots - highly mobile and versatile light vehicles - to watch the line of march. 'He would retire a short way from the route and hide in dense thickets, driving the inhabitants and cattle from the open country into the woods wherever he knew we intended to pass. If ever our cavalry incautiously ventured too far away in plundering and devastating the country, he would send all his charioteers out of the woods by well-known lanes and pathways and deliver very formidable attacks[20]'. This might be termed successful damage limitation, but Caesar went on to assault Cassivellaunus' stronghold, which was protected by forests and marshes, of great natural strength and excellently fortified. It is generally considered to have been Wheathampstead, near St Albans, and from the description must have been similar to Camulodunum, the Essex capital of the Trinovantes.

He comments that the Britons applied the term 'strongholds'[21] to densely wooded spots fortified with a rampart and trench, to which they would retire in order to escape the attacks of invaders. Ambresbury Banks and Loughton Camp, deep in Epping Forest, fit this description. Excavations have shown that Ambresbury was a probable refuge for people and their livestock in times of danger, with no evidence of permanent occupation.[22] The 'strongholds' appear to be the Iron Age fortifications generally known as hillforts, although this might seem a misnomer for Essex where they are found on ridges and high ground, but hardly hills. A line of them follows a rough north-south line along the valleys of the Lea, Stort and Cam: the Epping Forest examples, Wallbury Camp in Little Hallingbury, Ring Hill in Littlebury, and possibly Grimsditch Wood in Little Walden.

In east Essex, excavations at Asheldham Camp on the Dengie peninsula revealed the buried soil surface below the rampart, which showed that the 'hillfort' was constructed in an open grassland landscape with little evidence for tree cover in the vicinity. Elm, later to be so dominant on the Dengie, was absent. Although up to 90 per cent of the interior had been lost to quarrying, there was evidence for occupation and a possible wooden granary.[23] It seems that Asheldham may have been more a fortified settlement than a refuge.

At Little Waltham, ahead of the construction of a bypass, Paul Drury excavated a nucleated village of roundhouses. At the heart of the settlement lay a square building interpreted as a shrine, a feature found in many similar sites in southern Britain. The site had no defences and, interestingly, ditches found by Drury extended beyond the site into field boundaries in the vicinity which are still in use today.[24] At the Airport Catering Site at Stansted, virtually an entire village was discovered and excavated. Sited well into the Till, it began as two roundhouses and by around 50 BC had evolved into a village defended by a ditch and rampart. The village concentrated on livestock husbandry with grain bought from elsewhere, but was sufficiently prosperous to import amphoras of Italian wine. As at Little Waltham the

An Iron Age village discovered at the Airport Catering Site, Stansted Airport. A reconstruction painting by Frank Gardiner of how it may have looked around 50 BC, based on excavations by Essex County Council

focus of the settlement was a square shrine, which survived the decline of the village, continuing as a focus for offerings into the early Roman period.[25]

The veneration for water - rivers, springs and wetlands - so evident in the Bronze Age and earlier, notably at Flag Fen near Peterborough, but found in Essex with the siting of the Springfield monuments, and the ritual depositions in the Blackwater and the platform at Fenn Creek, continues through the Iron Age into the Roman period. Sacred wetland sites at Harlow and Ivy Chimneys, Witham, would develop into cult centres with temples. But the attractive aspects of this respect for the natural world may be tempered by evidence from Essex sites for the cult of the severed head. A successful Iron Age farmer might have displayed a rather different trophy on his steading than the weather-vane with a leaping hare of the annual FWAG award for conservation and farming we see today.

Camulodunum

Caesar's excuse for his costly forays into Britain had been an appeal for aid in a tribal dispute between the Catuvellauni and the Trinovantes, a conflict subsequently resolved by the conquest of the latter, probably by Cunobelin, Shakespeare's Cymbeline, and a mighty figure. He ruled a powerful state, which achieved supremacy over the bellicose tribes of south-east Britain, and enjoyed diplomatic links with Rome which brought trade and the import of luxury goods, such as the amphoras found at Stansted. He issued a coinage of high quality and it is estimated that he struck around a million gold coins.[8] His reign has been described as the culmination of Essex prehistory.[26]

Cunobelin ruled from his home at Camulodunum (the stronghold of Camulus, god of war). His fortified homestead lay at Gosbecks, just over a mile and a half to the south of Lexden. It stood at the head of what might be described as a vast inland promontory fort of some fifteen square miles, bounded by the Colne and the Roman River. To the east, the Colne was tidal with extensive mudflats and saltings and higher, to the north, the river flowed through a wide floodplain which would have been a marsh at most times of year. The eastern length of the Roman River would have been a similar natural barrier, but to the west, to the south of Gosbecks, it was just a relatively steep river valley. Here, dense thicket would be the strategic answer, but it would require management. The lime-dominated woodlands around Ambresbury Banks might deter charioteers, but certainly not infantry. A defensive barrier in the Roman River valley would require the removal of all large shade creating trees, encouraging the growth of a dense maquis of thorny scrub and gorse which would flourish on these sandy soils, a very different landscape to the enchanting valley of today.[27]

Across the promontory between the two rivers, and extending up the valley sides to north and south beyond, lay a series of dykes (ditch and rampart) totalling twelve to fifteen miles in length, the longest system of earthworks known from prehistoric Britain. They varied in size, but excavation has shown that the combined bank and ditch of the later dykes would have presented an unbroken slope of some 25 feet

(8 m), an impossible obstacle for chariots.[28] The dykes would also have provided an effective deterrent to cattle raiders, and a further function, perhaps the most important, may have been prestige - the visible evidence of power and wealth, monumentally displayed. Weather conditions in the mid 1970s produced exceptional cropmarks, revealing the former landscape that lay beyond the entrance through the dykes: a mesh of small fields and droveways. The focal point was a native farmstead within a fortified enclosure similar to the one excavated at Stansted, but three times as big. To the north of it, a spring-fed pond supplied a small brook which flowed out through the entrance in the dykes to join the Roman River. Focal point, huge farmstead and sacred spring, the site was a fitting home for Cunobelin.

Gosbecks in his time would have been a major place of assembly, perhaps in the area to the north of the pond where the cropmarks peter out, and a centre for religious and administrative functions, markets and fairs. Luxury goods from the Roman world would have been distributed from here. The centre of industrial production and Cunobelin's mint were located at Sheepen, lying to the south of the Colne and immediately west of the future Roman town.

The status of Camulodunum was established well before Cunobelin's long reign which lasted from circa 10 to 40 AD. The Lexden Tumulus, a likely burial place of a native king, dates from the late first century BC, and the Stanway burials begin around that time. The Heath Farm Dyke appears to have been the earliest, dating maybe from about 25 BC, followed by the Lexden and Sheepen Dykes. Cunobelin himself may have been responsible for Kidman's and Prettygate Dyke in its original form.[29]

Spectacular burial sites have been excavated in recent years at Stanway, to the west of the entrance to Camulodunum. Set within large enclosures and filled with imported goods of the highest quality, these were the graves of members of the royal house and high ranking aides, but not of Cunobelin himself. It seems probable that his burial place was the site of the future Gosbecks temple which lay inside a great square enclosure to the north of the homestead. It had a substantial ditch, some eleven feet deep (3.6 m), and resembles a high status burial site excavated at St Albans, the only site of this kind known in Britain outside Colchester.[30]

The grave goods found at Stanway are indicative of a massive trade with the continent. Evidence of the type of ships which carried these goods has survived on two bronze coins minted at Camulodunum early in the reign of Cunobelin.[31] These depict a tall vessel with steep sides, a single mast and a flat keel, eminently suitable for negotiating the shallow waters of the Essex estuaries. The picture accords with Caesar's description of the ships of the Veneti, a tribe occupying southern Brittany. 'The Gauls' own ships were built and rigged in a different manner from ours. They were made with much flatter bottoms, to help them to ride shallow water caused by shoals or ebb-tides. Exceptionally high bows and sterns fitted them for use in heavy seas and violent gales, and the hulls were made entirely of oak, to enable them to stand any amount of shocks and rough usage[32]'. This reads like a specification for the cog which developed into the dominant cargo vessel of the northern waters in the thirteenth and fifteenth centuries.[33] The high freeboard of the cog, like the ships of the Veneti, gave a distinct advantage in battle when fighting was still hand-to-hand. Caesar had found this to be so with his shallow galleys and devised means to overcome the disadvantage.

The Veneti were the strongest of the maritime tribes of Gaul and carried on a considerable trade with Britain. Knowledge as early as 57 BC of Caesar's plans to invade Britain may have provoked the Veneti into revolt with the ensuing naval war, which ended in an act of genocide by the clement future dictator.

These Gallic cogs, sailing into the Colne estuary, would have seen marshlands grazed by great flocks of sheep, much as recorded a thousand years later in Domesday Book.[34] Beyond, above high tide levels, lay the smoking red hills of the salt producing industry, a product vital for preserving meat, curing fish and eels, and for making cheeses from sheep's milk. All of these products are known to have been exported in later centuries and it is reasonable to suppose that they did so in the late Iron Age, providing a substantial contribution to Cunobelin's wealth.

The Lexden dykes and the Roman remains in Colchester fascinated early antiquarians, and in this century, particularly in recent years, have enabled archaeologists to develop an insight into how the area evolved in the late Iron Age and the Roman centuries. A measured survey of the dykes was first made in 1722, and later in the century the eminent Essex historian Philip Morant brought them to the attention of William Stukeley, the leading field antiquarian of the time, who published his survey in 1769.[35] At that time, it should be remembered, there was no concept of prehistory other than references in Latin and Greek histories and geographies to the native tribes and their customs beyond the limits of the Empire. They concluded, not unreasonably, that the monuments were the work of Cunobelin; the Lexden Tumulus was his burial place, the triple dykes a circus or racetrack for charioteers, and a large depression, now believed to be a quarry, was an amphitheatre.

In Morant's time much of the dyke system lay undisturbed on Lexden Heath, but in 1835 a later historian of the county wrote that 'Ancient entrenchments may yet be traced on Lexden-heath, which have been in some places nearly obliterated by the enclosure and cultivation of this district.....These works might be traced for several miles some time ago, particularly towards Mersea Island'.[36]

In this century Colchester has been fortunate in the archaeologists its antiquities have attracted. Around 1920, Mortimer Wheeler and Henry Laver, a local archaeologist, identified the vaults of Colchester Castle as the sub-structure of the Temple of Claudius. Rex Hull, Curator of the Colchester and Essex Museum from 1927 to 1963, brought a permanent archaeological presence to the town, excavating Sheepen ahead of the Colchester by-pass, and recording all evidence coming to light not only of Iron Age and Roman Colchester but over the county as a whole. Christopher Hawkes maintained a lifetime's interest, particularly in the dating riddle posed by the Lexden Dykes. In more recent years Philip Crummy, director of the Colchester Archaeological Trust, has directed numerous excavations ahead of development in central Colchester and its environs, including the Stanway burials, and has synthesized the massive information now available to the archaeologist into a coherent account for the layman of those years when Camulodunum/Colchester was central to events in Britain, and has followed the subsequent history and fortunes of the town through the later Empire and Dark Ages into the early Middle Ages.[37]

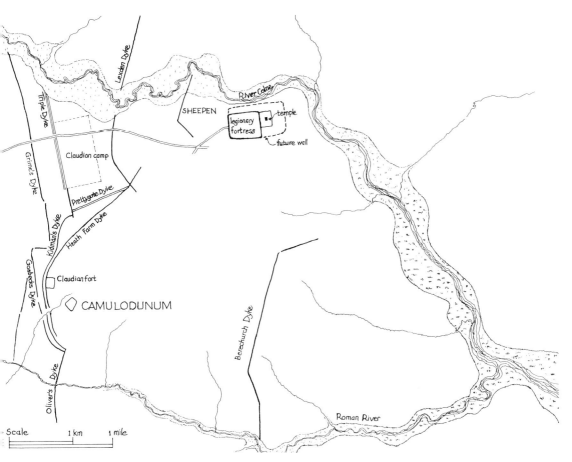

Camulodunum on the eve of Boudica's revolt of AD 60

CHAPTER FOUR

Roman Essex

IN AD 43 the Emperor Claudius launched an invasion intent on subduing the Britons and adding the island to the empire. His expedition met with success despite stiff opposition from the Catuvellauni-Trinovantes, and was joined by the Emperor himself, with reinforcements, for the capture of Camulodunum where he was formally saluted by the army as Imperator.[1] The ceremony with four legions, mounted auxiliaries and elephant corps on Lexden Heath, perhaps 30,000 men, must have been the most bizarre and spectacular tattoo seen in Essex before or since. Fortified politically by glory, the clash of arms and trumpetings of the elephants, Claudius returned to Rome. Legacies in the landscape of this event are the defences constructed by the legionaries around the army's encampment: westwards, the Triple Dykes, to the south, the reverse dyke paralleling Prettygate, and to the east, the existing Lexden Dyke.[2]

55

A small fort, known only from cropmarks, was built at Gosbecks abutting Heath Farm dyke, but the main permanent presence was a legionary fortress, constructed on the hilltop, south of the Colne and east of Sheepen. Its location, the site of future Colchester, tactfully away from the native capital of Camulodunum, suggests an accommodation with an element of the royal house, for high status burials continued at Stanway until AD 60.

A change in the treatment of the Trinovantes began after the invading force had departed, advancing far into midland, southern and western Britain. The legionary fortress became redundant and in AD 49 was converted into a colonia - a settlement for retired legionaries, intended to integrate them into civilian life and promote security - a long established practice. Colonia Victricensis initially proved a dismal failure in this respect, outraging those Trinovantes whose land was confiscated to provide the landholdings expected by the veterans. It has been estimated, on the basis of traditional allotments of this kind, that an area would be required equivalent to a circle around the town with a radius of 9 kilometres. Tacitus, the great Roman historian, describes the natives driven by the settlers from their homes and treated as prisoners and slaves. The huge temple being erected to Claudius (now divine) was seen as 'a blatant stronghold of alien rule, and its observances were a pretext to make the natives appointed as priests drain the whole country dry'.[3] Worse was to follow.

The Boudican Revolt

With the death of Claudius in AD 54 the Empire entered a phase of bad government. The youthful Emperor Nero had other interests, and the treatment of the Iceni tribe marked a return to the practices of the late Republic when ex-consuls saw the governorship of a province as a licence to plunder, a process winked at by their peers.[4] In AD 60 the procurator (imperial agent) was the greedy and incompetent Catus Decianus and the military governor, Suetonius Paulinus, was far away with the legions in Wales. Prasutagus, king of the Iceni, had willed half his estates to Nero in the hope that his wife and family would retain the rest. On his death, Decianus and his staff descended to pillage his kingdom, treating it as a conquered land. Leading Romans such as Seneca the Emperor's tutor, esteemed as a philosopher but venal, called in loans they had pressed on the inhabitants.[5]

Led by Boudica, Prasutagus' outraged widow, the tribe rose and marched on Camulodunum where, joined by dispossessed Trinovantes, they torched the Colonia Victricensis and massacred the inhabitants, continuing on to give the same treatment to London and St Albans, slaughtering every Roman and collaborator they could find. Paulinus returned, defeated Boudica, and pursued a policy of ferocious repression accompanied by famine. A new procurator, Classicianus, perceived that genocide was no solution and secured the replacement of Paulinus and the end of the revolt. Excavations in Colchester town centre have found a thick layer of incinerated debris, the 'Boudican destruction layer', preserving a rich seam of material from the everyday life of the town and evidence confirming the adaptation of the legionary fortress into the colonia.[6]

A policy of conciliation appears to have followed, doubtless uneasy on both sides. In AD 77 the able Agricola was appointed military governor. He pursued an active policy of Romanisation which had proved successful in other conquered provinces, and is described by his son-in-law Tacitus: 'to induce a people, hitherto scattered, uncivilized and therefore prone to fight, to grow pleasurably inured to peace and ease, Agricola gave private encouragement and official assistance to the building of temples, public squares and private mansions. ... Furthermore he trained the sons of the chiefs in the liberal arts and expressed a preference for British natural ability over the trained skill of the Gauls. The result was that in place of distaste for the Latin language came a passion to command it. In the same way, our national dress came into favour and the toga was everywhere to be seen. And so the Britons were gradually led on to the amenities that make vice agreeable - arcades, baths and sumptuous banquets. They spoke of such novelties as civilization, when really they were only a feature of enslavement[7]'. So Britain joined the Pax Romana. Tax revenues from a prosperous province were of more value to an emperor than plunder for the Roman aristocracy.

Colonia Victricensis was rebuilt as a showpiece town, defended by the walls which we can still see in substantial lengths, originally standing at least twenty feet (6 m) high. The dyke system was reinforced. Gryme's Dyke may date from this time[8], and Berechurch Dyke provided defence against an eastern attack.

Camulodunum (the Gosbecks area) entered a new phase with magnificent buildings, suggesting that it remained the cultural and spiritual centre of the Trinovantes under their Romanised aristocracy. The great ditched enclosure, which it seems likely contained the burial place of Cunobelin, was further enclosed by a monumental portico with a double row of columns within a perimeter wall. Inside, off-centre, stood a temple of the Romano-Celtic type: a tall square room surrounded by a covered ambulatory. Nearby a massive theatre was built, which could hold up to 5,000 people seated.[9] The sites of seven other temples of similar type are known in the area. There were four at Sheepen, now it seems a religious rather than industrial area; one in a prominent site outside the Balkerne Gate, the principal entry to the town. Another was excavated near Camulodunum, and plaques indicated that it was dedicated to Silvanus, god of woodland and hunting. A figurine of a stag was found, and it would seem that the area was still partially wooded.[10]

The Pax Romana

With the accession in AD 69 of Vespasian, earlier the conqueror of south-west Britain, the empire entered a period of good government, security and prosperity - a century that came to be regarded in later years as a golden age. The map of Essex, as it evolved at this time, is in many respects that of the county we know today. The three main inland corridors of communication were established: the London to Colchester road (A12) and the east-west route from Colchester to Bishops Stortford (A120), which extended in Roman times to St Albans. In the third corridor, running northwards from London through the Lea-Stort and Cam valleys to join the Icknield Way, the route of the Roman road is lost except for a cropmark in the park at Audley End. Many other roads survive in use, although rarely for any distance on their original straight courses, others as footpaths along hedgerows, and some only as cropmarks.

These were the roads that were planned and built by surveyors, but there were trackways and drove roads, which evidence from aerial photographs of Ardleigh and Gosbecks show were very different - winding and irregular like so many country roads and lanes we know today. It seems more than likely that some of our minor roads and green lanes formed part of the network of diverticulae of Roman times, or perhaps originated earlier still.[11]

With peace and stability, and a network of fine roads, towns rapidly developed as market centres for the countryside around them and as settlements for artisans

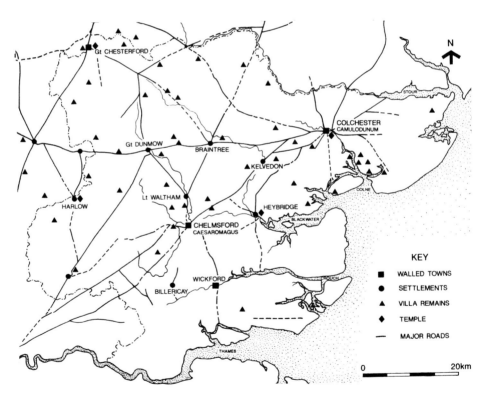

Roman Essex

and craftsmen. Ranging from 20 - 50 acres (8 - 20 ha) in size, they are mostly on nodal points in the main road system.[12] Many developed from late Iron Age hamlets and farmsteads, and at Chelmsford, for example, evidence for at least nine roundhouses has been found.[13] But around this time rectangular framed buildings, resting on sill plates, were superseding roundhouses and becoming the norm both in town and countryside. The evidence for such buildings can be difficult to detect in the soil and is easily erased by ploughing.[14] The buildings of the wealthy were generally of masonry, as were those for an administrative or religious purpose.

As rebuilt after its sack by Boudica, Colchester, which remained the principal town of the region, is a fine example of Roman civic planning, with its grid of streets, the Temple of Claudius restored in its huge precinct, and everywhere the orderliness of the right-angle. The other towns in Essex, all much smaller and mostly with earlier origins, tended to grow organically, focused on and around the main roads. The recent excavations of part of the Roman town of Heybridge, over an area of 49 acres (20 ha), revealed dense and complex archaeological remains with as much as a metre of stratified deposits in some parts. Evidence for the marketing of livestock and agrarian produce was apparent; hearths, ovens and kilns indicated crafts and manufacturing, and the footings of a large circular temple with ancillary buildings were found.[15] Gravel deposits defined a road layout that had little use for the right-angle.

As to the appearance of the towns in the landscape, it has proved possible to gain a fair picture of how Colchester looked from its inception as a legionary fortress through to its later decline.[16] The main entrance into the town from the west, the Balkerne Gate, incorporated a monumental arch erected for the colonia. The approach road, the Street of Tombs followed the Roman tradition of placing funerary monuments beside the road: mausolea and stelae such as the famed memorials to Longinus, a Thracian cavalry officer, and the centurion Facilis, both to be seen in Colchester Museum. Roman practice also suggests that evergreens would have been planted.

Villa estates

For many people, the villa (and perhaps Hadrian's wall) symbolizes Roman Britain. Examples showing spacious rooms, mosaic floors and luxurious bathhouses, set in bosky landscapes, can be visited to gain a vivid impression of the life of wealthy landowners, although unfortunately not in Essex. But villa sites abound here, unsurprisingly given the fertility of the soils and prosperity of the region.

A 'villa' has been defined as an agriculturally-based establishment with the principal residence constructed at least partly in masonry.[17] This covers a wide range of building types in size and quality; at the top, Fishbourne near Chichester, the palace of Cogidumnus, a local king who early saw the merits of throwing in his lot with the invaders; near the bottom, a farmstead such as that at Holt's Farm, Boreham, prosperous enough to be able to afford a bath-house. The Essex Sites and Monuments Record lists 69 sites of known or possible villas, and many more are likely to be added. Unfortunately only two have been excavated on a large scale to the standards of modern archaeology; these are the high status villa at Rivenhall and Holt's Farm, mentioned above, which was recently excavated ahead of mineral extraction.

Rivenhall was built in the late first century on the site of an early Roman building, itself with an Iron Age predecessor. The complex contained two large masonry buildings which were later remodelled and an aisled barn added. The buildings continued in use into the early Saxon period, and a medieval farmhouse and a church, which has its origins in the late Saxon period, stand on the site today. The excavators, Warwick and Kirsty Rodwell, studied the landscape context of the villa and concluded that once the principal settlement, the focus point of the estate, had been established (certainly by the Iron Age) it remained in domestic occupation until the present day with no evidence of discontinuity. Moreover, they suggested that the principal manor of Rivenhall might be equated with the Roman villa estate and might be delineated to a large extent by the parish boundaries.[18]

Except for a cluster around the Colne estuary, the great majority of Essex villas lie scattered across the Till. Only two sites are known south of a line drawn from Heybridge to Chelmsford, and then southwards along the A12. One of these at Dawes Heath, Thundersley, known from an aerial photograph and surface evidence, appears certain, but the other, at Wickford, may be a fortified settlement.

The question naturally arises as to whether, in the main, the villas were private mansions built on the estates of a native nobility induced by Agricola to become 'civilized'; as we have seen, Roman influence and a market for continental goods were in evidence well before the Claudian invasion. Alternatively, were they the homes of non-Britons, doing well from land seizures? Rivenhall, Warwick Rodwell concluded on the balance of probabilities, was the seat of a wealthy native. It lay well outside the area required to support the inhabitants of the colonia, and there was evidence of a native burial tradition. For a half century or so before the conquest, rich burials often contained vessels for the consumption of wine consisting of a bowl and jug, or 'patera and ewer', fashioned in metal. Patera and ewer burials became a regular practice around the time of the conquest and are concentrated in Essex and north Kent. They are generally accepted as 'native' burials and are often associated with barrows of the early Roman period. At Rivenhall a bronze patera and ewer was found in 1839 in Barrow Field, the site of a ploughed-out barrow near the villa.[19]

No less than five patera and ewer burials were found in the monumental cemetery known as the Bartlow Hills, which includes the largest burial mounds of the period in Europe.[20] Originally containing nine barrows dating from the late first to mid second centuries, the cemetery clearly belonged to a native family of enormous wealth. They are believed to have been the owners of the Ashdon villa, of which only the bath-house is known. A superb patera and ewer in the context of a sumptuous burial were found by the Stansted Archaeological team in 1988 at Duck End, near the site earlier noted for yielding palaeobotanical evidence of woodland clearance on the fringes of the plateau in the Bronze Age. Stamped pottery from Gaul dated the burial to around AD 140.[21]

These examples, though few, suggest that the native aristocracy survived the Boudican upheaval, to thrive in a period of better government when accommodation became the accepted policy. A particular group of villas, however, may have had non-native owners. These are grouped around the Colne estuary: Alresford, Fingringhoe, Brightlingsea (three), West Mersea, East Mersea (possible) and St Osyth. They lie on very choice sites, near to the colonia and with fine views over the estuaries and sea. Villas beside or overlooking the sea signalled status, wealth and taste for the Romans of this time - the Bay of Naples was studded with them - and here we may have a colony of high ranking foreigners within the area appropriated for the colonia.

A reconstruction of the Roman villa at Chignal St James as it may have appeared in the late third century AD, based on aerial photographs and excavations by Essex County Council. Watercolour by Frank Gardiner

The landscape

With the road network, small towns, Roman Colchester in its several phases, the scatter of villas - some like Chignall, with its geometry revealed in an aerial photograph[22], Rivenhall and Holt's Farm, scientifically excavated - all should add up, one might suppose, to give a picture of some coherence of the landscape of Essex under the Empire. But that would be an illusion. The pattern of rural development, where the great majority of the population dwelt in their elusive framed houses, remains a blur, as do their field systems and relationship to the wider landscape.[23] But one aspect is clear; the landscape was not dominated by woodland as was believed a few decades ago, and the thickets and woodlands referred to by Caesar would have come under pressure as the population rose in the first century of Roman rule.

Nevertheless, there are areas where the blur starts to focus. We have noted the results of Tom Williamson's fieldwalking exercise in the north-west corner of Essex which indicated a density of 1.2 settlement sites per square kilometre, and that clearance and cultivation extended over the heavy plateau clays. An interesting deduction from the scatter of sherds, spread with the contents of middens on the land as manure, was that infield-outfield farming was practised.[24] This involved an infield, heavily manured and kept under cultivation, and an outfield which was occasionally cultivated and manured, but relied on long periods of fallow to maintain fertility. The system was traditionally in use in 'Celtic' areas. At Stansted, the project team established that the area had been cleared for farming by this time, all but a small area in the north-east where there was no evidence of activity and is likely to have been managed woodland.

At the further end of the county, on the free draining brickearths of North Shoebury, excavations revealed evidence for cereal growing in narrow strip fields.[25] These were similar to a system of ditched strip fields at Slough House Farm, Great Totham, laid out in the late Iron Age together with a large enclosure which suggested a mix of arable farming and animal husbandry.[26]

At Great Holt's Farm, Boreham, excavation has revealed a Roman farmstead with ditches indicating the surrounding field system. It was laid out in the late first century on undeveloped ground, although there was evidence for occupation in the Bronze and early Iron Age. Early in the fourth century the farmhouse was replaced by an aisled building and a bath-house added; the fields were altered but kept to the previous alignment, and the correlation between these boundaries and those shown on modern maps appears too close to be coincidental and suggests continuity of cultivation or re-use of existing features.[27]

These are the bare bones, as it were, revealed by archaeology and much more information is to be expected in the future. Another aspect to be considered is the attitude to landscape features held by the inhabitants. The Celtic peoples were animists, as were the Italians at this time. Wetland sites - springs, brooks, marshes and rivers - were particularly revered. Two sites we have already noted, at Harlow and Witham, appear to have become pilgrimage centres. The Harlow shrine was sited on a gravel island in the Stort floodplain near to an important ford which linked the territories of the Catuvellauni and the Trinovantes. A Romano-Celtic temple of the standard type - a square cella with surrounding ambulatory - replaced an earlier roundhouse. Some 900 coins, many in mint condition, have been found from the pre-Roman period , and later offerings included weapons, jewellery and a remarkable assemblage of iron tools.[28] At Ivy Chimneys, Witham, a similar temple stood beside a large spring-fed pool, and a deep pit may have held a Jupiter column. This would explain why, in addition to coin hoards and other offerings, over 30 palaeolithic stone axes were found. These were believed to be 'fossilised' thunderbolts.[29]

Sacred groves were also important in the Celtic world, just as they were to the Mediterranean peoples. As woodland generally came under pressure one wonders whether their sacral importance permitted productive management, with only certain trees held to be inviolable. Accounts from the early post-Roman period on the continent describe the forcible conversion of pagan countrymen, and a frequent occurrence is a saint taking an axe to a great and venerated tree. So the answer may be in the affirmative. One might also wonder why the area of Epping Forest in the vicinity of Ambresbury Banks remained a tract of lime-dominated woodland throughout the Roman Period; perhaps as the setting for monumental tribal refuges it had a significance the Romans respected.

Another landscape feature to bear in mind is the private park. Owners of important villas may well have read the treatises on estate management by Varro and Columella which advocated an enclosed area near the house, stocked with deer, cattle, hares and even wild sheep.

The coast

The manufacturing of salt, which began as we have seen in the Bronze Age, flourished through into the early Roman period, turning much of the coastline at certain times into a smoky industrial landscape. By the end of the first century AD the industry went into decline, and it is doubtful if any red hills remained in operation after AD 200.[30] The most likely reason seems to be that inland sources of salt, with the benefit of the new road system, took over the market. The red hills were to take on a new function, however.

Already in the Iron Age, a woollen industry was supplied by marshland flocks and by the later Roman period the numbers of sheep were probably similar to those recorded in Domesday Book. A reference of AD 310 speaks of an 'innumerable multitude of gentle beasts.....laden with fleeces', and these flocks appear to have supported a high quality export market.[31] The Roman army required woollen tunics for the legionaries. Saltmarshes have advantages over inland pastures for sheep husbandry: they are less susceptible to drying out in summer, and the salt content limits the risk of footrot and liverfluke. Moreover the flavour of the meat is superb, although mutton would have been regarded as a by-product.

Sea levels lowered in the early Roman period, but the trend had reversed by the fourth century. Freshwater run off met higher tide levels with consequent flooding. The red hills provided high, well-drained refuges for shepherds and sheep, a use later attested to by Camden, writing in 1610, and it was even suggested at a later date that the hills had been constructed for this purpose.[32]

The later Roman period

In the reign of Marcus Aurelius, AD 161-180, the military situation on the frontiers grew sharply worse. Pressure from barbarian nations became almost overwhelming and henceforward the primary object of the state was military survival; the Pax Romana was over. By the fourth century, the principal source of revenue to support massive armed forces was a land tax which became increasingly oppressive and unfair. The worst sufferers were the agricultural poor - the 'free' men and women of the countryside - many of whom fled to seek protection from the owners of great estates where they became bound by law to the land in a way that foreshadowed the serfs of the Middle Ages.[33]

In Gaul there were the risings of the Bagaudae, tenants and slaves driven to revolt against landlords and authorities, and bloodily repressed, and vast areas were laid waste by invasions. Britain became seen as a source of supply, and in AD 359 Julian required a massive increase in exports to Gaul which required a fleet of some 600 ships. The eastern counties, with their productive soils and proximity to the continent, would have been especially burdened.[34] Agriculture was changing with the absorption of small farms into large estates (latifundia), and technology improving, with bigger field sizes for large scale crop production to meet export demands. Huge flocks of sheep were pastured, as we have seen, on the marshes.

Towards the end of the period there appears a marked divide in conditions between the east and west of Britain. In the west many towns were walled, new villas were being built and others enlarged, and mosaic floors laid. In the east there was widespread decline; towns were shrinking and few were equipped with masonry defences. Braintree and Chelmsford were contracting and, inside the walls of Colchester, crops were being grown and harvested as within many Gallic towns of this time. Two 'Saxon shore' forts guarded the coast, but with the one at Walton since lost to the sea , and Bradwell mostly so, we cannot know how effective they may have been at this late time.

As buildings outside the walls of Colchester began to disappear, a new feature appeared in the landscape. Over a small pagan cemetery, a large fourth century cemetery was superimposed with graves aligned east-west in the Christian manner. A church was constructed c 330 and used mainly for memorial services and funerary feasts as in the great extra-mural churches built over catacombs at Rome - an attractive custom akin to the wake. A timber building was built just to the west of the church to serve as a kitchen.[35] The site of the church has been consolidated and displayed as a monument. At Ivy Chimneys, Witham, the discovery of an octagonal font indicates the conversion of this ancient shrine to the new state religion.

In contrast to other Essex towns, Great Chesterford was twice provided with walls. The earlier circuit was replaced in the late fourth century by a much larger enclosure, the sole major fortification to be built in East Anglia in the later Roman period. This was 'no fancy of the local curia but an official construction undertaken on orders at the highest level'.[36] So perhaps a fortress rather than a 'town', guarding the vital point where the Stort-Cam gap meets the Icknield Way.

Turning to the farming landscape, the one excavation sizeable enough to give more than a small sample is at Mucking. It conforms to the trends described although it is unclear how typical it is. A farmstead on this long-settled site was not rebuilt after its destruction by fire in the later second century. Instead, the land became arable and the field system was remodelled into larger plots. By the end of the fourth century the land appears to have become waste.

The last years of Roman rule in eastern Britain produce a depressing picture of towns in decline, manufacturing near extinction, increasing threats of barbarian raids, and a thinning population of tied peasantry whose lives were governed by an oppressive bureaucracy and a small rich elite. One might think that for much of the population rule by Anglo-Saxon overlords may have been a change for the better.

CHAPTER FIVE

The Saxon kingdom

IF THE LAST decades of Roman rule appear murky in terms of written sources, the following two centuries approach the opaque. It is hardly surprising that historians coined the term Dark Ages. It is only in the early seventh century that southern Britain re-emerges into history, and in the eighth that the historian Bede tried to make some sense of what had gone before. The bare facts, but not their dating, are agreed. In the early years of the fifth century, imperial protection was withdrawn and the Britons advised to look to their own defence. Germanic mercenaries were hired, who in the course of time rebelled and following a short war secured a treaty which gave them control over a wide swathe of coastal territory in eastern and southern Britain. The conquest of the south-east, the midlands and north, followed in later stages. What is still not agreed is the fate of the native population, and over the last two centuries a multitude of interpretations of the meagre texts have been proffered, often illuminating the nature and prejudices of their advocates rather more than the subject.

A steady and continuing flow of information has come from the work of archaeologists which is shedding light on the late Roman years and the Anglo-Saxon adventus. Information is becoming knowledge, and the traditional view of an existing population largely displaced by an Anglo-Saxon mass migration is no longer tenable. The synthesis of the available evidence by Nick Higham seems to this writer to answer the many questions most satisfactorily, and form the best guide to the events of this difficult period.[1]

The mercenaries hired by the Romanised elite to take the place of Imperial units came from Denmark and Schleswig-Holstein. They had little or no previous contact with Rome and, unlike the Franks and Goths, had little or no respect for Roman systems of government and religion or, one presumes, for their employers. Before the revolt, the first immigrants would have observed the agrarian system by which the agricultural surplus was extracted from the peasantry. The subsequent destruction or flight of the British aristocracy over the areas they had seized left them in control of the renders in goods and labour paid by a numerous but socially and economically depressed native population. More Saxons came to join the new masters from the homelands, and power was now concentrated in the hands of local chieftains, with society re-focussed 'on the household and on a military elite dependent on the patronage of its chieftains, in direct control of the land, its workforce and its surplus'.[2] As a system it seems to have been a successful solution to the problems of the times, and the native population gradually assumed the language and culture of the newcomers to become the English.

Essex was in the first phase of Saxon conquest, which a Gallic chronicler recorded had taken place by AD 441.[3] The newcomers had rapidly acquired estates in full working order. These formed parts of small territories, which in time emerged as a unified East Saxon kingdom (Essex). In the seventh century the kingdom extended into Middlesex and Surrey, and remained independent until the mid ninth century. In 654 King Sigebert II, under the 'friendly and brotherly coun-sel' of the powerful Oswy, King of Northumbria, was baptized by St Cedd.[4] Cedd was consecrated bishop and founded minsters at Bradwell and Tilbury.

For the early Saxon period, information comes almost entirely from archaeol-ogy. Numerous sunken-floored buildings, a characteristic form at this time, have been found, often associated with existing settlements. Saxon burials and ceme-teries, as we have noted earlier, have been found on prehistoric sites where the earthworks were still visible - at the Brightlingsea urnfield, the Orsett enclosure and at Springfield Lyons, which the grave goods have indicated began in the late fifth century and continued well into the sixth.[5] On the lower Blackwater sites to the north-east of Heybridge, which have yielded so much information on the pre-historic and Roman periods, domestic occupation continued with evidence that this had become a centre for metalworking. Wells were also excavated, con-structed of timbers from mature 'wild' oaks growing from the end of the Roman period. This suggested that timber was plentiful, with enough to spare after house building for substantial well linings.[6]

The settlement at Mucking is the most extensive early Anglo-Saxon site exca-vated in England, with 53 posthole buildings and 203 sunken huts, not all in use at the same time but over a period beginning in the early fifth century and lasting to the beginning of the eighth. The village shifted over this period in a manner that has parallels across the North Sea, but not in this country.

In north-west Essex Tom Williamson found the Saxon period the most difficult in which to locate settlements. Saxon pottery has 'poor' visibility and some com-munities were aceramic, using wooden and leather vessels and utensils. Never-theless he concluded that there was a considerable contraction of land under cultivation in the post-Roman period with woodland growing up over abandoned farmland on the clay plateau land.[7] Whether this was typical is a matter of debate. Population levels were in decline in the late Roman period, and probably in the early seventh century 'Justinian's' plague reached England. Certainly by then there was no shortage of land, and the intensive farming required in the late Roman period was replaced by a largely pastoral regime with extensive land for rough grazing. How far this land would develop into wood-pasture would depend on the intensity of grazing and the requirements of the community for woodland products. At Stansted Airport there was only evidence for Saxon activ-ity on the southern margin, and the land to the north appears to have been effec-tively abandoned, developing with this area of flat interfluves into one of the most wooded areas recorded in the Essex Domesday Book.

The evidence of pollen and radiocarbon has shown that Epping Forest survived as a tract of woodland from the Neolithic to the early Saxon period.[8] But from 600 to 850 there was selective clearance and a dramatic decline in lime. This period, it seems, saw the establishment of wood-pasture management in a system of inter-commoning which lasted until the last century. Whether the many other areas of intercommoning in the Mid Essex Zone which survived in fragments to be recorded in the historic record date from this time, or whether they are relics from a yet earlier time, can only be a matter of conjecture. Other pollen records suggest no great regeneration of woodland in the post-Roman period, and this concurs with the evidence gathered from sites in Suffolk and Norfolk. However, apart from the coast and lower Blackwater valley for which there is now a wealth of information, sites in Essex yielding pollen cores are few and very far between, and they can hardly be seen as providing more than information on certain localities. Domesday Book shows Essex and Hertfordshire as relatively sylvan compared to their neighbours to the north. Whether this was just the position in the late Saxon period, or whether it reflects the pattern of earlier centuries, will only be known when far more palaeobotanical evidence becomes available.

Saxon estates

A middle Saxon date appears most likely for the establishment of the major boundaries and related field systems of the South Essex Plain, and their extension northwards onto the Warley-Horndon ridge to form the 'parallel parishes'. This implies control over a huge tract of land at that time, which later fragmented into the individual holdings recorded in Domesday Book. Elsewhere placenames suggest a similar fragmentation from an earlier single territory, for example the four Colnes (Earls, White, Wakes, Engaine), which by 1066 comprised five manors and five smallholdings. The Tolleshunts (Toll's spring) - D'Arcy, Knights and Major - share the personal name 'Toll' with Tollesbury, which again suggests the fission of a single estate. In 1066 the four future parishes contained twelve manors and four smallholdings.

The eight parishes of the Rodings (Hroda's people) comprised sixteen manors and two smallholdings in Domesday Book. They have been studied by Steven Bassett following all lines of approach - geographical, historical, archaeological and ecclesiastical - and he concludes that they originated as a single territorial unit.[9] It focusses on an eight kilometre stretch of the River Roding, and the boundaries to east and west mostly lie on the higher ground which forms the watersheds between the Roding and its adjacent rivers. It conforms to natural topography and there are many instances of local road lines and field systems appearing to flow uninterruptedly across parish boundaries. While the boundaries of parishes came to be established in the thirteenth century, following the boundaries of the manors included in each parish, it is likely that the whole territory of the Rodings had earlier comprised the parish of a minster, with the church situated in White Roding.

The available evidence then, largely derived from the happy survival of shared placenames, suggests the existence of huge estates in the early and middle Saxon periods, later fragmenting into the multiplicity of holdings recorded by the Domesday commissioners. Whether these were existing landholdings taken over by the conquering Saxons must remain a question, but it is a possibility and the interpretation of the events of the Adventus followed here makes that possibility likely.

It is probable that a great estate, almost certainly royal, focussed on the estuaries of the Blackwater and Colne. Brightlingsea was a royal vill, and able to command the labour resources to construct the causeway, about half a mile long, which links Mersea Island to the mainland. It was long thought to have been a Roman construction, but substantial oak piles, discovered when a water main was laid, were dated by dendrochronology and indicated that the causeway was built between AD 684 and 702. The motive for this massive work may have been to create a dry access to a minster in West Mersea on the orders of Sebbi the 'monk-king' who ruled from c 665-695.[10]

To the south in today's parish of Bradwell-juxta-Mare lay Ythancaestir, the former Roman shore fort of Othona, situated at the tip of a spit of land with creeks on either side.[11] A shell ridge partially blocked the mouth of the southern creek, creating a sheltered anchorage for ships trading with the important commercial centres of London and Ipswich, and across the Channel and North Sea. The Roman walls would have provided security for Cedd's minster, as did those of Reculver in Kent and Burgh in Norfolk for similar missionary churches, and the whole scene would have bustled with human life and activity, difficult to imagine now with St Peter's Church the only building, with sea birds for neighbours. Nevertheless, it is a moving site to visit and has become a place of pilgrimage.

On isolated sandbanks near Collins Creek in the Blackwater estuary, rows of timber posts have been dated by radiocarbon to AD 640-675 and 882-957. The rows, up to a kilometre in length, were fish-traps, known in Essex as kiddles. Withies were woven between the posts to form a dead hedge, and a pair of rows would come to a point facing seaward and end in a mesh trap. Huge quantities of timber would have been required as in the Mersea causeway. Similar structures are known to lie off Sales Point, Bradwell, and a kiddle was found by aerial survey off Mersea Island. As already noted, Rook Hall and Slough House Farms have yielded extensive evidence of ironworking, and environmental data from the wells indicated improved and perhaps intensified management of pasture and increased crop production during the early to middle Saxon period.[12]

Taken together, these different elements suggest a thriving economy in which the Blackwater estuary was not a barrier, but a unifying factor. The creeks, estuaries and seaways were the arteries of trade in a culture at home with water, navigation and nautical technology, the basis for the naval success of the later Anglo-Saxon kings.

The late Saxon period

The Danish raids and invasions left their mark on the pages of history rather than on the Essex landscape, although it is not difficult to picture the fleets of longships silently entering the creeks, or the conflagration at Benfleet in 894 when Alfred's army destroyed the camp and ships of the Danish commander, Hasten. Alfred's son, Edward the Elder, reclaimed Essex from the Danelaw and it is to him that we owe the boroughs of Colchester and Maldon. At Colchester he repaired the

Roman walls and would have insured that there was the population to defend them; at Maldon, in 916, he ordered the construction of a burh on the hilltop, a site that had been occupied in the Iron Age. The earthworks are no longer visible, but were still evident in the eighteenth century and a plan and sketched reconstruction survive. Archaeology has confirmed its position immediately to the west of the medieval town. The London road runs through its centre.

The site of the Battle of Maldon is known, and it is the only known battlefield in Essex. The events of that doomful but heroic day in 991 have survived in an important fragment of an epic poem. Byrhtnoth, Ealdorman of Essex, had drawn up his troops to oppose a Danish force which had landed and encamped on Northey Island which lies across the Blackwater estuary at the entry to Maldon. Fearing that if battle was not joined the Danes would sail off to attack elsewhere, he allowed them to cross the narrow causeway. Sadly, the gamble failed; Byrhtnoth was killed and his army eventually defeated. The causeway remains in use today, and although rising sea levels, the construction of a seawall, and a nearby area of landfill have altered the topography to landward, it is a site worth visiting.

This period saw the fission of the great estates and their replacement by the pattern of manors which would be recorded in Domesday Book. Fission also occurred in ecclesiastical organization with the building of proprietary chapels, the predecessors of the future parish churches, close to the manorial hall. Evidence of Saxon masonry construction or the postholes of timber buildings have been found in churches where archaeologists have had the opportunity to excavate early levels, but of the secular buildings, buried under later developments, little is known. At Springfield Lyons, however, the final phase on this remarkable site was a complex of buildings dated to the tenth and eleventh centuries by pottery and a silver coin of Aethelred II. Some thirteen buildings were found of varying size, and the number and range suggest that this was more than a simple farmstead, although a case has been made that three of the buildings, including the principal hall, belonged with the earlier cemetery.[13] The excavation was limited to the area of the cemetery, so it is not known if the whole of the complex was found. The most likely explanation for the abandonment that occurred is that the site shifted a short distance away to Cuton Hall, a farm identified as one of the three manors listed in the Domesday survey.[14]

It is to Domesday Book that we may turn for a view of the landscape at the end of the Anglo-Saxon kingdom, to seek for clues as to how it worked and what it looked like, always bearing in mind that it would never have occurred to William's commissioners that their fiscal findings would be put to such a bizarre use.

CHAPTER SIX

Audit and stocktaking :
the late Saxon landscape

DOMESDAY BOOK DESCRIBES Old English society under new management: 'foreign lords had taken over, but little else had changed'.[1] Essex was spared William's penchant for arousing terror by bloody devastation such as he employed in Buckinghamshire and Hertfordshire to secure the submission of London - unsuccessfully as it turned out - and later in the Harrying of the North. The coast may have suffered from his order to meet the threat of a Danish invasion by pre-emptive devastation in 1085, but the overall evidence is for a growing population and an expanding economy.

At Winchester in midwinter 1085, the Saxon Chronicle records, King William sent forth men all over England to each shire to inquire how much each landholder held and what it was worth. His purpose was twofold: first to assess all land for tax and, secondly, to establish who held it in rightful possession. In the confusion following the Conquest and the dispossession or death of most of the 'natural rulers', there were opportunities for the more ruthless and acquisitive of William's warrior adventurers to seize more land than he had granted. The Great Survey brought the Conquest to a conclusion, and approval of acquisition would ensure that the recorded 'claim would be upheld for ever by the hundred, the shire, the king's justices and the king'.[2] As a definitive register it became known as Domesday Book by analogy with the Day of Judgement.

The King was thorough, sending a second set of commissioners to check up on their predecessors' findings and to report any irregularities to him. Amazingly the survey was completed in less than twelve months, an achievement 'unmatched in Europe for many centuries, the product of a sophisticated and experienced English administration, fully exploited by the Conqueror's commanding energy'.[3] The circuit returns for Norfolk, Suffolk and Essex were not included in the main volume of the survey and form a second, often referred to as the Little Domesday Book, which was compiled after William's death. As a consequence it lacks the editing and codification undertaken in the main volume and contains details that might otherwise have been edited out.

The returns record statistics for 1066 and 1086, 'then and now', noting changes that had occurred between these dates. The return for Ely Abbey, which has survived, includes a copy of the Commissioners' brief.[4] Following the names of place and owner the inventory was to include the numbers and status of the work force, the area of productive land - arable, meadow and woodland, numbers of ploughs - 'both those in lordship and the mens', mills and fishponds. It concludes: 'what the total value was and is?...before 1066, when King William gave it, and now; and if more can be had than at present?' For the historian of landscape, the minute statistical detail is an extraordinary legacy for there was to be nothing comparable until L Dudley Stamp's survey carried out with voluntary field work in the 1930's, and there is still no comprehensive register of land such as the Conqueror demanded and received. Analysis of the Domesday returns permits an estimate of population at national, regional, sub-regional and, indeed, the local level, and most importantly for our purpose here, a general picture of the landscape in which these people lived and worked, again often cognizable at a local level. There are many caveats, inevitably, some of which we shall encounter.

Essex is fortunate in the work of Horace Round whose masterly analysis and structured synthesis of the Essex returns is available in the first volume of the Victoria County History. More recently, and available to hand, we have Ray Powell's *Essex in Domesday Book* which includes a summary of the information gleaned from the statistics, a gazetteer of manors, and this information delineated on the county map. It must be remembered that the area of Domesday Book Essex is substantially that of the county as it survived until 1965.

The population

Assessing the size of the Domesday population of England, a matter of endless debate, Sir Clifford Darby noted that estimates range from just over 1.2 million to just under 1.6 and concluded that around 1.5 million may not be far from the truth.[5]

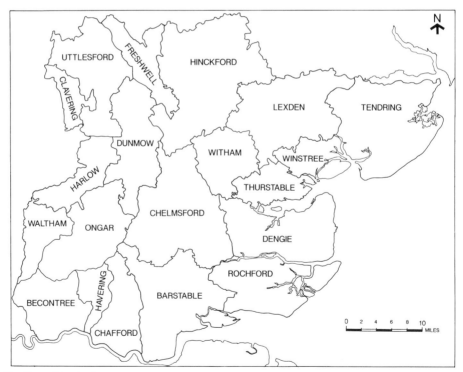

The Essex Hundreds

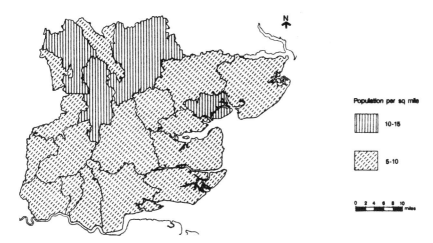

Population density in 1086 (after Darby, 1971)

The population recorded is interpreted as heads of households or males of working age. In Essex some 14,600 people are listed, of which 478 and 243 lived respectively in the boroughs of Colchester and Maldon, and there were about 300 of the new aristocracy. To arrive at a figure which includes families and dependants rests on the multiplying factor selected, but if we settle for 4.0 this gives a total of 59,600. However, Domesday Book does not record figures for the stewards, retainers and household staff of the manors and castles, the personnel of the building industry engaged on the construction of castles and ecclesiastical works, monks and their servants are not listed, and priests very rarely so.[6] An overall figure of 62,000 might reasonably include these people.[7]

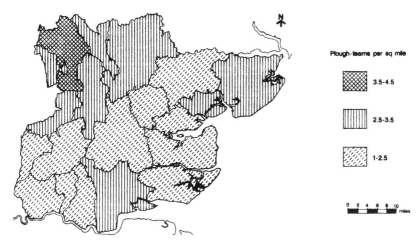

Plough-teams in 1086 (after Darby, 1971)

Ploughland

The Essex assessment of cultivated land is stated in terms of hides and virgates. While it is generally accepted that the virgate is 30 acres, and indeed a figure of 30 acres is frequently entered instead of a virgate, the area of the hide, usually reckoned at 120 acres, may give problems.[8] The hide originated as a unit of tax assessment and it would be unwise to use it as an exact measurement, most particularly at the local level.[9] The figures bear an inconsistent relationship to those of plough-teams, the other indicator of the extent of cultivated land. 'One thing is certain: it would be extremely rash to rely upon the hideage to give us any idea about the relative prosperity of different parts of the county in the eleventh century'.[10]

However, while accepting that the hide is not an exact figure and may vary considerably at the local level, aggregated figures for a total may be more reliable than those for the local or particular. If we employ the multiple of 120 to Darby's estimated total of 2,767 hides, we arrive at a total of 332,040 acres of cultivated land, or roughly one third of the county.

Turning then to plough-teams, Darby's figure of 3,865 suggests an average area of 86 acres per plough-team. This may seem a low figure if all the plough-teams were using a heavy plough, wheeled and fitted with a coulter to cut through the sod, with a mould-board to turn the furrow and a team of eight oxen to draw it. It is generally considered that such a team should be capable of achieving the necessary cultivations of a ploughland, which is equated with the hide of 120 acres. This would seem likely when the tenants combined with their oxen to plough the lord's demesne or to reclaim new land from the waste, but it would also seem probable that many cultivated their own land with smaller ploughs and fewer oxen.[11] One may recall the wheeled and coultered plough, drawn by a donkey, which concludes the Bayeux Tapestry.

There is also the factor of settlement pattern. In midland England nucleated villages with three-field systems were developing well before the Conquest and here, by efficient use of communal resources, plough-teams could be used to their maximum ability. In counties such as Essex, scattered settlement in hamlets and farmsteads appears to have been the norm, and this pattern would have made full communal co-operation often difficult and sometimes impossible.[12]

Given the probable diversity in the quality of ploughs and plough-teams, and the impediments to communal efficiency arising from dispersed settlement, the figure of 86 acres per plough-team seems not unreasonable. However, this is an average over the county and as with the hide, it would be most unwise to regard it as anything but a rough guide at the level of the individual manor.

The next consideration is the geographical distribution of this land. Reckoning the density of plough-teams to be a measure of prosperity, Darby aggregated the information for each hundred. As would be expected, higher densities occur on the Boulder Clay and the Tendring loams; but similar densities on the heavier clays of Winstree and Barstable may seem surprising. The gently sloping terrain with good surface run-off may account for Winstree, and free-draining river terraces in the south of the hundred explain Barstable. Uttlesford Hundred, with areas of exposed chalkland is the most prosperous. Generally one would expect the best land for the purpose to be ploughland even in the areas of higher density, for there was still the land available to allow a degree of choice.

To a modern eye the striking feature of the arable of 1086 would be the pattern of long parallel lines, twelve to fifteen feet apart, formed by ridge and furrow cultivation. This can still be seen in parts of England, particularly in the midlands, where the arable was turned over to pasture after the Black Death or by enclosure act, and has remained grazed ever since. Examples of ridge and furrow in Essex are rare and the outlines faint, suggesting that ploughing up in these cases was a short-lived expedient.

Meadows

Meadows comprised the rich grasslands of the alluvial floodplains of rivers and brooks, and were always regarded as a most valuable resource. In Essex they were familiar features of the landscape until the post-war years when local dairying virtually disappeared and the meads were then ploughed up and added to the arable or converted to willow plantations. In former times, under carefully controlled management, they were divided into tenurial strips growing a hay crop. After mowing in June the meadows were opened for common grazing until the autumn. Many illustrations of hay-making may be found in medieval manuscripts[13] and early fifteenth century Flemish miniatures depict the dense flower-rich texture of the swards. True meadows are now rare, particularly in predominantly arable counties such as Essex, and those which survive have frequently been 'improved' with fertiliser which diminishes their floristic variety and historic interest.

Domesday Book entries may include inland marsh and fen which, while unsuitable for grazing, would yield a nutritious crop of hay. The distribution of meadows is most frequent in the north of the county, reflecting the many vills sited beside the rivers and streams flowing south-eastward across the Till.[15]

The coastal marshes

The marshes are measured as 'pasture for x sheep', a peculiarity of the survey for Essex but hardly surprising as the value of this land lay in sheep products, in particular wool. Essex was well placed geographically to supply the spectacular expansion of the Flemish cloth industry which depended on England for its raw material.[16] Other products were skins, mutton and cheeses, perhaps the 'huge thicke cheeses' of later centuries.[17] The overall carrying capacity of the marshes is given as 18,000 sheep.

This valuable resource was mostly owned by manors in the coastal zone with only a very few located further inland, while those with the highest counts for grazing abutted or lay close to the marshes. At a later date, these detached portions of manors, or enclaves, were observed to be defined by ditches and drains. These were probably relics of a system under which a number of vills had rights in a common pasture; similar examples have been encountered in Fenland and elsewhere.[18]

The marshlands of 1086 were more extensive than those of today. The rise in sea levels had not yet required the building of dykes and the distinction between grazing marsh and saltmarsh would have been blurred. Myriads of red hills survived as grassy mounds, sometimes linked by turf causeways to provide a route of escape for the sheep if the marsh was inundated. There would have been much human activity : herding, milking, wildfowling and gathering shellfish, compared with the empty arable tracts of today, with only the occasional walker or bird-watcher on the sea-wall. The marshes viewed by the commissioners were not the lonely places they have become.

In the inter-tidal shallows of the Blackwater estuary and Mersea Island lay the extensive sea-hedges of the fisheries, made from brushwood woven around the stakes which are still to be seen. Radiocarbon has dated them to the late Saxon period and Domesday Book records fisheries for Goldhanger, Tollesbury, West Mersea and four for East Mersea.

Twenty two saltpans lay in the hundreds of Tendring, Winstree and Thurstable, but it may be that the Domesday record is incomplete as there was no report of salt working for certain places bearing 'salt' names such as Salcott on the Blackwater and Saltcote Farm on the Crouch.[19] Perhaps workings concealed by marsh vegetation in the labyrinthine creeks were not brought to the commissioners' attention.

Mills and vineyards

151 mills are recorded and, although it is always assumed that they were water-mills, some could have been driven by animals if a site lacked a ready supply of surface water. An eighth century watermill excavated at Tamworth[20] appears very similar to mills one encounters today in Crete and elsewhere in the Mediteranean (virtually all disused). The technology is simple: a jet of water propels a horizontal paddle wheel which turns by means of a vertical shaft a pair of stones in the mill house above. The buildings are tiny compared with the multi-storied structures dating from the eighteenth and nineteenth centuries which we are familiar with, but the dams and earthworks could be massive, as the mill dam at Thaxted (disused by the mid fourteenth century) shows. Possibly many of today's mills occupy sites in use in 1086, but long abandoned sites on rills above main rivers are also to be found, although dating is uncertain.

Nine vineyards are recorded. The cultivated vine may have been re-introduced by the Normans as both Suain of Essex at Rayleigh and Aubrey de Vere at Castle Hedingham had vineyards of six arpents - a French measure of about an acre.[21]

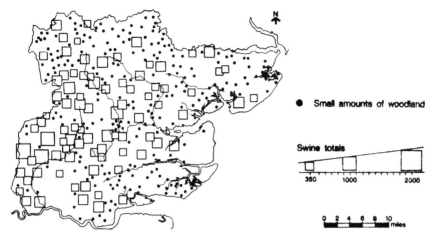

Distribution of woodland in 1086 (after Darby, 1971)

Woodlands

Mythology has descried Essex as a county covered by forest in Norman times. The reality was very different. The myth probably arose from a misunderstanding of the word 'forest' - in the Middle Ages it was a legal not descriptive term - and romantic stories of highwaymen lurking in Epping Forest. But the Domesday Book returns for woodland are the sections which give most problems. The curious form of measurement, 'woodland for x swine', suggests that its products of timber and underwood were not scarce, nor woodland a particularly valued resource. More-over, the figures appear indicative rather than measured and, where large areas are concerned, decidedly vague. It is difficult to believe that 1,000 pigs were let loose in the autumn to graze the woodlands of the manor of Debden, nor 2,200 over the three manors of Takeley, particularly as a good crop of acorns, the pigs' food, occurs infrequently and beech mast was limited to very few areas of the county. This would seem to confirm that 'woodland for x swine' is a formula of measurement only, and the presence or absence of pigs was an irrelevance.

It is clear, however, that Essex had marginally more woodland than most other counties. Oliver Rackham, making the best of the figures, has argued that roughly twenty per cent of Essex was then wooded, whereas over England as a whole it was an average of fifteen per cent.[22] However, this higher average arose from con-centrations in certain areas, and over much of Essex the density would have been similar to that of other counties of lowland England.

In 1086 the majority of woods were of the pasture type with trees growing in grassland. Coppice, the more intensive form of management, did not yet pre-dominate except in poorly wooded areas where scarcity required greater produc-tivity. A wood-pasture landscape can be seen today at Bush End, Hatfield Forest, where all the trees are pollards, but in the woodlands of 1086 pollards would have been limited to a sufficient number to produce underwood for local needs, while most trees would have been left free-growing to provide timber for the Normans' extensive building programme. Over the next two centuries as population growth required that more land be brought into cultivation, the wooded areas of Domesday Book would be converted to coppice woodland and survive as wood-pasture only in parks, forests and on commons.[23]

Despite its many uncertainties, Domesday Book does give a fair idea of the distribution and relative density of woodland and the reader's attention is drawn to the *Domesday Map of Essex* compiled by Ray Powell. While tracts of medium density are shown on both the Boulder and London Clays, the heaviest concentrations lie in the south-west in the Waltham and Ongar Hundreds, along the Warley, Thorndon, Ramsden ridge, and over the high, flat country from the Hallingburys through Takeley, Broxted and Debden to Wimbish. Land where cultivation had retreated in post-Roman times may have gone back to woodland. Rackham suggests that this happened around Hatfield Forest: 'In the eleventh century, the Forest-to-be was on the edge of an unusual survival for England: miles of near-continuous woodland, in which places like Molehill Green, Tye Green and Bamber's Green would still have been clearings'.[24] In south-west Essex the Rayleigh Hills, then as now, formed wooded eminences above the plain, and given its present sparse character, it is surprising to find that there was a concentration of woodland in the valley of the Salcott Brook.

As with land in the coastal marshes, we find enclaving: areas detached from the manors which held them. Sutton and Rawreth, for example, held enclaves in the Rayleigh Hills and the practice may have been more extensive than is readily apparent. Sometimes a later document may resolve a Domesday puzzle; Lawling, which lies on the sparse Dengie peninsula is recorded as having the high count of woodland for 800 pigs. An extent of 1310 shows that this was located elsewhere, in the relatively well wooded parishes of Danbury and Purleigh.[25]

Uncultivated land

If approximately one third of the land was arable, some twenty per cent was woodland, six per cent marshland and probably a similar area of meadow and fen, the remaining third comprised rough pastures and heathland. This land came to be known as 'waste' which is now a pejorative term, but was not so in the past. Most manors in 1086 owned some waste which together with woodland lay furthest from the manorial centre; an area of 'unimproved pasture which played a vital part in supporting the livestock which, as draught animals or producers of manure, provided an essential complement to the arable fields'.[26]

The nature of the heaths and pastures would be determined by the intensity of grazing. Trees and scrub will regenerate rapidly if grazing declines or ceases, and the commissioners may often have had difficulty in drawing a line between what might be considered as woodland and what constituted rough pasture bearing trees, but of too low a density to record. For an idea of the appearance of such landscapes we might turn to Dutch painters of the seventeenth century who reacted against idealised visions and sought to depict the reality of what today we would term semi-natural landscapes.[27]

Settlements

Domesday Book has much to tell us of the density and distribution of the population and manors in geographical terms, but at the local level the information is of limited use. Manors of status possessed a church, built near the hall and already an established feature of late Saxon Essex. These sites are generally self-evident as churches are stable features of the landscape, rarely moving away from where first built. Dependants, relatives and slaves would have lived in or near the manorial complex, and there would have been an open area for assembly and trade, the prototype of the village green. A second tier of manors lacked a church but are often identifiable as a farm bearing a name recognizable as that recorded by the commissioners. A third tier of holdings are the small estates, often held by free men before the Conquest, but then brought under Norman lordship. The sites of some are known, but many elude accurate location.

The location of settlement below the level of the manorial hall remains a mystery. The humble dwellings of villeins, bordars and cottars were short-lived and left little or no trace in the sub-soil for archaeologists to identify. They may underlie later farms and hamlets or cluster near the manor, but this remains conjecture. Consequently I have eschewed the term 'village' with its familiar imagery in favour of 'vill' which lacks such associations. Definition of settlement would come over the next two centuries as a response to population growth, the expansion of arable and the need to concentrate resources. Those years would see the establishment of towns, the digging of homestead moats, the formation of tofts around common grazing, and the clustering of cottages and smallholdings into hamlets, if indeed the hamlets did not pre-exist, which might sometimes have been the case.

Roads and trackways

Nearly all of today's villages and hamlets are recorded under the names of their manors, a total of 840 and almost all bearing English names, albeit sometimes qualified by the added appellation of their Norman overlord. All would have been connected, and it is likely that some of today's network of minor roads, country lanes and green ways, would appear familiar to a herdsman or carter of 1086. Modifications would happen, trackways diverted around deer parks and demesne fields, and new routes opened to farmsteads colonizing the rough pastures and wastes. The straight surveyors' roads which are characteristic of the Midlands are relatively unusual and are found where enclosure awards were made in the late eighteenth and early nineteenth centuries in the areas of heathland, the common-fields of north-west Essex, and commons and greens elsewhere. The road from Takeley Street to Bush End, cutting Hatfield Forest is a good example. These should be distinguished from the straight roads of much earlier date which occur in the Dengie peninsula and south Essex, and were a part of the scene in 1086.

The regional arteries built by the Romans remained then, as now, in use: Stane Street, the A120 from St Albans to Colchester, and the London to Colchester Road (A12). Many other stretches of Roman roads survive, but are rarely continuous over a distance; diverted maybe as their surfaces disintegrated to find gentler, meandering routes accommodated to contours. It is possible that following the conquest of Essex by Edward the Elder, efficient government may have required the maintenance of at least the principal roads - a long established duty of land-holders. We might conclude that some minor roads and green lanes are of Roman, or even of prehistoric date, and while none have yet been proved to be so, the density of former settlement makes it likely.[28]

Boundaries

It is often stated that parish boundary hedges date back to Saxon or even earlier times. In some cases this is so, but often it is not. Parishes did not exist in a formal sense in 1086 and when later established, were formed from groups of manors or holdings based on a church and the boundary of the parish naturally followed the perimetal boundary of the group. Manorial boundaries followed natural features such as rivers and brooks, existing features such as Roman roads, and were defined by field boundaries only where the fields of one manor abutted the land of another. In the planned landscapes of the Dengie and south Essex it seems likely that the bounds were precisely defined by hedges in 1086 except in the fens and wooded areas. Elsewhere, in the wastes, commons and heaths they may have been marked by pollard trees, erratic boulders or by the lie of the land enshrined in local custom. Personal observation of the date of hedges on the Till suggests that a good proportion of parish boundaries appear to date from medieval rather than earlier times.

CHAPTER SEVEN

The Conqueror's dispensation

WILLIAM'S GREAT SURVEY described, for purposes of taxation and record of land ownership, an existing landscape he had acquired by conquest and allotted to his followers as spoils of war. The imprint of the Norman kings on this landscape is still apparent in the earthworks and structures of the castles raised to subdue and overawe their new subjects, and in the surviving relics of the royal forest, whose legal extent once covered most of the county. These will be considered below, but first and more immediately apparent, is the legacy of the invaders and their descendants in the names of parishes, manors, farms and sometimes features such as woods.

'No county bears as strongly as Essex the imprint of the Norman Conquest', wrote P H Reaney, author of *The Place-Names of Essex*[1], 'many of the feudal and manorial names which preserve the memory of former land-holders are definitely Norman, some dating actually from the Conquest. The map of Essex is dotted with names which preserve - often in strange disguise - names of French towns and French families'. Two such parishes are Beaumont (Fulepett in 1086) and Pleshey, a post Conquest creation; Grays Thurrock is usually called simply Grays, from Henry de Grey, its lord in 1194. Helions Bumpstead, Woodham Ferrers, Shellow Bowells, Stondon Massey and Berners Roding all owe their added appellations to Domesday barons or undertenants. Reaney lists some 50 parishes with the manorial holder's name added or prefixed;[2] while most of these date from after 1086, they derive from the descendants of the new landholders.

It is certainly helpful that where a group of villages or hamlets with the same name occurs, to have each distinguished by an eponym or descriptive adjective. Take for example the Rodings (or Roothings), the settlement of the people of Hroda and the largest such cluster: Aythorpe Roding, from Aytrop (or Eutropius) c 1200; Berners Roding, held by Hugh de Berners in 1086; Leaden Roding, said to be the first church in the district roofed in lead; High Roding, from its high plateau position; Margaret Roding, from its patron saint; White Roding, the largest Roding and formerly called Great, from the whiteness of its church walls; Abbess Roding, a possession of Barking Abbey, and Beauchamp Roding, from the family of William de Beauchamp. Another example is Tolleshunt, Toll's spring, a group of three villages: Tolleshunt Major, formerly Magna or Great; Tolleshunt d'Arcy, from the Darcy family, and Tolleshunt Knights, perhaps the area of a knight's fee. Thus three appellations in the Rodings and one in the Tolleshunts derive from a follower of the Conqueror or his descendant.

At the local level numerous names, particularly of farms, derive from Domesday Book landholders. A good example is Robert Gernon, a major baron holding some 45 manors in Essex, whose family name is preserved in Theydon Garnon, Garnish Hall, Gernon Bushes and farms called Garnetts in Felsted, High Easter, Great Dunmow and Great Waltham. The name Gernon derives from grenon, 'moustaches' in Old French.

This brief discussion of a considerable subject serves to show the lasting enrichment brought by the influx of new families to an aspect of the countryside which we may value as important for identity and regional diversity. Doubtless many of the inhabitants of the time would have seen the matter differently.

Landscapes of surveillance and control

The castles of the Normans have mellowed through centuries of ruin and erosion to achieve a romantic beauty, and have come indeed to be viewed with affection as venerable features of the landscape. It is difficult now to visualise them as they were when raw and new, sinister and oppressive artefacts. Later castles would sometimes be built to be beautiful, but the Normans had more pressing matters on their minds.

Castles were the most important instruments in the subjugation of the country. The Saxon burhs were fortified towns, designed to shelter the population as well as for defence against invaders. Castles, very rare in England before the Conquest, were essentially different, being small and designed as a safe place from which a few men could dominate an area. Orderic Vitalis writing some six decades later, opined that the English would never have been conquered had they possessed castles of their own.[3]

The process by which the warrior adventurers took possession of the lands awarded them by the Conqueror has been reconstructed by R H C Davis.[4] The claimant would arrive at the shire court, where all landowners would be assembled at six-monthly intervals, and produce a sealed writ which would be opened, inspected and read aloud. Surrounded by a force of soldiers, resistance would be folly and doubtless locations and extents would be forthcoming. Boundaries would be extracted at local level, if necessary by terror. At first it would be unsafe to split up and 'for some years the Normans would have had to behave in the manner of all armies of occupation, living, eating and sleeping together in occupational units.' Housed in castles built in the principal towns and at strategic locations in the countryside, it is likely that they lived as the household knights of their overlord, exploiting their estates as absentee landlords for the time being.

Of the two Essex towns, Colchester's castle still stands, but Maldon's has vanished; it seems likely that one was built but possible clues, revealed by archaeology, do not yet provide a site. Elsewhere, castles appear the foci of the Essex estates of the overlords, the territorial magnates: Pleshey and Walden of the Mandevilles, Hedingham of the de Veres - with Canfield as an outpost - Rayleigh of Suain, Ongar of Eustace of Boulogne and Stansted of Gernon (he of the moustaches). It would seem likely that the essential elements were built first: the motte surmounted by a wooden tower, and the adjacent bailey protecting barracks, storehouses, stables and workshops. The need for speed would have ruled out the finely crafted carpentry of later timber castles. Earthworks would be raised by massed labour and crowned by palisades of timber from the extensive woodland resources, and these I suspect, were disguised as masonry as in the recent reconstruction at Wexford[5]: coated with cob, smoothed over and finished with limewash. The result: alien, effulgent and menacing, power was demonstrated and surveillance established over a wide tract of land. Perhaps, when time permitted, the tower was embellished with dragons and brightly painted as depicted on the Bayeux Tapestry.

The only Essex castle to find a mention in Domesday Book is Suain's Rayleigh which is of particular interest both for the intriguing history of its owners and for the monument itself, for which excavation has shown two phases of construction.[6] Robert FitzWymarc, Suain's father, was the only Essex lay magnate to retain the estates he held before the Conquest. Robert was a friend of Edward the Confessor and inevitably became involved in the power politics which attended the latter years of the childless old king. In 1052 Earl Godwin and his sons returned from exile and the French party fled, escaping 'north to Robert's castle'. Robert held Clavering, his largest Essex manor, where a monument known as Clavering Castle takes the form of a rectangular island over an acre in extent, surrounded by a massive fosse about 18 feet deep and 75 feet wide.[7] The few other pre-Conquest castles lie westwards on the Welsh border, so Clavering's claim to have the earliest castle in eastern England is a good one. Robert remained sheriff of Essex under William, and his son succeeded him, greatly increasing and consolidating his landholding in south-east Essex by seizures obtained in his capacity as sheriff.[8] By 1086 Suain was the greatest sheepmaster in Essex with grazing for over 4000 on the marshes.

Virtually his entire south-eastern fiefdom would have been visible on a clear day from the summit of the tower standing on his motte. Rayleigh Castle is sited on a spur of the Rayleigh-Hockley ridge with the motte standing some 50 feet above the general level, and the view from the tower would easily have cleared the tree line of the pastured woods and heaths which clothed the hills. Looking westwards, Suain would have observed the rectilinear patterns of the south Essex plain stretching to the wooded ridge of Upminster and Warley; northwards, beyond the woods of Burstead and Ramsden, the distinctive shape of Danbury would lie on the horizon; north-eastwards across the Crouch lay the planned landscape of the Dengie peninsula and in the far distance, if his sight was good and the light clear, he might just have discerned the great tower of Colchester Castle, some 25 miles away. Turning eastward, Suain would look across the gentle valley of the upper Roach with his extensive deer park to the ordered fields and lanes of Paglesham, Stambridge and the Wakerings and, in the distance, his valuable pastures in the Roach archipelago on the islands of Wallasea, Havengore, Potton and Foulness. Southward lay Canvey, and across the Thames estuary, the marshes of Kent and the North Downs.

In the twelfth century the castle underwent major reconstruction and extension with the level of the bailey raised and the enclosure walled. A large outer bailey was added, but this is not visible today having made way for later developments.[9]

In 1163 Suain's grandson Henry of Essex was disgraced, having allegedly fled in battle from the Welsh and abandoned the standard in his care. The matter was proved to the satisfaction of the king by trial by combat and Henry's estates and castle were forfeit to the crown. Henry survived and was allowed to become a monk. Rayleigh would seem to demonstrate two phases in castle development: first, a secure redoubt from which to exercise control, and secondly, a seigneurial stronghold which would impress one's peers as well as humbler inhabitants and also provide the space and setting for a more generous lifestyle.

The dates are not known for the initial construction of Essex castles, with the exception of Colchester where building work began in 1070 or 1071. Colchester is remarkable in other ways, the outer walls of the great tower being built around and against the massive podium of the temple of Claudius, the dimensions of which determined that it would be the largest in Britain, considerably exceeding the White Tower of London in size.[10] Despite its Roman walls, the town had been attacked and perhaps burned by a fleet of raiding Danes in 1069, an event which prompted William to grant the lordship of Colchester to his trusted steward Eudo with, one presumes, the injunction to construct a fortress as soon as possible.[11]

The ruins of the temple were traditionally believed to be those of the palace of King Coel. If anything survived of the superstructure it was swept away and walls 10 feet thick were built abutting the sides of the podium, the materials quarried from Roman remains in the town. In 1075 marauding Danes again threatened the town and battlements were built around the podium, the level that had been reached by the walls. When work resumed the battlements were incorporated into the structure and their outlines can still be seen.

The height we see today is much reduced from that attained by Eudo, the castle suffering plunder for building materials in the late seventeenth century, an act of destruction more characteristic of the later twentieth century until one reflects that Eudo did much the same, but in his case with the justification of strategic necessity. The original height was about 90 feet (27m) with the corner turrets reaching a further 15 - 20 feet (4.5-6.5m). The appearance of the great tower in the landscape when completed in about 1080 must have been stunning, a symbol of royal authority completely outclassing the strongholds of the barons, and if the size of the fortress was an indication of that of the garrison, a powerful deterrent to seaborne raiders.[12]

Colchester, as an urban castle, is similar to the Tower of London, Cambridge and Rochester, but differs by being sited within the town. These other examples were sited on the urban edge for ease of outside communication should the townsfolk rebel. The rural castles, centres of territorial control, were all of the motte and bailey type of which Pleshey is regarded as an exemplar. It is eminently photogenic, particularly from the air, where motte, baileys and town enclosure are seen compactly contained within a precise perimeter, a gourd shaped island in a sea of farmland. The early decline of the town to a small village ensured the survival of the massive earthworks and the absence of development outside the

Pleshey from the air (photo P. Rogers)

perimeter. A dramatic prospect of the motte can be seen from the viewing area beside The Street.

The first phase consisted of the motte and a single bailey which is now marked by the curve in Back Lane. Excavations of the upper bailey have dated its construction to the late twelfth century and this second phase was probably associated with the permission granted to William de Mandeville to re-fortify the castle in 1167. William's father, Geoffrey de Mandeville II, had fallen out with King Stephen in the civil war with Matilda and been forced to surrender his castles; Pleshey may have been 'slighted' as a result, or alternatively decommissioned when Henry II came to the throne and sought to reduce the numbers of castles in private hands. William may at this time have sought to repeat at Pleshey the success of the town planted by his family at Walden. This would give a date for the earthwork enclosing the town and most probably the deer park (Pleshey Little Park) which surrounded the town and castle.[13] The fields for the townsfolk lay adjacent to the west.

In a report on excavations carried out early in this century by the Morant Club of foundations discovered on the motte, Miller Christy made the point that the chalky boulder clay is an exceptionally stable material with a high angle of repose, and hence the excellent state of preservation of the Pleshey earthworks.[14] London clay is far less stable with a tendency to slump as can be seen at Hadleigh Castle. From the motte tower the whole Mandeville fiefdom in central Essex could be seen, and the North Downs are visible on a clear day from the surface of the motte.

The Mandevilles' other castle at Walden was sited on a strategic spur formed by two tributaries of the Cam. Here, in later centuries, a reverse process to that at Pleshey took place due to the prosperity of the town. The earthworks were shovelled into the ditches and built over, with the plan of the baileys preserved in the pattern of the streets. The rubble core of the keep survives, a romantic and melancholy ruin in the grounds of the excellent museum.

Hedingham Castle stands in a similarly commanding relationship to the valley of the Colne as Walden to that of the Cam. Like Walden its tower keep was built on the natural land surface, and it is described by the Royal Commission as 'among the finest and most complete examples of twelfth century military architecture in England. The condition of the tower is extraordinarily perfect'.[15] Faced with Barnack stone the tower stands 73 feet tall (22.2m) with two corner turrets extending a further 20 feet (6m). Hedingham meets well the traditional pictorial image of a stone castle and has no rivals nearer than the royal castle at Orford in Suffolk and the White Tower itself. The bailey earthworks, sculpted from the spur on which they stand, substantially remain and the pretty market town, now a village, with its Norman church lie at the foot just above the floodplain of the Colne.

Colchester, Pleshey and Hedingham are monuments of national importance, but others are also of considerable historic interest and are important features of

Castle Hedingham (G Virtue, 1831)

the landscape: Chipping Ongar, a fine tree-covered motte with a wet moat, presides over the planned market town and the valley of the Roding. Great Canfield, also tree-clad and well preserved lies in deep countryside, and mottes survive at Mount Bures, Great Easton and Stebbing. Lesser mounds and ringworks also occur which may date from this period, such as that at Elmdon.

The forest of Essex

The term Forest was used in the Middle Ages in a legal sense to denote a tract of land subject to special laws, devised to protect the king's deer and the deer's habitat, and to penalise those that infringed them. Its modern use to denote a large area covered by trees has given rise to considerable confusion, and continues to do so. This is particularly so because a mythology, invented to promote modern forestry, fostered the belief that the royal forests had suffered a long process of 'degradation' which, in the twentieth century, required re-planting and generous subsidy from the public purse to redress. This was far from the truth.

The main purpose of a forest was to supply venison for the consumption of the court or the king's friends. Venison was a commodity kept strictly for the royal and the rich, which was never sold on the market. The products of trees growing within a forest - timber and underwood - were the property of the landholder and his tenants, and were only the king's if the manor was royal. But forest law had a value other than venison for the king : it was a useful source of revenue from fines exacted by the forest courts, and when, several centuries later, Charles I tried to revive long dormant laws his interest did not lie in trees. The courts were administered by a special bureaucracy appointed by the crown headed, as far as Essex was concerned, by the Keeper of the Forest of Essex,[16] followed in various degrees of status by keepers, regarders, verderers and the skilled huntsmen who did the work. Sinecures and perquisites were a part of the system and one is reminded of the modern quango, providing rewards for followers believed to be loyal. For those not so employed, Forest Law was regarded as oppressive and became one of the many issues addressed in 1215 at Runnymede.

Forests were established on the continent at a much earlier date and introduced to England by the Conqueror. His successors, up to the time of King John, appear to have greatly extended their number and extent. By the time of the Angevins, the vast demesne acquired by William had been much reduced by grants of land given to loyal supporters by his sons and Stephen, and as a consequence forest law was used as a lucrative and welcome source of revenue from fines. Under Henry II forest law possibly covered one third of the kingdom, and a profitable flood of fines for 'waste of forest' and assarts, the conversion of woodland or waste into cultivated land, flowed into the exchequer.[17] The *Dialogus de Scaccario* (1177) laid down a common and fixed penalty for assarts in the royal forests: perpetual annual rents of one shilling per acre for land sown with wheat, and sixpence for oats. In the settlement of the dispute between Henry II and the Church which followed the murder of Thomas Becket, the papal legate conceded that clerks guilty of forest offences would be tried and punished in the royal courts.[18] As will be seen, two Essex religious houses would be fined for extending their demesnes.

It seems probable that there was a forest in Essex by 1104, and that it extended over much if not all of the county, as the crown was subsequently to claim. In 1141 Geoffrey de Mandeville, Earl of Essex, secured a charter from the Empress Matilda not only for a market for his manor of Walden, at the expense of the royal manor of Newport, but a pardon for all forest offences, wastes and assarts committed on his land, and permission to plough and cultivate the clearings freely. Aubrey de Vere, Earl of Oxford and owner of the great estate based on Hedingham, obtained a similar pardon in 1142.[19] Some were less fortunate. In 1167 Coggeshall Priory paid a fine of 34 pounds for wastes and assarts in breach of forest law, and in 1203 the Abbot of Waltham paid seven pounds for cultivating 100 acres.[20] In 1293 the Knights Templar were in trouble for selling timber from the Cressing woods, which was used as a pretext for their seizure by the crown.[21] When the woods were returned, it was on condition that other woods previously 'outside the regard of the forest' should now remain within it, in perpetuity. Where these were is not known, and the incident suggests some other motive at work than just royal sharp practice.

Not surprisingly, forest law was deeply unpopular. Knights, freeholders and religious houses combined to raise huge sums to secure the release of land, sometimes whole counties, from the restrictions of forest law. In 1204 the men of Essex paid 500 marks and five palfreys for 'the forest of Essex which is beyond the causeway between Colchester and Bishop's Stortford'.[22] But this settlement was only a preliminary for trials to come, and a legal battle raged for over a century as to the true extent of the forest over the rest of the county. Oral evidence was given by 'good and honest men', successive perambulations made, and at one point even the pope was involved; the advantage to each side ebbed and flowed, the crown giving way when politically weak or in need of money and support, and reneging when it felt itself strong.[23]

Eventually in 1327 the youthful Edward III, seeking to consolidate his support, confirmed the Charter of Forest which had been granted by his grandfather Edward I in 1301, but had subsequently prevailed on the pope to have quashed. Forest land was now confined to the royal manors and to the great forest in southwest Essex, where it had long been argued by the men of Essex it should rightfully have been.

The core areas of the remaining forests were tracts of common-land, generally well-wooded and attractive to deer. Hatfield and Writtle were royal manors and the legal extent of the forest included the whole area of the manor, although the 'physical' forest only covered a part. Kingswood was attached to Colchester, a royal borough, and the king owned the trees and grazing. Waltham Forest continued to cover a huge area of around 60,000 acres (24,280 ha), and contained three 'physical' forests: Epping, Wintry and Hainault. The king owned much of Hainault which lay next to the palace of Havering, a royal haunt, and although the crown owned almost none of Epping Forest it lay beside Waltham Abbey, a favourite royal monastery.

Harsh though the forest laws were in theory, being designed to protect the 'vert' as the deer's habitat as well as the deer themselves, the reality was that woodland management became condoned: timber was felled and underwood cut, and outside the core areas woodlands, heaths and wastes were steadily nibbled away to provide more land to grow crops for an expanding population.[24] The core areas survived, protected by systems of inter-commoning or royal ownership, but elsewhere one suspects that Edward's charter legalized a situation already de facto.

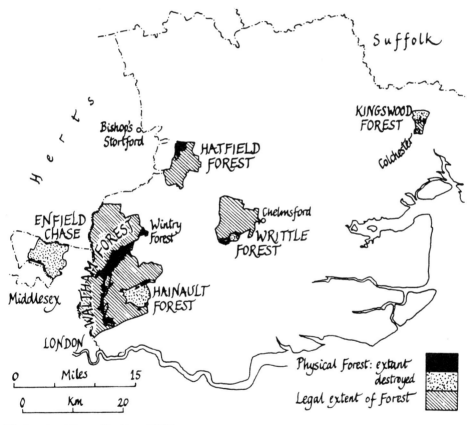

The forests of Essex (Rackham 1989)

CHAPTER EIGHT

The high Middle Ages

IN ECONOMIC AND social terms the single dominant characteristic of the two centuries which followed Domesday Book is expansion. In England, as over much of Europe during this period, new towns and markets sprang up and existing ones expanded. In 1086 there were two towns in Essex, while by 1250 there were more than thirty. Similarly, new industries were established while older ones developed and grew; more was being produced and more exchanged. Socially, the descendants of the Conqueror's army were becoming Englishmen; the *Dialogus de Scaccario* written in 1177 noted that 'nowadays, when English and Normans live close together and marry and are given in marriage to each other, the nations are so mixed that it can scarcely be decided (I mean in the case of the freemen) who is of English birth and who of Norman'.

A growing population required more food and this led to a progressive conversion of uncultivated land into arable, a retreat of common grazing, often to the land less attractive to cultivators and an intensification of management in the remaining areas of woodland. By 1300 a delicate balance existed between a high level of population and what could be supplied by the agricultural technology of the time.

Attitudes to landscape were changing. Norman aristocratic families maintained links with their kin overseas, particularly in the newly conquered kingdoms of southern Italy and Sicily.[1] Contacts with the Arab world brought awareness of the culture and science of antiquity, much of which had been lost in the Dark Ages in the west, and the paradisal tradition of parks and gardens. The pleasure grounds of the emirs around Palermo that were now the property of the adventurous Hauteville family must have seemed the Garden of Eden itself to a northern visitor. Two species of parkland fauna were transported to stock parks and royal forests in England: the fallow deer, originally from the near East, and the coney (rabbit), probably from Lusitania. Both adapted to a colder climate and thrived, in later centuries becoming feral, and nowadays something of a problem.

The interest of lords and great prelates was not limited to their new parks and pleasure grounds; in the thirteenth century many took an active and practical interest in the development and expansion of their demesnes. Scenes of farming activities had been depicted in late Anglo-Saxon manuscripts, and now the tradition revived and developed, and in time produced such masterpieces as the Luttrell Psalter and the Holkham Bible in which peasants, with their implements and stock, carts and mills are drawn with the accuracy that comes from direct observation. This, it would seem, is what the patrons expected.

By the early fourteenth century the balance between food supply and demand was becoming critical. Climatic deterioration, famines, epidemics and the Black Death in 1348 followed. The great period of expansion had ended effectively around 1300. Much of that landscape survives in Essex. The settlement pattern had crystallised into towns, villages and a scatter of hamlets and farmsteads.

Crofts, tofts and farmsteads dotted the edges of greens and the remaining commons and heaths like flotsam, marking the line left by the high tide of arable expansion. Scattered farmsteads were often moated, for this was the age of moat construction when anyone with the means and labour sought this status symbol. Woodland had retreated and was now a valuable resource, enclosed with ditches and banks, sometimes massive, to exclude livestock and deter further depredation. As a rule, woods were managed as coppice with standards, and pasture woodland was now to be found only on commons and in the many manorial parks. The core areas of Forest survived at Waltham (Epping and Wintry), Hainault, Writtle, Hatfield and Kingswood (to the north of Colchester). The clearance of land for cultivation had been pushed to its limits; demesnes had expanded, often with huge fields even by modern standards, while the peasantry tilled in scattered farms, crofts and small common-fields based on hamlets. Common-fields of the midland type, based on nucleated villages, had developed only in the extreme north-west of the county. Fields were generally hedged, and many of these hedgerows can be found if looked for. Some mark the boundaries of farms and manors, and the parishes which had been organised and defined by this time, probably 395 in number. Only on the heavy and barely tractable London clays of the Dengie and South Essex Plain do we find little change; the population remained low with little cause to alter the landscape.

The landscape of 1300 would seem in the main to be that depicted by Chapman and André in their Map of Essex of 1777. The distribution of settlement and the network of roads and lanes would seem much as they were on the eve of the Black Death, and indeed much as they are today where not overwhelmed by urban and industrial development. The great heaths were still there in 1777, but were regarded as retrograde and archaic by the agriculturalists of that time, and were enclosed over the four decades which followed. The scraps that survived have changed in character and the heathland landscapes of north-east Essex are now extinct. The manorial parks had gone, but their woods and boundaries often survived in farmland, and still do. In some cases as at Thorndon, Easton, Braxted and Copped Hall, early parks underlay the fashionable designed landscapes of later centuries.

Turning now to look at how this landscape evolved over the twelfth and thirteenth centuries, we will first consider the phenomenal growth in the number of towns, and why some prospered and others failed. The morphology of towns is properly a matter for townscape studies, and we are concerned here with the relationship of towns to the countryside around them and their impact on the landscape.

Markets and towns

Following the Conquest and the consolidation of the Norman kingdom, rising productivity and trade plus strong rule, freedom from invasion and a measure of

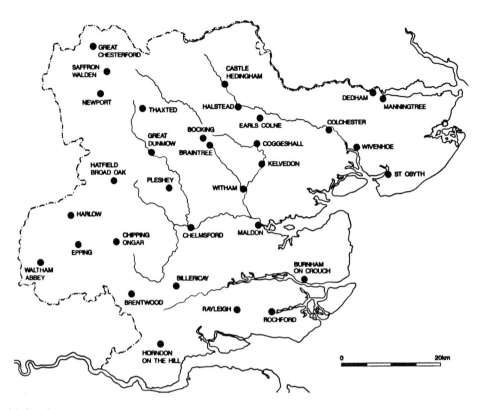

Medieval towns

stability led local magnates, both lay and ecclesiastical, to speculate in the founding of towns. In 1086 only Maldon and Colchester had the status of towns, but many local markets with what might be termed proto-towns must have already existed, some long established, for points of exchange for the surplus produced in the countryside were essential if taxes were to be paid and goods to be acquired that were not made locally. Incentives for the founding of towns lay in the returns from selling or leasing urban plots, in addition to income from market tolls. Against these benefits there was the cost of the charter, for the crown had also spotted new towns as a source of revenue, and from at least the late twelfth century, authorisation in the form of a charter was required to establish a new market. As early as 1141, the de Mandevilles had secured a charter to shut down the existing market at Newport and establish a new one beside their castle at Walden.

Some 24 markets are known to have existed prior to the year 1200. Most of these were held by prescription, or ancient custom, rather than royal charter. Between 1200 and 1249 charters for a further 54 were issued, the numbers peaking between

1225 and 1274 with 29 licensed. But in the long term the majority failed commercially, and during the period 1500 to 1640 only 27 had survived - three more than had been recorded in the years before 1200.[2]

Towns that were to flourish and prove long-lived were mostly sited on main roads, particularly at nodal points in the network, and at river crossings. In 1199 the Bishop of London secured a charter for a market at Braintree, a crossing point of two Roman roads, and also in the same year one for Chelmsford, where the enterprising prelate built a bridge and planted a town which thrived on trade diverted from its earlier route through the royal manor of Writtle. Great Dunmow (1227) was similarly well placed at the junction of two Roman roads. Braintree, Chelmsford and Dunmow were all founded on or beside the sites of former Roman towns. New foundations on the ancient roads radiating from London did well: the canons of Waltham Abbey planted Epping (1253) a mile away from the old manorial centre, while the Knights Templar planted Newland Street, Witham (1212) on the London to Colchester road near the sites of an Iron Age settlement and a Roman temple. The market was moved from the manorial centre beside the hill-fort at Chipping Hill.

Brentwood is similar to Epping, lying along the London road; there is no evidence for earlier settlement on the site which lay in woodland or waste on the southern edge of South Weald, but in 1221 the canons of St Osyth Priory received permission to build a chapel dedicated to St Thomas of Canterbury in the expectation of alms from pilgrims and travellers. A settlement was already growing following assarts in 1177, and probably a market was being held when a charter was obtained in 1227. Incidentally, it was in the Chapel of St Thomas that Hubert de Burgh, builder of Hadleigh Castle, sought sanctuary in 1232, eventually being starved into submission.

Another monastic foundation which proved a lasting success is Coggeshall. Situated only six miles from Witham, it is well-placed on Stane Street where the road from Earls Colne to Kelvedon crosses. The abbey was founded in 1142, a Cistercian house, with productive farming and landscape management a priority in the order's rule. The monks engineered flood control over the water meadows, diverting the River Blackwater into a new channel while leaving the old course as a drainage and overflow ditch. Extensive fishponds were dug and a large millpond. The monks' bridge is the oldest surviving brick bridge in Britain although the original work is not readily visible. The market was sited off the Roman road which ran along the river terrace to the north of the flood-plain. The parish church, centre of the earlier vill, lies on the edge of the medieval town.

Coggeshall Abbey was a relative newcomer in comparison with the abbey church of Waltham Holy Cross. A minster was built at Waltham in the seventh century, the first of three successive pre-Norman churches. The Norman church was an immense building, approximately 130 metres long from the western porch to the eastern wall, of which only the nave survives as the magnificent parish church. The site was venerated for a miraculous relic, a stone cross, and also as the rumoured burial place of Harold Godwinson, the last Saxon king and remembered as a former benefactor. Waltham had been a Saxon royal estate and place of assembly for the hundredal court, and had a long established fair and market, well-sited as a strategic point on a causeway crossing the marshy flood-plain of the Lea. The medieval town lay immediately to the south of the monastic precinct, while to the north lay the meadows of the grange. This land has remained open, with the shapes still visible of the fishponds which were formerly supplied by a sluice from the Cornmill stream. Both the artificial water-courses of the Cornmill and Lower Mill streams are still flowing and, viewed from the north, one can see a monastic landscape still dominated by its abbey church.

In a distinct category of their own, built with defences, were the castle towns, and of these there were four: Chipping Ongar, Hedingham, Walden and Pleshey. The area allotted for the new town was enclosed by a ditch and rampart crowned with a palisade, and the entries were controlled by gateways. These defining limits have mostly vanished; the approaches became developed in later centuries, and in the late twentieth are usually a suburban blur. At Castle Hedingham and in the northern approach to Saffron Walden there is still a good distinction between what is urban and what is country, and to our eyes agreeably bosky, but they would never have been so when these towns were young. Indeed the town perimeters, abutted by open arable fields, would at first have looked as raw and gaunt as their castles, until in course of time nature colonized the banks and the orchards of the burgesses grew up to soften the skyline.

Pleshey differed from the others in being surrounded by a deer park, with the fields of the townsfolk lying directly to the west. The town was ill-placed for long term viability, being sited well away from the main road network, and when the castle became derelict the town dwindled to a small village. This ensured the survival of the perimeter earthwork, although the park became farmland.

Walden, then known as Chipping Walden, was the most successful, lying beside the Cam valley, the important route through the chalk hills from London to the fenlands; but it owed its success to chicanery as well as siting. Geoffrey de Mandeville had acquired the charter from the Empress Matilda in 1141, a time when she needed support in her struggle with Stephen and was prepared to sacrifice the market at the royal manor of Newport to secure his loyalty. As Earl of Essex and castellan of the Tower of London Geoffrey could drive a hard bargain, which he did not keep. As we have seen earlier, he secured his estates from forest fines. A new road was built to divert traffic from the valley floor up into the town, and over the next century the town prospered sufficiently for Humphrey de Bohun - the de Bohuns had succeeded to the de Mandeville estates in Essex - to plan a major expansion to the south. This was enclosed by the earthwork which survives in the south-west corner of the medieval town, and has been traced elsewhere by archaeologists, and there is clear evidence for a gridded street plan.[3]

Unlike Pleshey, Castle Hedingham and Chipping Ongar were both well sited from a commercial viewpoint. Hedingham sits on a spur overlooking the Colne valley, the route from Cambridge and the Fenlands to Colchester, and Ongar lies astride the road from Woodford which follows the Roding valley northwards to Aythorpe Roding where it joins the Roman road to Dunmow.

Rayleigh, also a castle town, does not appear to have been enclosed by defences, although it is likely that the outer bailey of the castle would have served as a refuge for the townsfolk in an emergency. As the centre of the Rayleigh Hundred the settlement may have predated the building of the castle, and was sufficiently prosperous to survive its decommissioning when in the 1230s Hubert de Burgh built his new castle at Hadleigh.

Of the many settlements whose hopeful owners obtained charters, but failed to develop into viable towns, Kelvedon (1312) and Great Bardfield (1224) are good examples. Both are villages of architectural distinction, and when one considers the development which disgraced the centre of Witham in the 1960s, one may feel grateful that commercial success eluded its neighbour Kelvedon. In Roman times, Kelvedon was a town and of considerably higher status than the settlement at Witham, and it is to its earlier regular plan, as well as its gracious buildings, that Kelvedon owes its distinctly urban air. Great Bardfield is quite different, organic rather than regular, and with its village green and feeling of space it appears a classic pretty village. However, a block of buildings in the centre, bounded by Vine and Crown Streets, is infilled market, and it would seem that for a while it may have prospered as a small market town. The decline of its important manor and its remote position from principal roads rendered Bardfield economically unsustainable in the longer term.

Rural settlement

Essex is a county of dispersed rural settlement, generally in hamlets and scattered farmsteads. If the term 'village' means a settlement with church and manor house, pubs and basic shops, formerly surrounded by common-fields governed by manorial court or village assembly and worked by farms sited in the village, then the only Essex examples lie in the northwest corner of the county. This is the model general to central England and not applicable to most of Essex. But in practice 'village' is a term used very loosely, particularly by incomers who like it. Under the criteria listed above Thaxted would qualify as a village, were it not for its former charter and successful centuries as a market town; it is known (correctly) as a town by those who were born there, but as a village by those who have come there to live. Great Waltham and Ford End appear today as villages but their origins lay as hamlets. So one should perhaps not be pedantic when talking of villages. Towns too, as we have seen, can be complicated, particularly as in certain parts of England hamlets are referred to as townships. One may recall that relative status may sometimes seem odd; Chelmsford remains a town rather than a city, a status that St Davids, Pembrokeshire, has recently attained with a population smaller than that of Thaxted.

All of which is somewhat confusing. By 1300, however, it would seem that most rural settlements were hamlets, other than those aspiring, and sometimes succeeding, as towns. This is evident in the placenames which include the descriptive terms end, cross, street, green and tye, of which end and green are by far the most numerous. The huge parish of Great Waltham, second in size only to Writtle, demonstrates this form of settlement and is also of interest for aspects of its seignorial development.

Manor and hamlet

In 1086 Geoffrey de Mandeville held the three manors that were to form the parish of Great Waltham: Walthambury, much the largest, Chatham, and a small unidentified manor. Adjacent to the west he held High Easter. These were to form the cen-

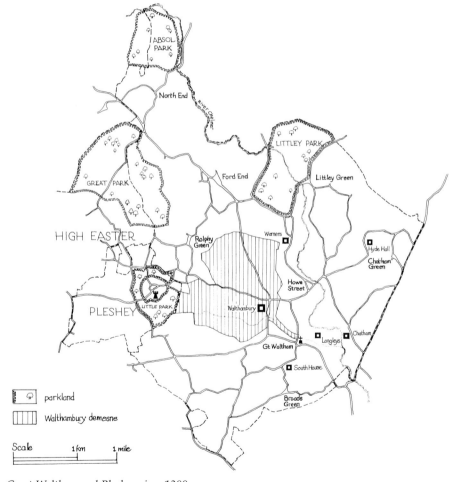

Great Waltham and Pleshey circa 1300

tre of his great fief in central Essex. The manorial centre of Walthambury lay beside the road running northwards from Chelmsford to Walden and Great Chesterford[4], but Geoffrey chose to build his castle a mile and a half to the west on the border with High Easter, a fatal decision for the long term viability of Pleshey as a town, but excellent for the future preservation of the town and castle earthworks. The land for the town fields was taken from High Easter and the town was surrounded by the Little Park.[5] Three other parks lay within the estate: Littley, Absol, and the Great Park, which was extended by a licence in 1320. In all, the parks comprized some 1475 acres (597 ha) reflecting high status - the de Mandevilles and their successors the de Bohuns were Earls of Essex - but there were also available stretches of well-wooded land; Domesday Book had recorded woodland for 1980 pigs.

Writing in 1768 Morant noted the following eight hamlets:

Church End, which became the village of Great Waltham
Chatham End, now Chatham Green
How Street - the spelling has changed to Howe
North End
Fourth End, now Ford End
South End, now Broad's Green
Littley Green
Rophey Green, now Rolphy Green

A parish map of 1816[6] shows the hamlets, other than the village, related to small, irregularly shaped fields. Between Ford End and the boundary of the former Great Park, much of the land is shown as strip farmed and adjacent closes, by their shape and names, were clearly once similar. With the aid of a written survey of 1563,[7] the area can be seen to have consisted of small common-fields: Frynswell, Stockcroft, Smetheley, Redon and Longfeld, with an average size of 37 acres (15 ha). This gives a clue to understanding a particular type of field pattern that occurs in association with hamlets, and it is indeed fortunate that these strip fields survived to be recorded on a map. Common-fields on the Midland model were very large and their management and rotations governed at village level, but these Ford End examples are small by comparison and their rotations must have been planned at the level of the hamlet. Common grazing in greens was generally retained as the core area of the hamlets.

In addition to the pre-Conquest manors of Walthambury and Chatham, the later sub-manors had been established of Warners, Hide Hall, South House, and Langleys; also the Rectory, which together with the advowson, had been granted by the de Mandevilles to their abbey at Walden. All available land was in productive use, farmed by the peasantry from their hamlets, or held in demesne or leased out by the manors. The boundaries of the huge Walthambury demesne are known; those of the other manors would have been very much smaller. Conspicuous wealth was displayed in the extent of the land reserved for the deer parks, by no

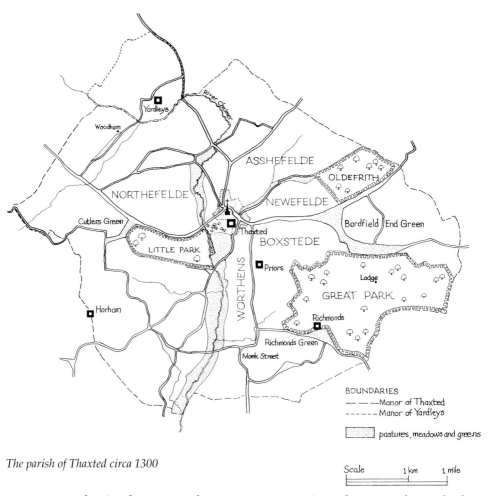

The parish of Thaxted circa 1300

BOUNDARIES
—— ——Manor of Thaxted
— — — — — Manor of Yardleys

pastures, meadows and greens

Scale   1 km   1 mile

means unproductive, but on a scale unnecessary at a time of pressure from a high population.

The manor of Thaxted was also large and of high status, and like Walthambury reserved extensive areas for deer parks despite the pressures to convert to arable. But it differed in being fully open-field in the Midland manner characteristic of north-west Essex. There was no exclusive demesne as at Walthambury, the manorial arable lying in the common-fields. We are fortunate in having Ken Newton's study *Thaxted in the Fourteenth Century* with his analysis and transcription of the survey made in 1393 to replace the records destroyed in the Peasants Revolt. There were three sub-manors: Horham, the largest, in existence in 1262; Priors, a pre-Conquest possession of the College of Stoke by Clare; and Richmonds, a very small manor, held by the keeper of the parks. Yardleys, a small Saxon manor, was independent but became included in the parish of Thaxted.

In Domesday Book Thaxted is reckoned at 11½ hides and 22½ acres. Newton was not unhappy with a hide of 120 acres, and thus a figure around 1,400 acres

(567 ha) of arable land. The parish of Thaxted measures 6,250 acres (2,530 ha), and after allowing for the meads, woodland for 1,000 pigs, and the area of Yardleys, it is clear that there was a considerable extent of land into which to expand. Five common-fields are named in the survey of 1393; they are Northefelde, Asshefelde, Worthens, Boxstede and Newefelde, the five being farmed on a three course rotation. The areas of the fields adjacent to the town were probably the core of the arable from which it advanced outward, reclaiming the waste, until the limits of the manor were reached and precise boundaries established with hedges. At some point in this process the parks were enclosed; the names Oldefrith and Southfrith (the Great Park) suggest that these comprised the woodland for 1,000 theoretical pigs; the Little Park, extending westward from the manor gardens, may have been more for amenity. Three hamlets around greens grew up, each a mile or more from the town: Cutlers, Bardfield End, and Richmonds, well-placed for farming the extended arable and also preserving relics of the waste essential for the grazing animals. In the thirteenth century, surrounded by tofts and small-holdings, the settlement around greens would have been denser than that shown on later maps which reflect the depopulation following the Black Death.

The loss of the common pasture of the waste to reclamation and emparking could give rise to problems.[8] Alternatives were found in greens, cropped for hay like the meads and then thrown open for grazing by the commoners, and in the broad roads which could function as linear greens; the latter were extensive on the Till and are shown on Chapman and André's Map of 1777. Many were enclosed into the arable during the French wars, and purprestures, cottage enclosures on the roadside waste, sprang up at that time. Examples of this linear pasture survive on the road from Cutlers Green to Debden. Additional pasture might also be available in the parks, land formerly commoned and now under the exclusive control of the manor.

Thaxted and Great Waltham would seem to provide two alternative models of manor and hamlet development under the pressures of early medieval expansion, respectively concentric and polyfocal. Thaxted developed outward from a core area, establishing hamlets on its outlying lands as they came under cultivation. Waltham comprised ten foci of which the manors, Walthambury and Chatham were two, each developing its own area, constrained only by the emparking of the more wooded land. Whether earlier settlement in the hamlets was shifting, or was focussed on the sites they have occupied since the thirteenth century, is a matter to which only archaeology may one day supply answers as the original buildings have vanished; relatively few domestic buidings survive anywhere from this time, and those that do are of high status.

Green settlement

Settlements based on greens appear ubiquitous north of the A12. Most of them, as at Waltham and Thaxted, appear to have been established or defined in the course of the twelfth and thirteenth centuries. But there is an older generation of greens sited beside the manor house and church, the focus of the estate and place of assembly and exchange, and a source of common grazing within the encircling penumbra of arable. Such greens may originally have been stockaded to give a measure of defence and safety for domestic animals in troubled times. An excellent example is Greenbury, the green beside the church at Writtle; other fine greens may be seen at Hadstock, Finchingfield and Broomfield, and small greens at Widdington, Wethersfield and many other villages.

An interesting example of a 'first generation' green which extended rather than dispersed is at Henham, a nucleated village formerly with common-fields. The manor house stood on a moated site some 200 metres northwest of the church, now separated by a field which appears to be the core site of the original settlement. From a small green beside the church, a linear green grew eastwards, sending out arms southwards, all fronted by a loose scatter of cottages set in tofts. Before development in recent years, with resulting urbanization, it was a village of great charm, some of which survives at the original end of Henham, with its church, farm, cottages and pub, against a backcloth of open country.

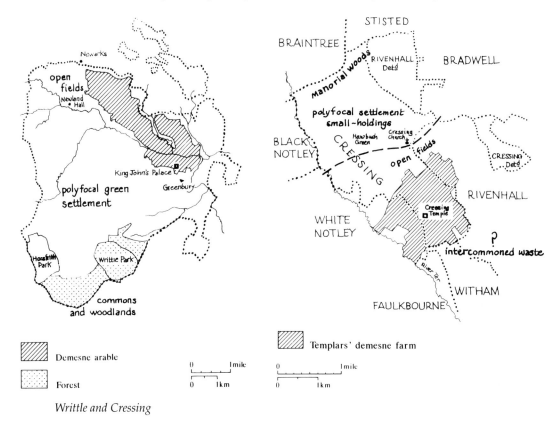

Writtle and Cressing

Two mid-Essex parishes stand in contrast to the nucleated common-field parishes of Thaxted and Henham, having more in common with the polyfocal parish of Great Waltham; these are Writtle and Cressing. In both, a network of linear and focal greens provided the permanent grassland for an arable patchwork of small strip-fields and individual crofts, a small scale 'peasant' landscape - the term 'peasant' is not here used pejoratively, as such systems were efficient in their time and supported vastly more families on the land than their successors today.

The royal manor of Writtle, which included the later parish of Roxwell, covered 13,568 acres [5,491ha] and may once have been larger, as prior to the Conquest the terra regis covered much of the later parishes of Chignall Smealy and Chignall St James. The manor divided into three zones: exclusive demesne in the northeast, a peasant zone in the centre which covered by far the largest area, and royal forest in the south. Surface geology is evident in these divisions; the demesne lay on fertile and productive boulder clay soils, the Forest on wretched soils of glacial outwash over Bagshot and Claygate deposits, and the central zone on a mixture of the two.

Ken Newton, in *The Manor of Writtle*, gives an analysis of the peasant zone which is useful for an understanding of similar areas in Cressing and elsewhere. On the evidence of medieval charters and manorial records, confirmed by late sixteenth century surveys, he gives a general picture of the Writtle tenants' holdings as one of small, often very small, enclosures. Thus, for example, the 270 acres [109 ha] of Shakestons Farm and 227 acres [92 ha] of Mountneys Farm were disposed respectively over 27 and 15 crofts. Both farms were ranked as sub-manors. Strip-fields based on the hamlet were evident; 'in this area of the manor (the southern) it is the sharing of the fields not by the community at large but by coparceners which is the characteristic in the documented period. It is a type of field-system consistent with a forested region, particularly as a late extension of the area of original clearance'.[9] How long fields in Writtle shared by coparceners endured, Newton found impossible to say, but by the time of a survey of 1564 they had wholly disappeared.

Turning to the demesne arable, Newton suspected that the lord had at some early stage taken over the original common-fields for his exclusive demesne, except those parts belonging to the other two manors, Newarks and Newland Hall, the tenants being compensated by assarts elsewhere. I have suggested instead that the peasant zone of Writtle was an ancient area of farming and settlement consolidated in the period of growth which followed the Conquest.[10] The lord's demesne already existed, lying to the north of Greenbury, the original focus, and in 1086 had twelve ploughs in lordship as against 64 ploughs among the men, some doubtless employed in cultivating the demesne. The demesne expanded northwards onto fertile land, and in 1209 King John's agents constructed the new manorial centre to the north of Greenbury, unencumbered by existing village development. From here reclamation continued until the limits were reached of manorial land, land which had supported the Chignall villa in imperial times. One might suspect that this land had lain, uncleared, in the Saxon demesne.

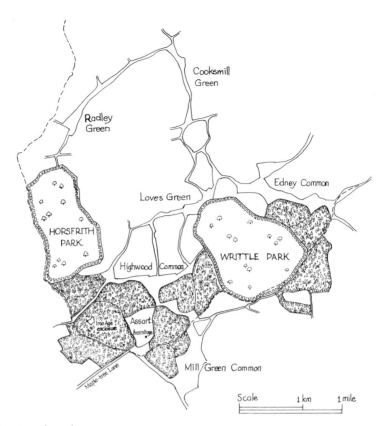

Writtle Forest, parks and greens

In the south of the manor lay the Forest on soils useless for sustainable cultivation, but growing good oak trees, an area of commoned wood-pasture. By 1300 it had been re-organised into compartmented coppice with standard woodland with strong enclosing banks, still with common grazing rights but regulated. Tenant control remained in the greens, while exclusive landlord control extended over the Horsefrith and Writtle parks.

It would seem that the community of Writtle had no shortage of land in its late Saxon condition. The manorial structure consisted of tenants farming small-holdings, while engaging in co-operative piecemeal assarting when the need arose, with extensive common pastures, part woodland or waste on the southern fringe of the manor. With population pressures, it would seem, all uses of land became defined by the year 1300.

The manor of Cressing shows some similarities to Writtle. Cressing was a post-Conquest creation, being granted to the Knights Templar by Queen Matilda, wife of King Stephen in 1137. Stephen added the royal manor of Witham and other benefactors gave land in Rivenhall and elsewhere in the neighbourhood.[11] The preceptory (headquarters) of the estate was located at Cressing Temple. The plan on p.100 shows the parish divided into two by a line running roughly eastwards from the church to the River Brain. To the north lay a polyfocal settlement of small-holdings, very similar to the peasant zone at Writtle, a patchwork of crofts, small farms with shared strip-fields, and woodlands subject to progressive clearance. There were five greens, two moated sites, and all the listed buildings of pre-1600 date in the parish other than the Temple itself. The parish church may pre-date the Templars as internal postholes may be evidence for an earlier building ,[12] and

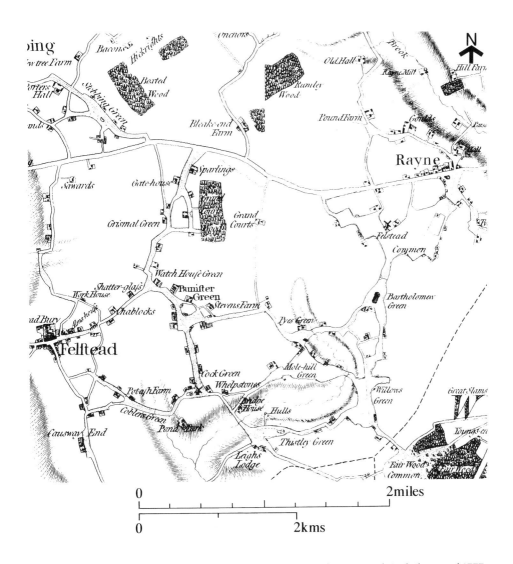

Green settlement in Felsted and adjacent parishes depicted on Chapman and André's map of 1777

Iron Age and Romano-British features in the adjacent field suggest a history of settlement. Northwards, along the parish boundary to Braintree and Stisted lay the manorial woods, of which a fragment survives as Lanham Wood; the presence of small-leaved lime indicates an ancient origin.

South of the line the farming was open-field, with a zone of mixed holdings, tenants and manor, lying between the line and the huge manorial demesne to the south. The manorial centre lay at Cressing Temple, a site occupied in Roman times but then deserted, as no archaeological evidence has been found for settlement in the Saxon period. From here the Templars carried out a programme of clearance, bringing waste and woodland into cultivation, and the stages of its progress were marked by the construction of the two great barns in the course of the thirteenth century. Further waste lay to the south of the demesne, probably intercommoned with the inhabitants of Rivenhall, Witham and Faulkbourne; this interpretation is supported by an inquiry into Templar property in 1307 which refers to eight acres of land lying waste in the common forest and twelve acres of wood.[13] To the north, demesne clearance reached the zone of mixed holdings on a line which includes Pettit Way, a lane which links Witham Road and Church Road. Hedge count averages gave seven and seven and a half species for the two sides of the lane, and its z-pattern suggests that it ran between two furlong blocks, one demesne, the other tenanted. It would seem that this was a boundary set out to define demesne land some time in the later thirteenth century.[14]

The most extensive polyfocal pattern of green settlement which survived to be mapped by Chapman and André in 1777 lay in the parish of Felsted. Eleven greens are named within the parish, and the pattern extended eastwards into the Leighs with Fair Wood Common and northwards into Stebbing and Rayne. Other examples, among many depicted on the map of 1777, are at Great Dunmow, with Parsonage and Dunmow Downs, at Bardfield Saling, and at Debden. All these examples, with that of Cressing, are sited on productive boulder clay soils, and whatever local variations may occur, the overall fertility of the land is no different from that of adjacent areas which show no evidence for, or survival of, green settlement. There is, therefore, no logic to be sought in the surface geology.

At Molehill Green, Broxted, analysis of hedges around long-vanished tofts indicated thirteenth century dating, which agrees with the case presented here that the precise definition of such greens took place as population pressure mounted in the two centuries preceding the Black Death. But this does not explain why areas of dispersed and polyfocal settlement occurred, so different from the common-field nucleated villages of much of lowland England. It has been suggested that these began long before the Middle Ages, in an area where the transition from Roman to Anglo-Saxon rule was early and less disruptive,[15] and it is tempting to seek parallels elsewhere, as in the townlands of early Christian Ireland.[16] The hamlets of Great Waltham with their associated strip-fields have a certain resemblance to rundale, a common-field system of the west of Ireland based on a clachan, a loose cluster of dwellings and outbuildings.[17]

Heaths and commons

Southeast of Cressing and Witham, across the River Blackwater, lay the great heath of Tiptree. Morant, writing of the reign of King John, refers to 'this great waste in the forest .... from an Inquisition taken in February 1401 we learn that the freeholders, or tenants, of Inworth, Messing, Layer, Brackstead, the town of Maldon, Totham, Tollesbury, and Tolleshunt, had common of pasture for their cattle here and estovers of the trees and under-wood growing upon this waste, for the building and repairing of the houses and hedges belonging to their tenements, and sufficient fuel for firing, as belonging to their lands and tenements in the vills or places aforesaid, and had ever enjoyed the same. But the Abbess of Barking, the Abbot of Coxall, and Reginald de Graie, Lord of Ruthen, who possessed maners in the adjoining parishes of Tollesbury, Tolleshunt-major, and Brackstead, had grievously incroached upon a great part of this waste'.

It would seem that the heath was already reduced from its extent in King John's day by predatory neighbours; compartments for woods had been formed on the Braxted/Beacon Hill ridge and in 1342 the Countess of Pembroke obtained a licence for her park at Great Braxted. But the heath as depicted by Chapman and André may not differ much from that described in the inquisition of 1401; there were many commoners to protest their rights. Later, in the reign of Henry VIII, Common of Pasture was affirmed by an order in council and the parishes of Wigborough, Goldhanger, Heybridge, Langford, Wickham and Kelvedon (in part) added. This appears a regularization of an existing situation. Management was carefully defined: pigs must be ringed and goats were banned; the commoners had the right to cut broom, furze and thorn, and underwood (coppice) for fuel and building repairs, and if there was insufficient, to lop and crop pollards, and to shred unpollarded trees.[19] Shredding involved cutting off lateral growth from a tree, leaving a clear stem for timber.

As was generally the case with the Essex heathlands, Tiptree Heath lay on poor soils formed by glacial outwash, fluvial sands and gravels, and merging into the London Clays of the Coastal Zone. The boundaries of the Witham, Thurstable and Winstree Hundreds met in the middle of the heath.

The heaths that lay around Colchester, particularly extensive on the western and northern sides, appear to be directly related to parishes and bear their names. Virtually every parish within a five mile radius had a considerable area of this type of rough pasture. Moving through the Mid-Essex Zone to the southwest, there were huge commons, recorded on the eve of their enclosure by Chapman and André, the largest being the intercommoned tract we now call Epping Forest. It appears to have been a more populated area than the heathlands with relatively dense settlement abutting the edges of the commons, notably at Nazeing, Parndon and Harlow.

overleaf: Tiptree Heath as depicted in 1777 by Chapman and André

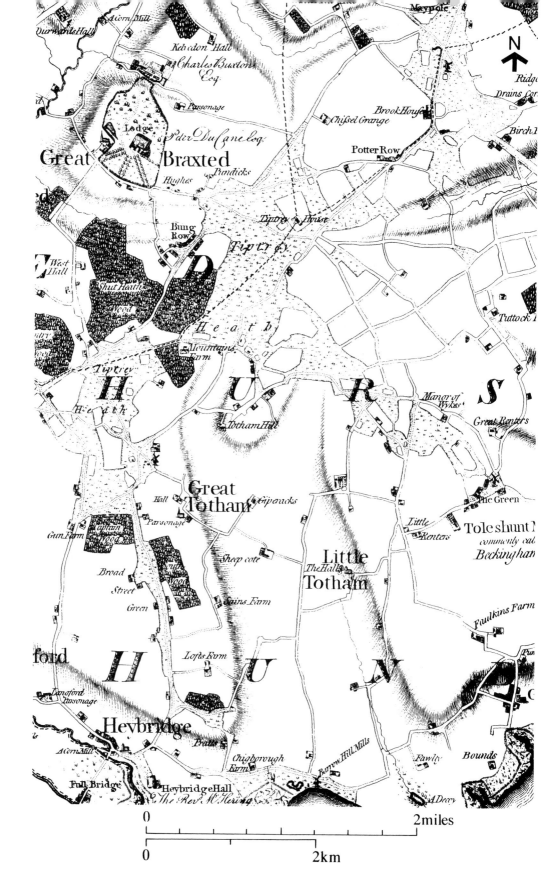

Parish and church

The thirteenth century saw the parish system fully established. Its purpose at that stage was purely ecclesiastical; civil matters at the local level were the concern of the manorial courts, and it was not until the reign of Henry VIII that parishes were required to accept civil responsibilities, and in due course replaced the manor as the unit responsible for local government. The widely stated view that parishes represent ancient tracts of discrete territory is, therefore, erroneous; such antiquity as they possess lies in the territorial components that made up the medieval manor.

In the later Saxon period churches were built by thegns for the inhabitants of their estates and as a mark of their personal wealth, status and piety, and sometimes guilt. The church was the private property of its founder and the priest one of his servants. Small estates, lacking the means to support a church and priest, tended to look to a neighbour who had one, and this arrangement evolved into a proto-parish. The earlier minster churches, which had carried out pastoral duties over wide areas, were targets for the heathen Danes and those that recovered were little more than private churches. At least 300 churches and chapels were in existence in Essex before 1200, and about 400 churches and 70 chapels before 1300.[20] In the twelfth century a powerful and reforming papacy took measures to bring the parish clergy under diocesan control; in 1179 Alexander III decreed that bishops would institute to churches and that the patron's role was merely to present a priest - he was no longer to be regarded as the proprietor.

Thus by the thirteenth century the parochial system in Essex was fully developed in the form which would last with only minor changes until the nineteenth century.[21] Roughly, there was a ratio of one church or chapel to two manors (excluding sub-manors). Their extent and boundaries are shown on the First Edition OS 6 inch maps, surveyed about two decades after the tithe award maps and incomparably better in cartographical terms; most importantly, they depict the parishes before the rationalization of the late nineteenth century when many features deemed to be untidy by the administrative mind were understandably replaced. These features include detached areas, some of which may be early small estates, and are clearly of considerable interest in seeking to interpret how a landscape has evolved.

Turning now to some examples of parishes based on manors whose development has been considered earlier, Thaxted and Yardleys are a good instance of a large and small manor forming a parish. The neighbouring parish of Debden comprized two medium sized manors: Debden and Amberden, and similarly Widdington, with Priors Hall and Widdington Hall. Cressing parish was based on the manor of Cressing Temple, a post-Conquest royal creation formed from the northern area of the largest Witham manor (also granted to the Knights Templar). Two other holdings formed a part of the Templars' manor: Lanham, an adjacent estate remained a detached part of Rivenhall parish, while Sheepcotes, an outlying farm, was a detached part of Cressing parish, sometimes known as Little Cressing.

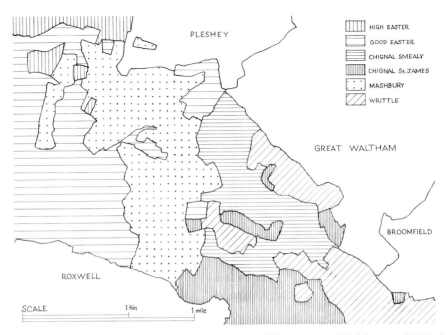

PLESHEY

GREAT WALTHAM

BROOMFIELD

ROXWELL

	HIGH EASTER
	GOOD EASTER
	CHIGNAL SMEALY
	CHIGNAL St.JAMES
	MASHBURY
	WRITTLE

SCALE   1 Km   1 mile

Parish boundaries on the border between the huge parishes of Great Waltham and Writtle.

The parish of Great Waltham comprised the three manors held by Geoffrey de Mandeville in 1086, less a small area subtracted for the new town of Pleshey. The boundaries appear rational - a Roman road and the Chelmer form part - except for the tract of land lying between Great Waltham, Pleshey and High Easter to the north, and Writtle and Roxwell to the south. Here lay the small parishes of Mashbury, Chignall St James and Chignall Smealy, all fragmented, and mixed with detached areas of the Easters and Writtle they present the appearance of a crazy archipelago.

Churches, being mostly of manorial origin, generally lie beside, or within easy walking distance of the hall. Isolated churches today are generally so because the manor has at some time migrated or disappeared. South of the A12 churches are sometimes sited on hill tops; notably Danbury, beside the Iron Age hillfort. On the Till they follow their manors, sited for a reliable water supply on springlines and river terraces, and so lie below the plane of the plateau, although on the southern reaches of the Boulder Clays, in the Easters and Rodings, the gentle topography gives the churches a prominence in the landscape that is generally denied to those further north. Saffron Walden and Thaxted are unusual for north Essex, being sited on eminences; Walden owes its position to the new town beside the castle it was built to serve; Thaxted may have been built on a new site in about 1340, replacing an older church beside the manor, but this a matter that only archaeology may perhaps one day resolve.

An unusual site is that of Great Waltham which lies over half a mile (1 km) from the manor (Walthambury). With the course of the main road diverting around the graveyard, the site may well be older in its origins than the parish church.

And so to consider the buildings themselves. The twelfth and thirteenth centuries in England witnessed an ecclesiastical building programme such as seen neither before nor since. It is sometimes suggested that a sinister purpose was the motive: a deliberate display of Norman cultural superiority over the conquered English as well as the raw power we have seen demonstrated, for practical reasons of conquest and survival, in their castles. But it is not evident that the Conqueror's warrior adventurers saw themselves as culturally superior, nor indeed as Normans - the term was coined and applied retrospectively in the next century by Orderic Vitalis.[22] Although the capacity of the 'Normans' to assimilate culturally into their conquests is most evident in Sicily and Ireland, it would appear that a century after the Conquest native-born prelates and landholders regarded themselves as English subjects of the king of England. This was borne out by the solid support given by the English barons and bishops to Henry II in his bitter quarrel with Thomas Becket, whose backing lay abroad. It may be wrong, therefore, to see the building and rebuilding of churches as 'political', but rather as an element of the exuberant and expansive mood we have noted in the economic life of post-Domesday England, expressed in the medium of the re-invented and dynamic Romanesque style, in due course evolving into Gothic.

All of which may seem peripheral to the consideration of landscape, but churches have proved to be the most permanent of buildings, built to the highest affordable quality. The motivation that lay behind them is as relevant as it is for other long-lasting features in the landscape.

It would appear that on the sites of many early churches the first buildings were of wood, and these were subsequently rebuilt in stone. By the eleventh century masonry structures had become the rule. Only one example, Greensted Church, has famously survived, unique in its log construction and believed to be the oldest timber building still in use. Its dating has ranged widely, but has now been defined by dendrochronology to somewhere between 1063 and 1100. Despite much speculation, however, Greensted remains something of an enigma. Why was it built in timber at this late date? Is it an anomaly, or a representative of a building type once common?

But if masonry had become the accepted medium for church walling, a group of bell towers display the art of the carpenter in spectacular fashion. At Navestock, Margaretting, Stock and Blackmore, the tower stands on four main posts with an ambulatory around, making a centrally planned building, attached to but structurally independent of the church. Comparisons with stave churches come to mind, and other possible links. Pevsner admired them, finding 'their sturdy directness extremely impressive, and they are wholly out of the ordinary'.[23] When he was writing, in the early 1950s, there was little evidence to suggest dating other than the fifteenth century. Since then Navestock has been carbon-dated to the late twelfth century, so the type begins in the Romanesque and continues through to the late fifteenth century with the building of the noble tower for the Augustinian priory at Blackmore, described by Pevsner as 'one of the most impressive, if not the most impressive, of all timber towers of England'.[24]

Pevsner's problem with the dating of timber structures was, at the time he was writing, a universal one. A comprehensive typology for stone building had been in place since the early nineteenth century, when Rickman coined the terms for the phases of Gothic that are still in use. But for carpentry there was no source of reference, and unless a timber structure contained decorative detail the historian was at sea. This situation was rectified by Cecil Hewett, who single-handedly constructed a typological framework for the development of medieval carpentry, publishing his conclusions in the late 1960s. Hewett showed that many buildings

The late fifteenth century belfry of Blackmore Church, formerly an Augustinian friary

(including Navestock church) were considerably older than had been supposed and also achieved a belated recognition of the importance of the carpenter's art in the study of medieval architecture.

Less spectacular than the bell towers, but fortunately numerous, are the timber belfries which stand on or near the west end of the roof, but in fact stand on posts visible inside. The range of dates appear to cover a span similar to that of the bell towers. At Bradwell-juxta-Coggeshall Hewett found firm evidence for ascribing the belfry to the original building of the church (Norman), and considers that one can safely assume that west-gable turrets and free timber towers were not uncommon in the Norman period.[25]

Cistercian abbeys, sited in the countryside rather than towns, provided a capella juxta portas (gate chapel) for the use of their parishioners. Two survive - although their abbey churches were destroyed at the Reformation - one at Little Coggeshall and the other at Tilty, near Thaxted. As we have seen earlier, the Coggeshall monks re-introduced the art of brick making in Britain. In the chapel and in the monks' domestic buildings, converted into a house at the Dissolution, brick dressings are used instead of imported freestone. The domestic buildings date from about 1185 onwards and the chapel from around 1225. One wonders if the decision to make their own bricks stemmed from seeing the extensive re-use

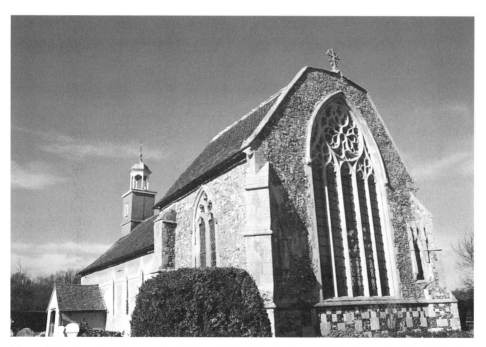

The early fourteenth century east window of Tilty Church, the capella juxta porta of the Cistercian abbey

111

of Roman brick at Colchester, particularly at St Botolph's priory; it would have been much cheaper than stone.

Of the main buildings of Tilty Abbey, a few lengths of rubble walling are all that remain. But the chapel survives intact, and the only later additions are the small porch and delightful belfry and cupola. The nave is Early English with lancet windows, similar to those at Little Coggeshall and similar also in plan, being originally single-cell with nave and chancel in one. In the early fourteenth century a sumptuous chancel was added, wider and much taller than the nave with a huge east window, all in the Curvilinear style at its finest. It is an architectural collision that breaks all rules and, perhaps as a result, is superb. How it came about is unknown; perhaps an ambitious abbot keen to leave his mark, or a rich man's gift, or the beginning of a rebuilding scheme for the whole church. If the latter case, we must be thankful that funds ran out or impetus flagged. Its remote setting, against woodland in the valley of the upper Chelmer, is just right for a church which can justly claim to be the prettiest in Essex.

The dominant church towers so characteristic of the wealthier regions - the Cotswolds, Somerset, East Anglia and Essex - belong to the later Middle Ages, and we will return to them. Of this period, two cannot escape mention: the magnificent crossing tower of Great Tey (Norman with Roman brick dressings), a landmark in a somewhat level landscape, and Corringham, monumental early Norman in a charming village scene. Hidden away from a setting of undistinguished urban sprawl and vast petroleum refineries, Corringham never fails to surprise; it is indeed a locus amoenus.

Landscapes of lords and prelates

Over much of Essex the landscape of the High Middle Ages underlies that of today, evident in boundaries, highways and the pattern of settlement, and on certain favoured sites such as Hatfield Forest the medieval scene survives in working order and is managed accordingly. But if we look for secular buildings of this time we are not so fortunate. A few buildings of high status are to be found, but virtually all else has vanished from the landscape or been replaced by later buildings. Some fine halls have survived, with or without their aisles, and some superb barns, but their surroundings have changed from those of their youth, and their context is that of a later age. To envisage the purprise of the great manors we may turn to the documentary record and to archaeology. By good fortune we have Ken Newton's study of the manor of Thaxted[26] and Philip Rahtz's excavation report on King John's palace at Writtle.[27]

At the Conquest Thaxted was granted to Richard FitzGilbert, founder of the great feudal dynasty which held the Honour of Clare. In the early fourteenth century the manor was alienated, then subjected to lengthy legal battles, and in 1372 it was divided among four heirs. The great complex of manorial buildings, described by Newton, with extensive gardens and three parks, belongs to the happier days when Thaxted was a seat of the Lords of Clare. The complex was bounded by Town Street to the north and Park Street to the east, and is described in a survey of 1348.[28] The great outer gateway, 'with chambers above and below', stood close to the site of the future moothall, and led directly into the outer courtyard where the principal outbuildings were ranged - the grange, stables, smithy, granary, bakery and brewery, 'la Pressourhous' where wine was pressed, the pound and the piggery. A further gateway, near a building called the 'knightes Chamber', led to the inner court, across which lay the core of the complex - the great hall with its domestic offices, a great upper chamber and the 'Countesses Chambre', and a separate building called the 'Quarelleshall' with a number of smaller chambers at either end of it. This, Newton considered, was the likely building where the courts of the manor were held. Across another court on the south side of the great hall lay another gateway into Park Street beside 'Swynfordchambre'.

Westwards, over the brow of the hill where the mill of 1810 now stands, and stretching down to the Chelmer, lay the gardens of the manor - 'Countesse Gardyn', 'Bolforde Gardyn', and 'la Burton'. Along the river, dammed to power the former Saxon mill, lay a sheet of water, doubtless teeming with fish and wildfowl, and rising up the facing hill lay the wood-pasture of the Little Park. This was land reserved in the landscape for the amenity of the manor, to provide a pleasing prospect for the gardens; economic logic would have suggested its incorporation into the arable fields, but medieval parks were not just deer farms. One might envisage pavilions, and perhaps a lodge with a banqueting room standing amongst the pollard oaks, with a view northwards from its galleries across the sparkle of water to the blossoms or fruit (according to the season) of the orchards in the manor gardens; a visiting cousin from Sicily might feel a familiar ambience.

With litigations and divisions, and lacking a resident family, the manorial buildings went into decline. The 1393 survey noted houses in the lower court which were ruinous for lack of repair. Bailiff's accounts for 1377-78 and 1380-81 record returns for agistment of 'divers beasts sent out into the little park'; its value was now for grazing rents. In the next century the manor's frontage to the market place was developed, a reflection of the borough's prosperity. In the centre of this range stands the Recorder's House with the arms of Edward IV carved on the coves below its first floor oriels. At some time early in the sixteenth century Sir John Cutte rebuilt the sub-manor of Horham Hall on a grand scale, which then became the manor of Thaxted. Of the old manor, only a hall attached to the former gatehouse now remains, itself concealed by later buildings.

Of the great manor house of Writtle, only the moat remains. 'The king's house at Writtle' was built in 1211 on open land well away from the old manor at Greenbury beside the church. The new site abutted the huge arable demesne, expanding northward, with unlimited space for the farming enclosure and storage of crops, meadows for grazing were immediately to hand, and a brook to supply the moat and three fishponds. The moated enclosure contained the small palace to accommodate royal visits. Whether King John ever visited is unknown but it seems likely, as he was in Essex in the course of his war with the barons (1215-1216) when he took both Hedingham and Colchester castles - one activity John was good at. Visits are recorded by both Henry III and Edward I, and the illustration below shows the palace receiving Edward and his young second wife, Margaret of France, in 1305. The king was old and irascible, and all is shown in good order and very tidy.

The moated area contained the great hall, the king's private chambers, a large service area and separate kitchen, chapel, and gatehouse with accommodation over. The layout and dimensions were elucidated by Rahtz in his excavation, and these are interpreted in the reconstruction by using structures which survive elsewhere, mainly in Essex.[29]

The precise location of the buildings serving the demesne, sited outside the moated area, is not known; but a survey of 1419 lists all the buildings in use and is likely to describe the farm as it had developed in the period of high demesne farming.[30] There was a house for the caretaker of the manor called the Squire's Chamber, a gatehouse with a room over, and houses for the bailiff, cowherd and warrener. There were stables, yards and byres for cows and oxen, a hay barn and a barn with a dovecote. The Squire's Chamber and the dovecote were noted as being roofed with tiles, as were all the buildings within the moat, but otherwise thatch was used.

If this active king felt an inclination for exercise, away from matters of state and plans to hammer the Scots, Writtle Park lay just over two miles away.

King John's palace at Writtle on the occasion of the visit in 1305 of Edward I and his young second wife, Margaret of France. This reconstruction by Frank Gardiner is based on excavations of the moated enclosure carried out in 1955-57 by Philip Rahtz and evidence from surviving buildings of similar date .

Thaxted and Writtle were high status manors, as also were Southchurch Hall and Cressing Temple, of which a good deal is now known. But of those of lower status, no material, documentary or archaeological, has yet been studied to guide a description or reconstruction. But such material may well exist in inquisitions and surveys, as when a partition between heirs occurred, preserved in the royal records when so much material was destroyed in the Peasants' Revolt.

Looking outward from the manor complex, the thirteenth century saw the active interest of many lords and prelates in the development of their demesne farms, and this has left its record in the landscape.

Demesne farming

The decision of landowners to manage their demesnes in hand followed the notorious inflation under King John, brought about by an influx of silver from wool exports, and leading to a fall in rental income in terms of real value.[31] Leasing had been a general practice in the twelfth century; now demesne land that had been relinquished was taken back and added to by expansion onto the waste. Landowners became entrepreneurs, seeking direct access to profits, and while the rise in population supplied an increasing demand for casual labour, the servile obligations of villeinage were re-imposed and defined.[32] Landlords' rights to enclose waste and common pasture were increased by the Statute of Merton in 1235.

A new administrative class developed to manage the demesnes, with stewards, auditors and long-serving reeves. Lordships became more effective and management more efficient, although there could inevitably be problems of accountability. Treatises were written on estate management and accounting, notably that of Walter of Henley. The countryside, its inhabitants and their labours were of interest to patrons, as noted earlier, and a new realism appeared in the work of sculptors; plant forms were depicted with the freshness that comes from direct observation.

The manor of the Knights Templar at Cressing is a good example of land reclamation and entrepreneurial farming. The order was exempt from the obligation to pay tithes, and since this valuable privilege lay with the land rather than the owner, it survived the dissolution of the Templars, and their successors the Hospitallers, to be recorded on the tithe award for Cressing and neighbouring parishes into which the estate extended.[33] The exemption lay only with land in hand - land leased out was excluded and it would appear a reasonable conclusion that the tithe-free land represents the Templars' demesne at its greatest extent in the thirteenth century.

The development of the parish has been considered earlier. The manorial woods lay abutting the northern boundary, and the manor had strips in small commonfields around the church. To the south lay the preceptory, the demesne home farm, on land reclaimed in the course of the thirteenth century from the great area of waste which lay between Cressing and Witham. Worked from the new estate centre,

Cressing Temple, this was farming at its most intensive and productive. The two great barns could comfortably accommodate the entire harvest, and their respective dates reflect the progress of turning the waste into farmland;[34] dendro-dates for the Barley Barn are 1205-35, and 1257-90 for the Wheat Barn.[35]

The field plan can be readily reconstructed as the lanes that formed many of the boundaries appear to have followed pre-existing trackways and linear features that had survived from a much earlier time.[36] These, it appears, were made use of in the new plan rather than ignored. The lanes have become metalled roads and the fields, which were sub-divided in the later Middle Ages or Tudor times, have reverted in recent years to their original dimensions. So the fields surrounding the Temple today are not very different from those of the 13th century. They are certainly large, even by the standards of 'prairie farming'; the Templars' North Field was 76 acres (31 ha), Bannerly 110 acres (45 ha), and the largest, Whistocks, approached 300 acres (121 ha), a compact holding in what would appear to have been a common-field in both Cressing and Rivenhall.

The Temple estate was concerned with medieval 'agribusiness'; there was no deer park that might have seemed a misuse of productive resources required for the war against the infidel. But there was a considerable warren, divided into Great and Lower, on the sandy river terrace above the Brain - land attractive to rabbits for easy burrowing. Rabbits (known as coneys until the nineteenth century) had been native to Britain in post-glacial times but became extinct. Re-introduction by the Normans, they were kept in enclosed warrens or 'coney-garths' under the watchful eye of a warrener. To begin with they were delicate southern

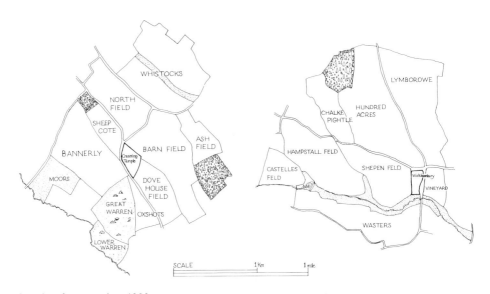

Cressing demesne circa 1300   *Walthambury demesne circa 1300*

animals who took time to adapt to the northern climate, and were given artificial hillocks (pillow-mounds) to burrow into. There was a rapid spread of warrens across England in the period 1230-50, and by 1300 they were numerous. The value of rabbits lay more in the skins than the meat, and gave rise to an export trade.[37]

Today Cressing Temple is renowned for its two great barns, monuments to the achievement of medieval carpenters, and also to the importance attached to capital investment by a leading monastic order. As buildings in the landscape and as internal spaces the barns are awesome and, although designed to fulfill a purely utilitarian purpose, the knights must have felt a surge of pride in these symbols of their managerial efficiency.

At Walthambury, the demesne farm with huge fields covered a discrete area and had some similarity to Cressing, although it is uncertain how and when it came about. At Writtle the exclusive demesne arable lay in the north of the manor. At Thaxted the demesne land lay in the common-fields and cannot be separately defined, as the proportions of tenants' holdings are not defined in the surveys and the sub-manors worked the fields in common with the parent manor.[38] Much remains to be discovered elsewhere, through the study of later estate maps and earlier surveys.

The thirteenth century was a period in which landlords became directly concerned in the management and development of their estates, an interest not again seen to a comparable degree until the eighteenth century. By the second quarter of the fourteenth century, however, retrenchment and leasehold had become the trend.[39] This appears to have been for a number of reasons, some of which stemmed from the bureaucratic tendencies which arose as great estates developed: a top-heavy apparatus to oversee manorial officials, particularly on scattered demesnes, and an understandable reluctance of the man on the spot to take risks.[40] With demesnes expanded to their limits, perhaps inertia set in. Then there were the famines due to harvest failures in 1315, 1316 and 1321 and the terrible murrain of 1319-21, portents of the calamities to follow and very discouraging. So contraction in demesne farming set in, and was well under way before the Black Death gave a new bargaining power to labourers, whom the lord might prefer to leave to his tenants to handle provided his rents were paid. By 1348 at Thaxted only 47 of the 1,160 acres (469 ha) of the demesne remained in hand, and there were no remaining livestock of the lord's own. By 1361, the disintegration of the old manorial order was almost complete and the demesne in the sense of a home farm was no more.[41]

Woodlands and parks

Domesday Essex is often described as a well-wooded county, and woodland may indeed have covered one fifth of its area. But this high figure was boosted by areas of dense woodland, mainly in west Essex, while elsewhere the extent was probably much the same as in other lowland counties. At that time most woodland was of the wood-pasture type and unenclosed. Conversion to arable over the next two centuries gave the remaining woodland a scarcity value; its products were essential to both the local and the wider economy, and market forces ensured its survival. Enclosure by the manor followed, with the wood-pasture converted either into managed woods with grazing excluded, or into parks where grazing remained the priority. Both woods and parks were under the exclusive control of the lord. Wood-pasture also survived on commons, unenclosed but regulated by custom and with defined boundaries.

Medieval woods were managed as coppice (underwood) to provide fuel, charcoal, fencing and the materials for a wide range of products, and timber trees, usually oak, for buildings and other structural works. Enclosure was by means of a bank, often of considerable size, and a deep ditch - not a boundary that could be surreptitiously shifted. The top of the bank was fenced by means of a hedge, and the entrances had lockable gates. Management, under the direction of a woodward, was intensive, but necessarily concerned with the maintenance of a self-renewing resource. Underwood, regularly cut to the stool, regrew to be cut again when the woodward considered the growth sufficient. Timber trees provided the seedlings which would grow to replace them. 'Sustainability', a concept fashionable today, governed the management of medieval woods.

A rich flora is characteristic of ancient coppices, which may contain certain plants that do not occur in recently established woods. A few woods may be primary - continuously wooded since post-glacial warming. Here there will be species inherited from the original wildwood. Old secondary woods may have acquired all but the least mobile of these plants. In recent woods one will find only those plants which colonize new sites or may have survived from a previous use of the land. 'The plant communities of the ancient wood will have had perhaps a thousand years in which to come to terms with management, often with the mixed-coppice system which provides a series of habitats favouring a rich and complex flora. The continuous cycle of felling and regrowth provides a home for plants with varying requirements for shade, while the mixture of tree species ensures that some areas, for instance under ash trees, will always be suitable for plants that cannot stand heavy shade.

Apart from their botanical value, ancient woods are important landscape features, tending to lie away from settlements along parish boundaries, with sinuous outlines, and qualities stemming from their individual tree communities: variations in texture, colour, and response to seasonal change. All are different with their own particular character. Many have that indefinable quality that only comes with time and long survival, and in the historic landscape of a parish may be seen as complementary to its medieval church.

That is if the wood has survived unscathed the destructive years following 1950, when some were erased to make way for farming and others were wrecked by coniferization; in all, including additional losses to development, road building and wartime airfields, the toll is around 50 per cent. But a considerable number have survived, and there are now many where visitors are welcome and traditional management practices are followed, with the coppices at various stages of regrowth. These include Hatfield Forest, the Hockley Woods, Blake's Wood (Danbury), and Garnett's Wood (Barnston). Many woods are owned by the Essex Wildlife Trust, including Shadwell Wood (Ashdon), where the rich flora - which includes oxlips and wood anemones - forms a mosaic of plant communities, reflecting the variation in the glacial soils beneath, unblended by later ploughing.

Chalkney Wood, an important lime wood near Earls Colne, has an interesting history. Its outline has remained unchanged since it was depicted on a map of 1598.[43] The map records that the wood was used by its owners, the Earls of Oxford, as a park for keeping wild swine, which had escaped. Consequently, in the reign of Henry VIII, the earl had 'caused them to be destroied for the greate damage and hurte the Contrie susteined by them'. So the use ceased and the wood had a tranquil existence over many centuries until its northern half fell into the hands of the Forestry Commission. This was in the Commission's post-war triumphalist phase when ancient woodland was regarded as scrub awaiting improvement. Accordingly the existing tree cover was felled, the regrowth poisoned, and the whole area covered with conifers which grew poorly. In 1976 the Planning Committee of Essex County Council purchased the southern area, mindful of its historical and botanical importance, the threat posed by its neighbour, and the need at that time for woodlands to visit .[44] Twenty years on, an extraordinary change has come about. A new generation of foresters has reversed the policy of its predecessors and progressively removed the conifers to favour the old vegetation, which had survived eradication and fought back against the aliens. The wood is an entity again, the northern area improves each year, and in the southern, coppicing of lime, hornbeam and sweet chestnut continues as it has since it was resumed in the late 1970s. At Shardlowes Wood, near Gosfield, the Forestry Authority is implementing a similar programme of rehabilitation.

In parks the existing tradition of wood-pasture was continued. The purpose was to enclose and fence a tract of land for the keeping of semi-wild animals, in particular the fallow deer, newly introduced in all probability from Sicily. A second purpose was prestige; a park was a status symbol for the rich and newly rich, and the very rich might have several in one manor. A third purpose, or benefit, was that in most cases the owner had complete control, free from rights of commoning such as continued in the forests. As parks became fashionable the king realised that as with markets and towns, there was money to be made, and required that a licence be obtained to empark, or to extend a park. From the early thirteenth century a substantial record survives of licences granted.

In Essex about 160 medieval parks are known to have existed, a high number - only Hertfordshire is higher - possibly because parks conflicted with forest law and licences were more systematically sought than in non-forest counties.[45] The distribution bears some relationship to wooded areas; parks were usually made out of existing woodlands or contained an element of woodland. Deer required some shelter, brakes for the does, and a supply of water from brook or spring, not a difficult specification to meet over much of Essex in the early Middle Ages. The area selected was enclosed with a ditch and high bank, sometimes with an inside ditch to increase the interior height. On the bank stood the park pale, a tall fence made of cleft-oak palings, expensive to build and to maintain - park records frequently refer to repairs. Stone was a preferred material in counties where it was available. Early parks are compact in shape with characteristic rounded corners to minimise the length of the perimeter, with its initial and continuing costs.

The wood-pasture tradition continued in parks, ultimately to be 'discovered' and appreciated by eighteenth century landscape designers. Although parks contained timber trees, allowed to grow bigger than those in woods, trees generally were pollarded, yielding crops of faggots. Where the higher productivity of coppice was required, compartments were introduced for periodic fencing to exclude the deer, while a laund, an open treeless area, provided richer pasture and a place for hunting. Parks sometimes contained fishponds, and records frequently refer to the agistment of sheep and cattle.

At the highest point, with the best views over the park, stood the lodge. Here the parker conducted the day to day business and saw to the orderly running of the park. The Thaxted survey of 1393 contains a charter of the mid thirteenth century granted to the keeper of the three parks, who in return for his duties held the largest free estate within the manor. The holding acquired the status of a manor which was to take its name from the Richmond family, whose members were the parkers in the fourteenth and fifteenth centuries. Of a lower status were the keepers of the gates who paid no rent for their dwellings and smallholdings. Instead they maintained the enclosures of the parks as well as attending to the gates, and were also charged with bringing to safety any who lost their way in the park at night.[46].

Some lodges were also standings, buildings with galleries to observe the chase. Lodge Farm, Galleywood, is a lodge-standing converted into a farmhouse when the park was turned into farmland.[47] Like Henry VIII's standing in Epping Forest (Queen Elizabeth's Hunting Lodge), it had open galleries and a large room for entertainment, a reminder that in the society of chivalry, hunting and hawking, together with the martial arts, were a part of normal life.

Ongar Great Park is an exemplar for those seeking the traces of lost parks. It lay forgotten in the countryside to the west of North Weald, its lineaments preserved in hedgerows and relict woodland, until its discovery by Oliver Rackham. It is the oldest recorded park in Britain, being mentioned in a will of 1045,[48] and is huge, about the size of Hatfield Forest, with rounded corners. How long it lasted in operation is not known, but the landscape around was fashioned to it; the greens of North Weald abutted it and parish boundaries followed the pale. Sadly, Ongar Park Wood was destroyed long before its importance was known, but the fragment that remains has preserved a length of the enclosing earthwork on which stood the pale. It is impressive and now a scheduled monument. The boundary of the whole park survives otherwise as a hedgerow. The boundaries of other ancient parks survive in this way, because the pattern of land was shaped up to and not through them. Rayleigh is an example, the only Essex park mentioned in Domesday Book.

Parks that survived as parks in the long term often did so because they offered a setting for a fine new house with amenities - 'prospects', ancient trees, no near neighbours and, for an arriviste, an air of respectability - and in these cases the manor house moved to the site of the lodge. This was the case with Copped Hall, Braxted, Quendon and Easton (destroyed to make a wartime airfield). Quendon is unique in Essex, being still a deer park. At Weald and Thorndon the parks lay close to the house. Thorndon has a fascinating history to which we shall return, with later overlays of designed landscapes and the enclosure of an adjacent common into the park, which preserved some spectacular pollard oaks.

Thorndon and Weald are owned by Essex County Council and managed with full regard to their importance as historic landscapes. Weald is of particular interest because although altered by later fashions, interesting in themselves, it contains an area of wood-pasture maintained by grazing, and looking much as it would have done in the days of its earlier owners, the abbots of Waltham, or even when its Iron Age hillfort was built.[49]

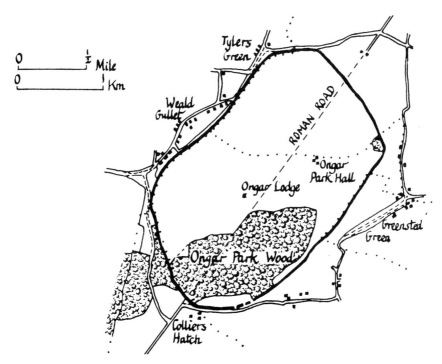

Ongar Great Park (Rackham 1989)

Royal forests

In 1238 the tenancy of the royal manors of Hatfield and Writtle, with their forests, was granted by Henry III to Isabel de Bruce in exchange for her share in her father's estate, the late Earl of Chester. In due course they were inherited by her great grandson, Robert the Bruce, who was crowned King of Scotland in 1306. For this treason the estates were forfeit and granted to Humphrey de Bohun, the king's brother-in-law, and remained with the de Bohuns for 200 years.

The king retained rights, and in 1336 confiscated the woods of Hatfield and Writtle from John de Bohun for his lifetime for wasting 'le Heghwode' (High Wood, Writtle) 'to the harm of the king and his beasts', and at Hatfield there were four charcoal hearths, leading to 'the destruction of the forest and the detriment and escape of the king's beasts'.[50] John's attempt at commercialization appears to have been discovered when the king's steward sold 100 oaks from Hatfield, and he was convicted by the forest court.

It may be that the compartmentation of Hatfield and Writtle took place under the de Bohuns, with the coppices embanked to protect the regrowth from browsing, for it may be more than a coincidence that there were seventeen coppices in Hatfield and 17 'quarters' in the de Bohun park at Walden.[51] Whether or not this was the case, it would seem certain that the two forests were shaped into the pattern of land use we see today during the tenure of the de Bruces or the later de Bohuns.

Farmstead and smallholding

In neighbouring south Cambridgeshire we see an open landscape where the farmsteads have traditionally lain in villages, and mostly continued to do so after late enclosure of the common-fields. On the Essex Till we find a contrast with settlements in small ends and greens, and the intervening landscape filled with scattered farms. From the seventeenth century onwards wide highway verges were often colonized by licensed purprestures.[52] The result is a landscape that appears well settled, although few of its inhabitants now have any connection with the land.

The scattered farms seem mostly to date from the sixteenth and seventeenth centuries, while a few may date from the later Middle Ages. Many were rebuilt or refaced in brick in times of farming prosperity. These later centuries seem to have been a time of consolidation, when the isolated steading became the norm and the yeoman holdings enlarged at the expense of smallholdings. The tenant holdings of the Middle Ages were very different.

The Thaxted survey of 1348 lists only six tenants with holdings which ranged from 60 acres up to the largest of 82. The next group, of twenty tenants held from twelve to 32 acres, and the biggest group of 66 held from one to nine acres.[53] The 1393 survey, under Wodham, lists Margaret de Rauf as holding one messuage and 60 acres of farmland, and eighteen acres elsewhere.[54] Margaret's home must be

Woodhams, a moated farmstead in the north of the parish. Also listed under Wodham are William Hirde, the keeper of the lord's swine, with twenty acres, and a
number of smallholders with a few acres. These probably clustered along the track
to Woodhams, which has very wide verges. So where we now have an isolated
farmstead, there was once a hamlet. Elsewhere, apart from the three sub-manors,
settlement accompanying the expansion of the manor onto the waste appears to
have been around the greens and the hamlet of Monk street.

It has been calculated that the minimum area required for a medieval family to
survive on farming alone was 10-15 acres.[55] Thus the majority of Thaxted tenants
must have worked as craftsmen, artisans, retailers or labourers in addition to cultivating their smallholdings. In 1993 a medieval farm was excavated near Stebbingford Farm, Felsted, on the route of the proposed A120 trunk road. The area
excavated was 2.5 acres, revealing the farmstead and sufficient evidence of its surroundings to conclude that this was a self-contained holding of middle status, laid
out with a degree of deliberate planning in the mid twelfth century on 'empty'
land.[56] The three buildings were interpreted as dwelling house, byre, and kitchen
or store; a garden lay nearby with fruit trees and beds for vegetables and herbs.
Cereals, predominantly wheat, were grown in the fields, and the evidence from

*A reconstruction of the farmstead at Stebbingford in the thirteenth century by Peter Froste, based
on excavations by Essex County Council*

bones suggests that horses and livestock were kept, including cattle, sheep, pigs and poultry. The farm generated sufficient surplus to sell or exchange for pottery, wine and shellfish. Occupation ended in the mid fourteenth century.

Round Wood, a similar site, was excavated in the course of the Stansted Airport Archaeological Project. It too had three buildings, interpreted as house, kitchen and granary, and a preliminary assessment of the pottery showed that the site was operating in the thirteenth century, but was abandoned in the course of the fourteenth.[57]

At Saffron Walden, the survival of manuscripts and surveys compiled for the Benedictine Abbey of Walden enabled Dorothy Cromarty to reconstruct the management of the abbey's estate, and the pattern of settlement and landholding on the heavy clay lands, colonized in the twelfth and thirteenth centuries.[58] The western boundary of the parish lies along the north-flowing Cam, into which flow two tributary streams, creating lateral valleys. On the slopes of the three valleys the chalk is exposed - land that would be the first choice for farming. The second choice would be the glacial clay plateau, mostly above the 300 foot contour line, into which the valleys are incised. There are thus two geomorphological areas, each giving rise to a different development and its own landscape. The first is of the type termed 'champion', the second 'bocage' or 'wooded'.

In 1086 the future parish of Walden (7,500 acres) was a single de Mandeville manor of 28 hides and one virgate; at the rough and ready approximation of 120 acres to the hide, this gives a cultivated area of 3,390 acres. The chalkland areas were already under the plough. In the years that followed, the castle was built on the strategic spur between the tributaries, and the town developed beside it. Beside the river, one and a half miles to the west, lay the abbey, founded in 1136, and its village of Brookwalden, with its demesne in the surrounding fields. The lay manor of Chepyng Walden was based in the castle and its holdings lay in the fields around the town. This was an open landscape of strip farming in huge fields and so it remained until late enclosure, apart from the land required from the sixteenth century onwards for the development of parkland for Audley End, the mansion on the site of the former abbey.

Land for expansion could only be found up on the clay plateau, and here a landscape evolved characteristic of enclosure from waste and woodland; fields were of many different sizes, some subdivided into strips, and interlaced with sizable areas of pasture and woodland. Seven sub-manors developed originating in the subinfeudation of the uncultivated tracts of the de Bohun lands (successors to the de Mandevilles) in the late twelfth and early thirteenth centuries.[59] Four of these were acquired by the abbey: Mattens, Pounces, Butlers and St Aylotts. St Aylotts held 407 acres with 49 in open-fields; the manor's enclosed arable lay in large fields ranging from 25 to 56 acres. Pasture lay in small closes of a few acres, except for one of eighteen acres. Mattens and Pounces contained villein as well as demesne land, with small open-fields of about twenty acres, but also with large enclosed fields.

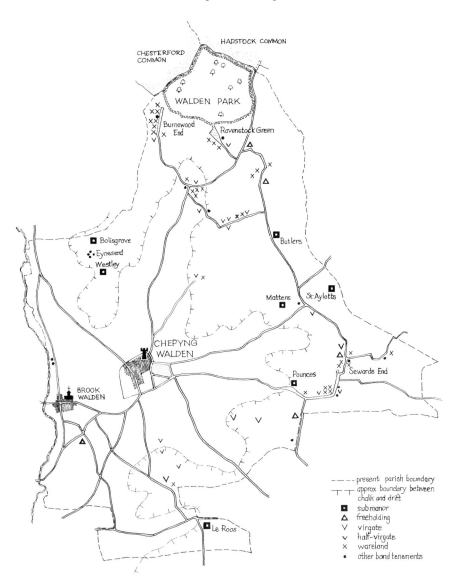

The parish of Saffron Walden in 1400

In addition to the sub-manors and their tenants' cottages, there were many other messuages, some in hamlets, some in groups of two or three, and others isolated. Four freeholders had crofts of up to ten acres as well as strips in the open-fields of Walden and Little Walden. Thirty others, described as holders of virgates or half-virgates, mostly had mixed holdings with home crofts of up to five acres and strips in the open-fields. A large group of cottagers held 'wareland', which appears to conform to a fixed standard of three, six or ten acres. These lay pre-dominantly in the hamlets of Little Walden, Burnewood End, Ravenstock Green, and Sewards End.

The woodlands of the parish all lay on the plateau. The de Bohuns' park, with its wooded quarters, enclosed the northern tip of the parish, and three woods belonging to the abbey, totalling 358 acres, lay close to the boundary with Ashdon.

Cromarty's analysis is of the situation in 1400, but it reflects the settlement pattern achieved before the calamities that culminated in the Black Death. Little would have happened in the years that followed except, perhaps, retreat. Certainly retreat followed in subsequent centuries with the disappearance of the smallholdings. Two hamlets, Little Walden and Sewards End, survived and thrived but the others declined or vanished. Eynesend had disappeared by the time of Chapman and André's map of 1777, as had the two sub-manors of Bolisgrove and Mattens, and an un-named hamlet lying south-east of Little Walden had reduced to a single farmstead by the time of the first edition OS six inch map. It has now gone and only the lane, a bridleway, remains. The plateau areas of the parish were far more densely populated in the fourteenth century than today, and the contrast with 'champion' south Cambridgeshire yet more marked.

Cromarty's study is a model for future research into the history of the tract of wooded land which at the time of Domesday Book stretched southwards from Walden, through Wimbish, Debden and Broxted, to Takeley and the Hallingburys. A most valuable project for future research would be to field walk the Walden claylands in the manner pursued by Tom Williamson over the land to the west of the Cam. In this way a prehistorical dimension could be added to Cromarty's historical account of a recolonization.

Moated sites

For many people the homestead moat, together with the castle, church tower and village green is the embodiment of medieval England in the landscape. It is then surprising that so little is known about moats, why and when they became fashionable, their purpose or purposes, and what logic lies behind their distribution. It has been suggested that the earliest moats were circular in emulation of mottes, but it is not known whether the moats of motte and bailey castles were intended to be water-filled when first built, or whether water was a fortuitous result of building on clay soils. However that may be, there is hard evidence of the development of one early site in Essex : the palace built by King John at Writtle in 1211, which we have looked at earlier. Tiptofts Manor, Wimbish, built early in the thirteenth century and magnificent in the landscape with its great sweeping roof and gabled cross-wings, stands within a rectangular moated enclosure, similar to Writtle. The neighbouring manor of St Aylotts was similarly moated, at least 200 years earlier than the splendid rural retreat of the abbot of Walden that stands on the site. But otherwise, the many sites which one can reasonably suppose to date from the early Middle Ages, particularly in peripheral areas, are lacking in secure dates.

Some caution therefore is needed in assuming that the occupation of a site and the construction of its moat occurred at the same time. There is some consensus, however, that in the national context the majority of homestead moats, particularly in isolated assarted areas, were constructed between 1275 and 1350.[60] There was social disorder from the stresses incurred by Edward I's wars of conquest, and natural disasters followed in that unhappy time. The security offered by a moat and internal palisade would have been comforting for those who could afford it.

But it should be kept in mind that moat building enjoyed a revival in the later Middle Ages and early Tudor period as a status symbol, and a new owner of an older, unmoated site, might have felt moved to add one, or improve a moat that already existed. The manors of earlier times appear to have been sited where there was a good water supply and natural drainage, in which a slope would be an advantage; security would be provided by a deep ditch and stout fencing.

Cressing Temple is a case in point, where the contours precluded the construction of a continuous moated enclosure. When the new Tudor mansion came to be built, it seems likely that sections of the defensive ditches of the earlier manor were widened to give the desired moated effect. At the remarkable manorial complex of Colville Hall, White Roding, the same process may have happened as it also lies on a sloping site; but if so, it was at an earlier date. It was acquired by Sir Anthony Browne, Master of Horse to Henry VIII, who extended the site and added a formal gateway, approached through an outer moat, or fishponds. An interesting feature of Colville is that a spring cools the cellars before joining the moats.

If a moat was a requisite when a new site was planned, then a level area was selected as in the case of Writtle, or late medieval sites such as Rookwood Hall, Abbess Roding, or Netherhall, Roydon. This allowed the moat a continuous surface within a formal orthogonal plan.

Lengths of moat, possibly constructed at a late date for show, occur on ancient sites, and to assume that there was formerly a total enclosure may be a will-o'-the-wisp. The two pre-Conquest manors at Widdington are a case in point. Widdington Hall sports a moat beside its fine courthall wing - the approach seen by the tenants - and at Prior's Hall a moat abuts two sides of the great barn, built when William of Wykham's agents took over and re-equipped the manor in the late fourteenth century. Nearby in Debden, is Amberden Hall, also a pre-Conquest manor. The present house dates from Tudor times and stands outside a large rectangular moated enclosure, which raises the question: did an earlier house stand within the enclosure? Or was the enclosure for an orchard or garden - perhaps a Tudor landscape feature? It is likely that the house was originally much bigger, and its approach between two great fishponds is prestigious.

The development of these three manors is unclear, and raises many questions that only archaeology might find answers to. The distribution of moats as a whole raises much wider questions. In 1978 the Moated Sites Research Group brought together what knowledge and conclusions had been reached at that time.[61] A total of 5,307 sites were known of in Britain, of which 548 were in Essex and 507 in Suffolk; of the other counties, only Yorkshire with 320 had more than 300 sites. The largest concentration lay on the Boulder Clays of Essex and Suffolk. With the establishment of county Sites and Monuments Records, the numbers are all likely to have grown since 1978, and in Essex now stand at 855 (1997).

Within Essex, the concentration of sites in the west of the county gives a very loose correlation with the well-wooded areas of 1086, and also with the surviving distribution of pre c1400 aisled halls.[62] The highest density lies within the trapezium bounded by the M11, A120, A130 and A414, which includes the Rodings, Easters, Hatfield, Matching, Moreton and the Lavers. Northwards of this area, the correlation with Domesday Book woodland is closer, with a high density particularly in Wimbish and parts of neighbouring parishes.

The most common moat form in Essex is the simple rectangular plan as at Writtle and Tiptofts, but there exists all manner of variants, some regular and some irregular, and many partially moated sites. There are examples of more complex forms: concentric and double moats, extended arms, and linked fishponds.[63] The

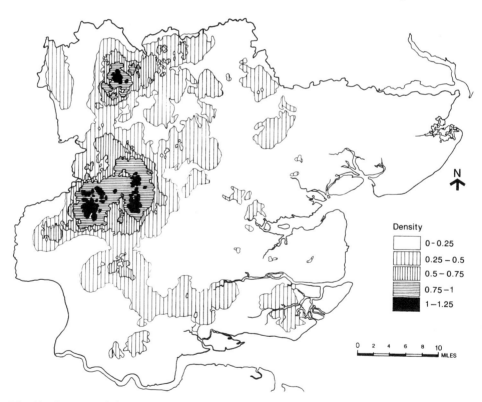

Density

☐	0 – 0.25
⊞	0.25 – 0.5
⊞	0.5 – 0.75
☰	0.75 – 1
■	1 – 1.25

0 2 4 6 8 10
MILES

The distribution and density of moated sites in Essex (source: the Essex Sites and Monuments Record)

128

enclosures vary in size from 20 metres square to 15 acres (6 ha), but an area of 0.5-1.0 acre (0.2-0.4 ha) is more common. Moats were not all enclosures for home-steads; some surrounded orchards and gardens. Sometimes the farm was included with the domestic buildings within the moated area, and sometimes it lay outside, as at Writtle.

Essex and Suffolk are the obvious counties in which to study moats - their forms, age, distribution and context. So far, in Essex, we have an inventory, one full excavation report (Writtle), and the paper prepared by John Hedges for the 1978 survey which summarized the state of knowledge at that time, and to which little has since been added. So this rich and fascinating field invites study, both to understand how this class of monument developed and how it related to the development of its surrounding area, and also, and not least, why such a prepon-derance of sites should occur in Essex.

The landscape of Park Farm, Thaxted, formerly the Little Park, depicted in an oil painting by Alec Hunter in 1948. In the fourteenth century the land was wood-pasture with the gardens and orchards of the manor covering the field where the mill stands. The brick tower mill (1810) is probably on the site of the Church Mill which appears by the fourteenth century to have superseded the earlier watermill. The hedges, planted in the Tudor period, were removed in the 1960s, but in recent years have been replaced by extensive new hedgerow planting to a richer mix of species than that advocated by Thomas Tusser. Park Farm won the coveted annual Conservation Award in 1997

CHAPTER NINE

The later Middle Ages

Calamities and opportunities

The climate of the eleventh and twelfth centuries has been called the 'Little Optimum'. By the late thirteenth it was deteriorating. Evidence from deserted medieval villages shows raised house platforms, new drainage ditches - regularly cleaned, cobbled floors and stone paving.[1] 'A physical chill settled on the fourteenth century at its very start, initiating the miseries to come. The Baltic sea froze over twice, in 1303 and 1306-07; years followed of unseasonable cold, storms and rains.[2]' Contemporaries could not know that it was the onset of what is sometimes called the Little Ice Age, which would last until about 1700. Harvest failures occurred in 1315, 1316 and 1321, bringing famine, and in 1319-21 the great sheep murrain swept flocks. It was a time of social disorder, and those who lived in isolated areas and could afford it built moats.[3] In 1348 bubonic plague arrived. No wonder that many believed that the Apocalypse was imminent, and the Four Horsemen loosed. The English peasantry, unlike the unhappy French, were spared the ravages of war, but famine, plague and death were all too evident.

The Great Pestilence

Bubonic plague, known as the Black Death or Great Pestilence, had returned from central Asia after an absence of 700 years. Known as Justinian's Plague, it had raged in England in the mid seventh century. Its effects were as devastating in rural areas as in towns. In 1350 the population of males in Great Waltham had dropped from 187 to 104, a loss of 45 per cent. Animals as well as humans were vulnerable; the bacillus spread via rodents to cats and dogs, and farmyard animals, but apparently not to horses.[4] The plague was pandemic - bubonic in summer and pneumonic in winter - and perhaps 40 per cent of the population died in the first occurrence. But the pestilence kept returning, and was likely to carry off young people who had not the immunity of the survivors of previous attacks. It is likely that over 40-50 years the population halved, and numbers would not fully recover until the eighteenth century. At Writtle in 1328 there were 408 decenners (males over twelve) over two thirds of the manor, suggesting a total of 612. In 1382 there were 268 over the whole manor, a number which declined to 192 in 1411. The number remained low and only reached 277 in 1492.[5]

The poll tax return for Essex in 1377, which included all people over fourteen, numbered 47,962.[6] This suggests a total population for the county may have been 89,000. The population before the Black Death and the earlier famines, probably lay between 130,000 and 170,000 representing a loss respectively of around 40 or 50 per cent.[7] From a situation of stress, where population growth had outrun its resources and the clearance of productive land had been pushed to its limits, peasants were now in a position that favoured them - labour was in short supply and there was no shortage of land. In Thaxted since 1361 labour services had only been demanded at a time of emergency, as in the rebuilding of the windmill after it was thrown down by a storm, and by 1380 no services were being exacted.[8] Expectations improved, and in the Peasants' Revolt of 1381 the fundamental grievances were the bond of villeinage, the lack of legal and political rights, and the right to commute services to rent. The revolt failed but the economic forces already propelling commutation and the decline of villeinage continued. By 1397 the whole manor of Writtle was leased out.[9]

The men of Essex had played a leading role in the Revolt. It would seem that they were well organised, and their programme included the destruction of the manorial records which were the legal basis for bond services. We may sympathise, their actions were not those of Luddites, but the destruction is a sadness for the historian. Villeinage was now perceived as arduous and humiliating; Essex men looked to Suffolk where a high proportion of the population were recorded as freemen at the Conquest, and across the estuary to Kent with its ancient tradition of free tenure. For a while lords struggled through the courts to force the return of bondmen who had fled, but in practice it appears that labour services gradually lapsed and had faded away by the second decade of the fourteenth century.

Cloth, farming and London

Notwithstanding the social tensions and repressions of the later fourteenth and early fifteenth centuries, Essex was embarking on a period of unparalleled prosperity. The Lay Subsidy of 1334 is an indicator of relative economic status at that time, although the assessments were fixed in 1306 before the decline of demesne 'high farming'. If London and Middlesex are disregarded, Essex lay a little below the middle at £11 per square mile.[10] The Lay Subsidy of 1515, however, showed that in the intervening years the status of Essex had changed dramatically. It has been called 'a sophisticated measure of the true wealth of the community', based on annual income, the capital value of moveable goods, and wages. Essex, at £102 per 1,000 acres, was the third highest.[11] The factors behind this extraordinary change were proximity to London and the rise of the cloth industry.

During this period London and its suburbs Westminster and Southwark were growing phenomenally, whereas other ancient centres such as York, Lincoln and Oxford remained static. 'Essex was in the business of supplying this expanding and immensely wealthy market on its doorstep with necessities and luxuries.[12]' Besides supplying grain for London's mills, dairy products, beef and hides were in demand. An ordinance of the late fourteenth century prohibited the slaughter of cattle nearer to the City than Knightsbridge to the west and Stratford to the east, where a lively market and butchery industry grew up. South-west Essex had the advantage of proximity, and its soils formed from London Clay, Bagshot and Claygate Beds, were more suitable for pasturage than arable. Faggots were required for London's bakeries, and the demand was reflected in woodland management that favoured hornbeam and in the intensification of pollard densities in Epping Forest. From the marshes came cheeses, mutton and fleeces, and from the estuary, fish and shellfish.

A small cloth industry was already established in Colchester, Coggeshall and Maldon in the late thirteenth century. It was stimulated by fiscal measures under Edward III, and in 1388 a settlement with the Hansa opened up markets in the Baltic and Prussia. From a position of producing only a fraction of the output of Suffolk and Kent, Essex production rose to equal that of Suffolk and double that of Kent - a prodigious expansion achieved between the 1350s and the 1390s. The reason for this has been studied by John McCann, who concluded that it lay in the availability of a large new labour force, itself the result of peasant dissatisfactions with their social and economic conditions on the manor.[13]

Lords who knew that their bondmen had fled to other manors to work for better wages sought their return through the coercive mechanisms of the courts, which the state supported. However, the cloth industry was another matter; it was producing valuable taxes for the crown, and central government had no interest in depriving it of its essential labour force. The conflict appears to have resolved itself in time. As customary labour services lapsed and there was no recovery in population levels, lords were glad to find tenants for land that would otherwise be waste. From the 1420s the smallholder had freedom and prosperity, and no incentive to leave the land for the cloth industry, which continued at a high level in Essex but did not expand further.[14]

The greatest concentration of cloth production was in the north-east of the county in and around Colchester, with outlying centres at Halstead, Bocking, Braintree, Maldon and Chelmsford, but there are records of weavers, fullers and drapers in many towns and villages, mostly lying to the north of Stane Street (the A120).

The prosperous fifteenth century

If the fourteenth century was a time of natural disasters followed by social tensions, the fifteenth developed into one of unparalleled prosperity for the people of Essex. As we have seen, there was a thriving market for farming and woodland products, a developing symbiosis between London and the Essex coast, and a booming cloth industry. The latter brought the additional and invaluable benefit of a cottage industry in spinning, attested to by the frequency of holes for warping pegs on the internal faces of timber studding. Figures for a later time, which may not greatly differ, suggest that 25,000 spinners were required to supply 4,000 Essex weavers, and others spun for London.[15] Wives and daughters could double the family income. The general prosperity is evident in the many buildings that survive from this time, the homes of farmers, smallholders and townspeople, as well as monuments to piety and civic pride, and the mansions of the rich.

Buildings in the landscape

In an earlier chapter, we saw Rayleigh Castle as demonstrating two phases in castle development: at first, a secure redoubt from which to exercise control, then later, a seigniorial stronghold built to impress one's peers as well as humbler folk, and also providing the space and setting for a generous lifestyle. After the disgrace of Henry of Essex, Rayleigh came into royal hands and soon after 1200 King John gave it to Hubert de Burgh, who is thought to have used its stone in the 1230s to build his new castle on a spur below the Hadleigh Downs, to guard and survey the Thames estuary. Documents dating between 1279 and 1303 refer to the motte as used for pasture, and in 1394 Richard II gave permission for the townsfolk to quarry the foundations for such stone that Hubert had left in place.[16]

In the 1360s, William of Wykham rebuilt Hadleigh as a royal castle of some magnificence and also something of a puzzle. A tall curtain wall linking cylindrical towers did not complete its circuit but dropped to form a base for a timber superstructure. It was not for lack of money, for the interior buildings included a great hall, chapel and suites for the king and queen. More likely it was

Hadleigh Castle as reconstructed by William of Wykham in the later fourteenth century, viewed from the deer park looking southwards over the sheep pastures of Canvey Island to the Thames estuary. Watercolour by Frank Gardiner

intended as a splendid royal residence, styled as a castle - it would have been unlikely to frighten the French, but it might have impressed them. One may recall Bodiam - Hadleigh's near contemporary - a country mansion built as a castle, and set in an artificial lake within a carefully designed landscape.

Wykham had no need to devise a suitable setting. Hubert had chosen a site with noble prospects. From its eminence, the castle looked out over its harbour and tidemill, across the marshland flats of Canvey to the estuary and to the North Downs beyond. Seen from the estuary, it stood against the backcloth of Hadleigh Downs, then the wood-pasture of the castle's deer park. The castle ruins have long suffered from the instability of London Clay on slopes, but Constable found it an impressive site, and so it is today, both for the castle's remains and for the long views which it was first built to observe.

Pleshey remained an important seat, held in the late fourteenth century by the Duke of Gloucester, who was duly murdered by his nephew, Richard II. Excavations on the motte by the Morant Club early in this century, revealed the foundations of an interesting building, rectangular in plan and measuring 67 by 56 feet (20 by 17m). On all sides were rectangular projections to form towers.[17] The stone walls nowhere exceeded 15 inches (380 mm) in width, and one concludes that this was a timber framed building, faced with stone, not only designed to be commodious, but also to form a feature in the landscape that would impress and delight. One is reminded that it was approaching the age of the castles depicted in that remarkable illustrated gazetteer of castellar architecture, the Très Riches Heures of the Duc de Berry, elaborately detailed and multi-towered, with complex skylines capped by gilded finials.[18]

By this time, it seems, the castle was effectively obsolete for purposes of warfare; its architecture remained the badge of rank not only for the aristocrat, but also for the arriviste. Licences to crenellate were issued by the Crown to favoured servants to show that they had attained the respectability to be owners of castles. In 1439 Sir John Montgomery, a leading soldier who had served at Agincourt, began to add a castellated brick house to his timber framed manor house at Faulkbourne. At Nether Hall, Roydon, in the 1460s Thomas Colt, a lawyer who had served Edward IV, decided that his manor built around two courts was not grand enough, and built himself a miniature castle on a new axis to the north of the old enclosures, and surrounded it with a moat. Its gate house, in red-brick with blue diaper patterns, survives as a splendid, jagged ruin. Traces of ridge and furrow show that it was laid out over former open-fields.[19]

The techniques used at Nether Hall suggest that a Fleming was in charge, and there are records of Dutch and Flemish brickmakers at work on several sites in Essex in the fifteenth century.[20] By 1500, English craftsmen had mastered the techniques and brick building proliferated in Essex for mansions and church work. Essex is the county to study the history of early brickwork in England, and it is easy to see why it caught on in an area that lacked its own resources of freestone but had abundant brickearth. The marks of annual shuttering in church walls show how

The gatehouse of Nether Hall, Roydon, built in the 1460s (survey by David Andrews)

slow, by comparison, rubble walling was to build, and moulded bricks could soon achieve the intricate dressings and tracery that had previously required imported freestone. Moreover, trading contacts with the Low Countries would have established cultural links and awareness of the sophisticated brick tradition there.

Turning to church building, it is generally in the cloth producing areas in the north of the county that one finds the finest examples of the Perpendicular style. Pevsner singled out three - Saffron Walden, Thaxted and Dedham - which can stand up to a comparison with Long Melford and Lavenham in Suffolk, or the best and grandest in Norfolk.[21] He considered Dedham of c1500, 'wholly Suffolk in character'. Its 130 foot tower dominates the Dedham Vale just as it did in Constable's time. Saffron Walden, rebuilt c1450-1525, reflects the wealth brought by the saffron crocus, and superseded the castle as the dominating building of the town. Its spire, designed by Rickman, was added in 1831. Thaxted, begun c1340, has a certain mystery attending its development. Unusually for a Till church, it is sited on the top of a hill and with its spire, 181 feet high, visible for miles around - not a building that could be missed. As with Dedham and Walden, the wealth existed to complete the church in stone when others might have opted for brick. The nave originally stood higher than the chancel, and openings with steps down were built on either side of the present high altar. A reference to an inscription referring to a miracle suggests there may once have been a shrine, and where there was a shrine there were pilgrims with offerings.[22]

In north-east Essex there are notable examples of flint and freestone flushwork displayed in the towers of Dedham and Brightlingsea churches, and the incomparable gatehouses of St Osyth Priory and St John's Abbey, Colchester. This fine art also graces the south porch and tower battlements of Chelmsford Cathedral.

The emergence of a prosperous middle class of merchants, clothiers and yeoman farmers is evident in the large number of timber-framed buildings surviving from the late medieval and Tudor periods. The quality that would enable a building to last and adapt to change was no longer limited to the level of the rich manor or monastic order. A newly-created database of Essex listed buildings gives a figure of 21 for the thirteenth century, 152 for the fourteenth, and 552 for the fifteenth.[23] The figures are indicative only, as dating requires internal access and

The spectacular flint and freestone flushwork displayed in the gatehouse of St Osyth's Priory

even if this is obtained, timbers and joints may be hidden. Nevertheless, the number of early buildings continues to grow. A well-known civic building of the period, Thaxted's so-called Guildhall (in fact a market hall), has been securely dated by dendrochronology to around 1450. Originally built with twin gables and market stalls on the first as well as ground floor, the quality of its carpentry has enabled its survival through modification, mutilation, adaptation to new uses, and the crazy insertion of brick nogging which nearly brought about its collapse. A veteran of distinction.

The landscape fabric

With a population now reduced to a little less than one and a half times that of 1086, pressure on the landscape had eased, while near at hand the growth of London provided a ready market for its farming, coastal and woodland products. As lords sought tenants, smallholders found freedom and prosperity, and a yeoman class began to emerge in a stable landscape. Until the eighteenth century, when once again interest grew in farm development - crops, rotations and machinery - there was little motive for change other than consolidation, and it appears, enhancement. For this reason, surviving estate maps of the late sixteenth and seventeenth centuries are relevant as a guide to the fabric of the landscape that had evolved in the course of the fifteenth. In aesthetic terms it would appear the most pleasing seen in Essex before or since.

Most notable among early Essex map-makers were John Walker of West Hanningfield and his son, John, who worked in the years around 1600, mostly in central Essex. Within certain cartographical conventions, the accuracy and detail of their work requires little imagination to bring their landscapes to life, and here we are concerned with the individual features depicted - the buildings will be considered in a later chapter. Former common-fields, already small, are shown now divided into closes, while elsewhere amalgamation of small fields or crofts has left hedgerow trees standing, useful for shade where stock farming predominated.[24]. Hedgerow timber was clearly considered a valuable resource, for virtually all hedges are shown with trees, carefully spaced. Park pales, fences and precise positions of gates are depicted. Many former tofts and crofts are empty small enclosures, while others have been absorbed into neighbouring land. It is a relaxed landscape, of which many features remain with us, but the enhancement of demesne land by planting which appears to have been a characteristic of this time has left little trace in the landscape. Fortunately there are the estate maps of the Walkers and their successors.[25]

The working landscape of the Walkers' time was celebrated by Thomas Tusser (1524-80), a native of Rivenhall. Although he failed as a practical farmer, he became famous for his poem: 'Hundreth Good Points of Husbandrie' describing farming practices and management. On hedge planting he gave the following advice: 'The berries of hawthorne, acrones, ashkeys, mixed and then wrought up in a rope of straw will serve.... make a trench at the top of the ditch and lay in some fat soil and then lay the rope all along and cover it with good soile.... keepe cattle from bruising them, and cut the young springs by the earth, so they will branch and grow thicke'.[26]

One of the finest estate maps is the Walker map, dated 1598, of West and East Horndon, Dunton and Bulphan, covering 2,585 acres (1,045 ha). It was commissioned by Sir John Petre, who acquired the estate following the death of his father, Sir William, in 1572, and established his own seat at Thorndon Hall. We are concerned here with the siting of the hall and its surrounding landscape; although the map shows Sir John's alterations to the hall, one can reasonably suppose that at this early stage of his ownership, the landscape remained much as it was when he acquired it. In the early fifteenth century, the West Horndon estate had been held by Sir John Fitz-Lewis, a London vintner and goldsmith, who built a brick mansion for which he had a licence to crenellate. His grandson and his bride 'had the misfortune, on their wedding-night, to be consumed in the flames which destroyed West Horndon Hall'.[27] This sad event followed the restoration of the family estates by Henry VII, so a part of the hall shown by Walker, and its overall planning, dates from the late fifteenth century.

West Horndon is one of the parallel parishes lying north-south across the Warley-Horndon ridge - an ancient allotment of land which gave each community a share of the different resources: wood-pasture, slope (for arable), flat plain and fen. The hall is sited on the edge of the ridge above the church, and is either on or near the site of the Saxon manor. The map is packed with interesting information on buildings, the pattern of settlement, and details of the landscape. The house, unusually for the fifteenth and sixteenth centuries, is not built around a courtyard and instead presents an east-west facade, some 260 feet long, which would have given fine views over the South Essex Plain to the principal rooms, and conversely, seen from the south, the long complex would have presented a noble and impressive form on the skyline.

Immediately to the north lies the 'oulde parke' and to the north-east, the linear village of Herongate with its greens bounded by tofts, many of them empty of cottages. Southwards the land rapidly slopes down to the plain with its ancient rectilinear field patterns, governed by long north-south axes. Along these boundaries lie narrow strips of woodland termed shaws. Some are shown fenced which would allow management as coppice, but others consist of standing trees, open to grazing and browsing, and clearly long established features. The short lengths that survive contain oaks, in contrast to the field boundaries of the plain where elm is dominant. The estate had no shortage of timber and underwood, and one must conclude that the shaws were planted at some time in the fifteenth century for reasons of amenity, to enhance the landscape as seen from the hall.

Mature, unfenced shaws are depicted on other Walker maps; for example, at Ingatestone and South Hanningfield,[28] and on the small estate of Little Leighs Hall, which shows a small former park with an open shaw along the length of its northern boundary.[29]

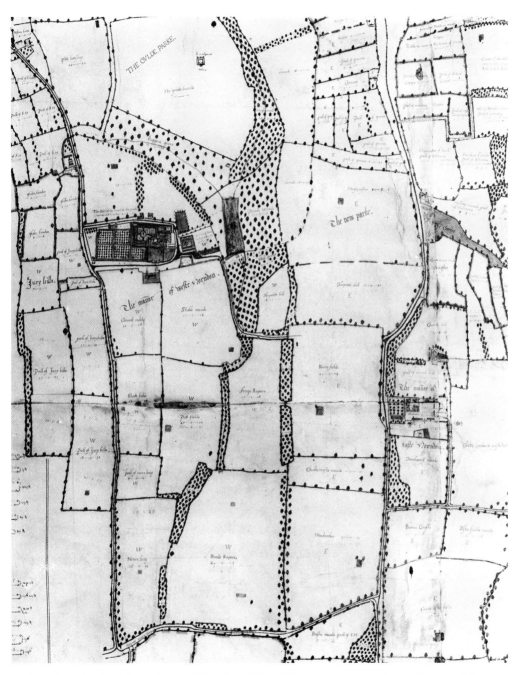

Old Thorndon Hall, formerly West Horndon Hall, and its surrounding landscape shown on John Walker's estate map of 1598 (ERO D/DP P5)

Following the decline of demesne high farming, the huge fields of the home farm at Cressing Temple were subdivided. The date is not known, but it was most likely to have been under the Hospitallers, when the land may have been leased out. A written survey of the manor, dated to 1656,[30] lists sixteen springs, the alternative term for shaw, generally used in the northern half of the county. The largest spring is just over two acres in size, while most are just under one, and they are named from the adjacent fields. All are coppice, and the survey gives the growth in years of the underwood. A map of 1727 of New House Farm, Cressing, which lay on land formerly part of the Templar demesne, shows springs bounding the former Ash Field, now subdivided into three.[31] These had vanished by 1800 when the Ordnance surveyors produced their first draft survey of Essex. A map of 1794 of Cressing Temple Manor, the reduced core of the demesne, shows no springs surviving,[32] which is hardly surprising as prices for corn had gone through the roof and the plough now ruled the landscape.

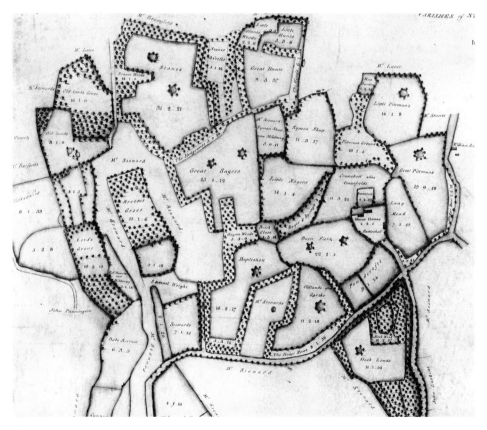

The demesne land of Battels Hall in Stapleford Abbots and Lambourne in an estate map of c 1800, copied from a map of 1655 (ERO D/DM P18)

A map of the Walthambury demesne in 1643 shows it as very similar to the Cressing Temple demesne described in the survey of 1656; its huge former fields divided into smaller units with springs along old and new boundaries, all open and unfenced.[33] Another map, dated 1655, of the manor and demesne lands of Battels Hall in Stapleford and Lambourne shows an extraordinarily complex pattern of springs, which closer analysis and field names suggest was planted along existing field boundaries, themselves following the enclosure of former arable fields.[34] It was now a sylvan and pastural landscape, with ponds placed centrally in the larger fields and ringed with trees. Only a few of the many springs are shown open, and it may be that this is a late example of a proud owner following an established fashion.

It is possible to draw some conclusions from these four examples. First, in the fifteenth century, freed from the pressures that propelled high farming in the thirteenth and the social tensions of the fourteenth, landowners could relax and enjoy the amenities of their demesnes and seek ways to enhance them. West Horndon, Cressing Temple and Walthambury were important estates which would give a lead; their springs and shaws appear to have originated in the fourteenth century, and began a fashion that was to prove long lasting, indeed until the eighteenth century when other pressures favoured the maximization of land under corn. Secondly, springs and shaws only occurred on demesnes or land over which the landlord had firm control and, importantly, where he lived. Thirdly, it appears likely that they were an introduction into the Essex scene and their origin lay south of the River Thames.

Shaws are a traditional feature of the Weald of Sussex and Kent, and date at least from the Middle Ages and probably well before. Moreover, they were general to the landscape fabric and not limited to demesnes, and nor were they subject to changes in fashion - at least until the monocultural mania following World War Two. They are often two rods wide (33 feet), with four to five standards of oak or elm in a 30 yard stretch, and overall contain at least fifteen species of tree and shrub. Hawthorn, hazel and maple are common, and hornbeam in Kent. Fruit trees are also common and include bullace, crab apple, wild pear, cherry and damson.[35]

Of the very few springs that survive in Essex today, two can be seen from the M11 travelling northwards on the left, just past the Bank of England works at Debden. They are Broadfield Shaw and Long Shaw; both once lay within the demesne of Loughton Hall. While Broadfield Shaw is long established coppice with standards, Long Shaw has a very different character; it contains apple and crab apple trees and also some ancient oak and hornbeam pollards, which indicate that the present wood was once wood-pasture. It is reasonable to conclude that Long Shaw was established in the seventeenth or early eighteenth century, while Broadfield Shaw is far older.[36]

The oak content of the West Horndon shaws makes it certain that they were planted, and it seems likely that the other examples we have considered were also established in this way, although it may have included seeding from adjacent hedgerows. Some examples, however, could have been strips of retained woodland. This may be the case with Bovingdon Rows, a narrow woodland lying to the north of Bovingdon Hall, Bocking. It lay within the Monks' Park, which subsequently is identified with the 400 acres of woodland attached to Bovingdon Hall.[37] An estate map of 1803 shows Bovingdon Wood, an ancient lime woodland which formed the northern area of the park, and to the south a collection of springs with irregular outlines which suggest they were relict rather than planted.[38] Bovingdon Wood is probably primary (continuously wooded since recolonization following the end of the Devensian cold phase), but Bovingdon Rows is old secondary since the outline of two ditched enclosures are visible in the woodland floor, occupying a substantial area of the present wood. Moreover, lime is absent although it is abundant in nearby woods. So we have here evidence of former clearance followed by recolonization, perhaps post-Roman, or even earlier, and then clearance again, but leaving wooded strips.

It was during this time that Chepping Walden was developing into a centre for the production of saffron, its fame leading in the next century to the substitution of 'Saffron' for its affix. Nowadays saffron is just another cooking spice (and expensive), but in the fourteenth to seventeenth centuries it was regarded as valuable for both culinary and medicinal use, and probably even more so as a dye. Harrison devoted a lengthy section to a discussion of its origins, cultivation and many uses, but for him it was of course a local industry.[39] He believed it to have been introduced in the reign of Edward III and to have become commonly grown by the time of Richard II. This would accord with a market demand for its use in the Essex cloth industry. The earliest factual record in Walden comes from 1444, when an agreement between the abbot and vicar established saffron as a titheable commodity.[40]

While Walden was the focus of the industry, and centre for the processing and marketing of the product, its cultivation covered a much wider area which has been established by the study of field names and references in wills. But certainly the saffron plants coloured the landscape around the town with their pale to mid-purple flowers - the dye came from the stigmas. In 1586 William Camden wrote of Walden being situated midst fields smiling with the beautiful crocus, and visiting Audley End in 1654, John Evelyn recorded 'Saffron Walden, famous for the abundance of Saffron there cultivated and esteemed the best'.

CHAPTER TEN

Tudor and Stuart Essex

THE SIXTEENTH AND seventeenth centuries loom heavily, often flamboyantly and sometimes cruelly, in the national history, but the Essex landscape lay mostly undisturbed. A massive change in land ownership followed the Dissolution, but for the yeomen and cottagers it was little more than a change of landlords. Evictions to make room for sheep, a national problem Wolsey sought to address, were not evident (or have left no trace) in the Essex scene. There is little for the observer of landscape to record other than the buildings in the countryside, from the dwellings of the humble to the mansions of the rich (mostly newly so) and their attendant parks.

First we must consider the progress of brick. It was now the material of fashion, evidenced by its use by Wolsey for his palace at Hampton Court, for which he had the choice of any material then available. The early Tudor period saw the final flourish of church rebuilding, addition and adornment before the chill of the Reformation froze all joy in these symbols of community pride. The skills of craftsmen in brick excelled in Essex; Pevsner reckoned some 30 church towers built in brick, 'the most magnificent, tall, often adorned with trefoiled corbel friezes and stepped battlements, are probably those of Ingatestone, Rochford, and Layer Marney'.[1] There are the additions of many porches, often with stepped gables, and even reconstructions such as the nave of St Osyth.

An interesting account of a new brick mansion comes from a survey, dated 1530, of the Manor House at Henham, built by Robert Radcliffe (1483-1542) who prospered under Henry VIII, being created Earl of Sussex at the Field of the Cloth of Gold in 1529 and Great Chamberlain in 1540. The house is described as standing a mile from the village in the midst of Henham Park which was enclosed with a pale and was 'high and dry champion grounde and competently wooded very comodyous and parken where in be redd dear'.[2] A three-storied turreted gatehouse led to a court, across which lay the Chamber of Presence (60 by 18 feet in plan) with adjoining rooms looking into the garden, 'very commodious for flavours of the herbs and view into the same'. On either side of the gatehouse were galleries with oriel windows and chimneys, and at the western end, a chapel (50 by 20 feet). There were two ranges of kitchens, and so on, all very new and grand.

With its gatehouse and turrets, Henham lay typically within the domestic castle genre - or house decked out with castellar trimmings - as seen earlier at Nether Hall, and at its grandest, Hampton Court. What is new is the siting. The old manor house was abandoned and the new complex constructed in the verdant setting of the existing deer park, on high ground with space and fine views, and distanced from the community.[3] But its life was not long; it became redundant as a seat when a later owner moved to Boreham, and while it appears, still emparked, on John Norden's county map of 1594, it had vanished when John Oliver prepared his of 1696. Today, Lodge Farm stands on or near its site.

A parkland setting, like castellar references, conveyed a sense of pedigree and respectability to the new men of the age and the upwardly mobile, of whom the archetype was Richard Rich, a man devoid of any credit in the eyes of his contemporaries and posterity. He landed the plum job of Chancellor of the Court of Augmentations, where he could take his pick of the spoils of the Dissolution. It has been said that when the abbey lands passed through his hands, many of them stuck to his fingers. In Essex he acquired at least 100 manors and made his seat at Leez (or Leighs) where he built a mansion in the ruins of the priory. He already owned Absol, Little Leighs and Littley Parks and Pleshey Great Park in the area, but they were not enough for Rich. He extended Littley Park northwards and created two new parks, Pond and Leez, over farmland, thus cocooning himself in parky respectability. A fine map of 1775 in the Essex Record Office of Pond Park, by then long disparked, shows a hedged and wooded landscape that certainly

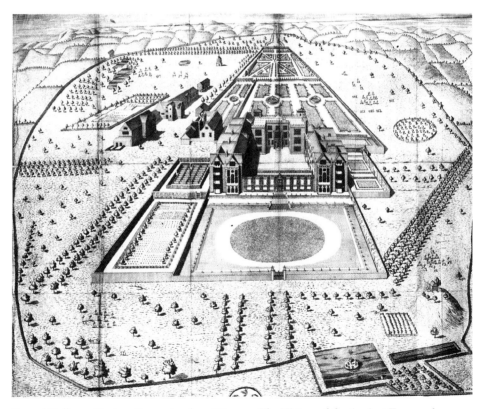

Copped Hall near Epping. Engraving from J Farmer, The History of the Ancient Town and once famous Abbey of Waltham in the County of Essex, from the Foundation to the Present Time, 1735

144

pre-dated Rich. The pattern suggests a post-Black Death hedged field layout over former arable. The fields are studded with trees, indicating a pasture regime, probably planted when the land was emparked to give an appearance of wood-pasture.[3]

A bird's eye view print of Copped Hall of 1735[4] shows the mansion built by Sir Thomas Heneage between 1564 and 1567, on the site of an earlier house where Princess Mary was held under house arrest, within the park formerly owned by the abbots of Waltham, licensed in 1293. Extensive formal gardens and avenues of a later date are depicted, but these overlie the earlier landscape of scattered trees - medieval wood-pasture. Other examples of the new mansion sited out in the deer park are Easton Lodge, built in the 1590s by Henry Maynard, and Hill Hall, Theydon Mount, where Sir Thomas Smith's pile stands on the skyline above the junction of the M11 and M25.

For the planning and appearance of mansions and manor houses, and their appurtenances, at the end of the sixteenth century we are fortunate that a number are shown on Walker maps. At Thorndon Hall, where we have considered the siting and landscape, Sir John Petre embarked on a programme of remodelling between 1575 and 1595 for which detailed annual accounts survive. The map of 1598 shows three towers rising above the chimney stacks: the lead-capped High and Bell Towers, and the battlemented Great Tower. Entry is through a pretty gatehouse to a large court where a considerable party, arriving or departing could assemble. Behind, to the north-east, lies a service court with bakehouse and stables, built in 1589-90.[5] Built at the same time, to the east, lies a massive range of farm buildings and more stables, with a large enclosure for 'strangers' horses' lying to the north. Immediately behind the house to the north-west lies a huge formal sunken garden, with banqueting house, and to the west, extensive orchards and two dovecotes. All except the farm complex are enclosed with brick walls.

In 1763 the house was demolished when the ninth Lord Petre built his new Thorndon Hall a mile and a quarter to the north. The sunken garden and house foundations now lie under a wood, and their inhabitants are badgers and bats, but it is a site that is certainly worth a visit. It lies between the two Thorndon Country Parks, and the adjacent field pattern of 1598 has been re-established. The extent and siting of the mansion can be appreciated, and the fine views southwards enjoyed much as they were by Sir John Petre and his predecessors.

It is in the field of vernacular architecture that the Walkers' maps are perhaps most valuable, as the pictorial conventions of the age show the building types and their materials in a way that was denied when cartography developed. Some 62 per cent of dwellings were one-storeyed cottages, and some surviving examples have been identified. These could be described more accurately as one and a half storeyed, as they are of sufficient height to allow upper rooms in the roof at either end of a small open hall; the type can be spotted today by small windows in the end gables. They are substantial structures, more so than similar buildings of the seventeenth century, although it may be that the survivors represent the upper end of the range. Virtually all are shown with brick chimneys or smoke-hoods, and a high proportion have tiled roofs, although the ratio of thatch to tile varied from area to area.

Next in number to cottages are open-hall houses with one two-storeyed cross-wing. Only large and important medieval houses had two crosswings, and many of this type have been found to have had the second crosswing added in late Elizabethan or early Stuart times. Another type, which became fashionable from the third quarter of the fifteenth century, is the long-jettied rectangular house which continued to be built well into the seventeenth century. The Walkers show no Wealden type houses, although over 30 are known in Essex and more are likely to be discovered.

Chimneys are virtually ubiquitous, built in brick with only a few in cottages made of wood. Writing in 1587, William Harrison numbered the things that 'old men yet dwelling in the village where I remain [Radwinter] have noted to be marvelously altered in England within their sound remembrance... One is the multitude of chimneys lately erected, whereas in their young days there were not above two or three, if so many, in most uplandish towns of the realm (the religious houses and manor places always excepted, and peradventure some great personages), but each one made his fire against a reredos [back of an open hearth] in the hall, where he dined and dressed his meat'.[6]

The maps show a few purprestures on highway waste, features which would become commonplace in the next two centuries. *Purpresture*, a medieval term, has two meanings: first, an illegal enclosure, and secondly, a payment to a feudal superior for liberty to enclose land or erect a building upon it. In Elizabeth's reign, hastily built cottages were frequently presented to the courts, who either ordered their removal or seizure, or less often, allowed them to remain after payment for licences, this giving copyhold title.[7] Lords seldom granted licences before the seventeenth century, when they required that the tenant maintain the adjacent road in addition to his rent. The plots in this early form of ribbon development are narrow and very long, giving space for a garden and small orchard, and enclosed by a hawthorn hedge.

Returning to the opposite end of the social spectrum, the maps show many manor houses, still of timber framed construction with gables a main feature and often with oriel windows - sophisticated vernacular architecture at its most attractive, and one may feel a deep regret that so little has survived.[8] One that has is Spains Hall, Finchingfield, built for Robert Kempe c1585, incorporating buildings from a moated house of the first half of the fifteenth century. Kempe's new frontage was built in red brick with six curving gables, pleasantly informal and unregimented. A spectacular feature of the site was a series of eight monumental fishponds with a ninth forming a huge extension to the moat.[9] The earthworks are still impressive although the water areas are much reduced.

The Walkers' map of Ingatestone depicts Ingatestone Hall, the seat of Sir William Petre (1505-72), diplomat and councillor to four monarchs.[10] A contem-

Spains Hall, Finchingfield

porary of Rich and following a similar legal and governmental career, Petre was regarded in his own time and by posterity as the antithesis of Rich - a highly efficient but honourable man in a time when rogues were the winners. The main courtyard of Ingatestone survives less the west wing which contained the great hall. Pevsner describes it as 'as one of the most characteristic of its period in England', before Elizabethan striving for systematisation. The courtyard is pleasingly irregular, reminding one that asymmetry is a tradition as ordered and valid as classical symmetry. Happily, Ingatestone Hall remains the seat of Petre's descendants.

Perhaps the most extraordinary building of the sixteenth century in Essex is Layer Marney Towers; to quote Pevsner again, 'of all the gatehouses of Essex and indeed of England, a showpiece of crazy height'. Begun c1520, its owner Lord Marney died in 1523 and his son in 1525, and their projected mansion was never begun, but from the evidence of their gatehouse one presumes it was intended to be very grand indeed.

Extraordinary buildings certainly arose in the latter half of the sixteenth century as magnates turned away from the native tradition and built mansions heaped with ill-digested Mannerist forms and motifs, imported from France and the Netherlands. Fortunately Essex was spared, and when Thomas Howard embarked on the building of his mansion at Audley End a new architecture had evolved that was grand but not bombastic, and expressed stability as much as wealth. Howard had inherited the estate from his grandfather, Thomas Audley, who had received the buildings and lands of Walden Abbey for his ruthless service to Henry VIII. Audley had incorporated the abbey buildings into his mansion, retaining the cloister and adapting the nave. But this was not good enough for Howard who required a building that would encourage frequent royal visits, and in 1605 he commissioned the building of one of the largest mansions ever built in Britain. In date and style it was similar to Robert Cecil's Hatfield House; but whereas Cecil was content with brick, Howard required stone which had to be brought from a distance at great cost.

Work on the gardens probably began about 1614, creating rectangular walled enclosures. The entrance court to the west was enormous with the approach road flanked by double avenues of lime trees and crossing the River Cam, now dammed and turned into a formal canal.[10] The monastic fishponds were retained and lined with trees, and formal avenues planted over the parkland to the east. This landscape was to be totally remodelled in the eighteenth century and virtually nothing remains of it. A plan prepared by Bridgeman in about 1730 shows much of the Jacobean layout still intact and is of particular interest for the detail it gives of the park.[11] The medieval park lay far away at the northern end of the parish, and the park beside the house was created over the abbey's home farm, almost certainly by Audley, and it is a wood-pasture landscape with the familiar irregular pattern of scattered trees. Some clearly were retained when field boundaries were removed, but the majority must have been planted or were the result of natural regeneration, carefully selected and protected from browsing in their early years.

With Howard's Audley End we have entered the seventeenth century, a period when peoples' thoughts became concerned with other matters than enhancement of the landscape, at least until the later years when sanity prevailed, and there is little to record. A memorable record of the Civil War in Essex is the panorama of the siege of Colchester in 1648,[12] a bird's-eye view of the 'Line of Circumvallation' which recalls the spectacular earthworks of an earlier age in the area. These huge works left little trace; perhaps, understandably, the inhabitants sought to erase the reminder of an unpleasant experience.

In the course of the century, the number of parks dropped dramatically. In his map of the county in 1594 John Norden showed 50 parks, while in 1696 on John Oliver's map there were 24. Of parks referred to earlier, Henham and Walden had gone, but Rich's trio at Leez survived. At Thaxted the Little Park had become Park Farm in 1596,[13] and a map of 1737 shows the Great Park laid out to form two farms at some earlier date.[14] Horham Hall had become the Manor of Thaxted, but by 1696 it too had lost its park. Park palings were expensive to maintain, and the rents from tenant farmers an attractive alternative. As a result only those parks that formed the setting and environs of country houses were retained.

The seventeenth century also saw a decline in the quality of the timber used by carpenters. The Granary at Cressing Temple, erected in 1623, is strikingly inferior in this respect to the two great barns built in the thirteenth century despite it being a showy building on the approach to the Great House. About 50 per cent of the timbers are reused from medieval buildings on the site which had been pulled down, new timbers do not appear to have come from well-managed woodland, and a significant proportion of the larger timbers are of elm rather than oak - in surviving medieval buildings in Essex it is very exceptional to find either reused timbers or elm.[15]

This would seem to suggest a shortage of good quality timber and a reduction in woodland. The evidence of the Walker and other estate maps, however, shows that trees were abundant at this time, growing in woodlands, hedgerows, springs, shaws and parks. It is also possible that the common elm was a relatively recent introduction to the hedgerows of the area.

There has to be a different explanation, and the following possibilities are suggested. First, timber framed construction remained the general rule in London until after the Great Fire of 1666 and this could have led to high prices for quality oak. Secondly, other markets for oak, such as staves for barrels, may have been competitive, and thirdly, the demands of London's bakeries for faggots, and other industries for charcoal, could have stimulated the growing of underwood at the expense of timber, and as we have seen, the Cressing springs were coppices. Lastly, the Granary could make do with second best in terms of appearance as the timbers were concealed beneath an external coat of plaster. Other possible explanations would be welcome.

CHAPTER ELEVEN

Georgian landscapes

IN 1670, IT has been estimated, the population of Essex stood at 120,000; by 1723 it had reached 135,000, and in 1801 it had grown to 227,682.[1] As the eighteenth century progressed, the need to feed the growing population stimulated interest, investment and experiment in farming to an extent not seen since the thirteenth century. In this Essex landowners and farmers played their part, but the movement to enclose commons and open-fields which so altered the face of the Midland counties had relatively little effect over much of Essex, the land being long enclosed. In the areas we have termed the Former Heathlands and the Chalk Uplands, however, the effect of parliamentary enclosure acts was profound.

Parallel to the interest in the functional landscape, new perceptions and sensibilities led to developments in the 'ideal' landscapes of gardens and parklands, and in this too Essex played its part.

Designed landscapes

Earlier, we have noted the planned enhancement of demesnes with springs and shaws, an introduction of a feature traditionally found south of the Thames, primarily for reasons of amenity . In the reign of James I, direct cultural contacts with the Continent saw the importation of the formal styles for gardens and parks that were fashionable in France and Italy, and their influence is clearly seen in the landscaping of Howard's Audley End. At New Hall, Boreham, a great avenue was planted in 1624 by John Tradescant for George Villiers, Duke of Buckingham, which survives (replanted) although cut by the railway and A12.

By the early eighteenth century, literary figures such as Pope and Addison were reacting against formality in landscape and seeking a naturalistic approach. This developed into a creative ferment of ideas and experiment, in which diverse directions were explored and developed, lasting until the death of the leading figures in the 1740s.[2] As the importance of their achievements has come to be appreciated and the role of key players assessed, the role of Robert James, eighth Lord Petre, as both horticulturalist and landscape designer has been unjustly neglected. By the age of sixteen, in 1729, he had taken on the management of his grandmother's gardens at Thorndon and the 'stoves' or hothouses were reckoned outstanding. At eighteen, he had made his mark amongst the most eminent botanists, plantsmen and landscapers of the day, and was elected a Fellow of the Royal Society.[3] Sadly, he died at the age of 29 in 1742.

A part of the great design of 1733 by Robert James, 8th Lord Petre for Thorndon Park and Gardens, drawn by the surveyor Bourginion (ERO D/DP P23). It is interesting to compare with the Walker map on page 139 The plan retains the woodland to the east of the house as wood-pasture, and hedgerow trees beyond, while the mill pond is re-shaped as a formal lake. The mount for a dovehouse, to the west of the house, remains a feature of the site today

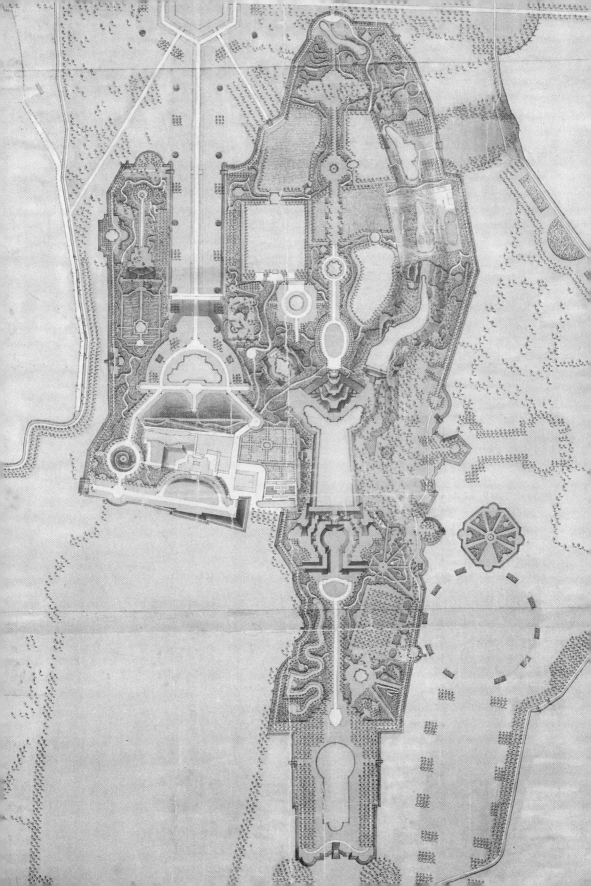

His nursery at Thorndon developed with his stoves rivalled only by those of the Chelsea Physic Garden and the Oxford Botanic Garden. Trees and shrubs were raised from seed on a prodigious scale, both natives and exotics sent by his contacts abroad, especially in the New World. As a landscape designer, his finished plans survive for Worksop, Nottinghamshire, and his own estate at Thorndon, both drawn by the French surveyor Bourginion. Although in each design an element of formality remains in the use of a grand axis, the landscapes appear to explode into a myriad of localities, some open and others enclosed, some geometrical while others are irregular or serpentine. At Worksop, clumps extend into the fields of the functional landscape following the approach of Switzer at Grimsthorpe, 'why may not a whole estate be thrown into a kind of garden by frequent plantations?',[4] and at Thorndon fields are included in the design. In his use of clumps he anticipated not only Brown's designs but William Kent's work at Euston in Suffolk.[5]

At Thorndon, the main axis extends northwards from the house through the wood-pasture of park and commons, marked by small formal clumps, reflecting in a different manner the long boundaries with their shaws extending southwards across the plain. In his planting, Petre made full use of the exotic trees he had raised. His great friend and colleague, the horticulturalist Peter Collinson, described how in 1740, 20,000 European trees were planted, together with 10,000 'Americans' and some 'Asians', and to walk in the thickets of Thorndon was like being in North America - and to be at table was like being in South America with up to a dozen pineapples fresh from the stoves.[6] At the northern end of the avenue he raised two flanking mounts, which he planted with larch and evergreens, topped with cedars of Lebanon, and also the mount to the west of the house, in the centre of the orchards that had been depicted on the Walker map. He was also noted for his skills in transplanting; Collinson wrote that 'Lord Petre, who was the ornament and delight of the age he lived in, removed, in the spring of 1734, 24 fully-grown elms about 60 ft. high, and 2 ft. in diameter: all grew finely, and now [1764] are not known from the old trees they were planted to match'.[7]

Since the house itself was now seriously out of tune with the Palladian style of the time, a design was commissioned from Giacomo Leoni and work began on rebuilding. This included the magnificent six-columned Corinthian portico which was later moved to grace the new Thorndon Hall. Immediately to the south, a great lawn was made which entailed the demolition of the old church and its replacement by St Nicholas, Ingrave.

Following his tragically early death leaving an infant son, there was no one to carry on Petre's plans and the work of improvements to the house and park halted. Fortunately, Collinson was able to arrange the dispersal of the contents of the nursery to other great estates who were eager to receive them. Visiting Thorndon in 1762, he found a desolate scene, with the house falling down, the nurseries overgrown and the stoves empty. Only traces of the works survive today, notably the mounts and the Octagon Plantation.

Robert James, Lord Petre, was renowned amongst his contemporaries for his mastery of all the sciences and skills involved in plantsmanship and landscape design, but in particular for his use of trees and shrubs to create contrasts of form, colour and texture - 'painting with living pencils', as Collinson put it. Pope's friend, John Spence, wrote that 'Mr Pope and Mr Kent were the first that practised painting in gardening. But Lord Petre carried it further than either of them'.[8] Now he is again recognized for his contribution to what we may consider the most creative and exciting time ever in the design of landscapes.

Compared with the grandeur of Thorndon, Bower Hall, Steeple Bumpstead, seems homely. It is known only from a delightful bird's eye view painting, which the costumes suggest was painted c1755, full of interesting information on the landscape, gardens and vernacular farm buildings.[9] A three-storey house in brick, built in about 1710 and embellished with pilasters in the giant Doric order, has formal enclosed gardens which include two trim geometrical parterres with clipped conical yews, features that may seem somewhat old-fashioned at this date. But they serve as a reminder that styles for the surrounds of great houses and the gardens of enterprising individuals were not yet typical of those of the conservative majority of the gentry. Yet, an up to date element has been added to the park in an informal scatter of small clumps. They are composed of young trees and contrast

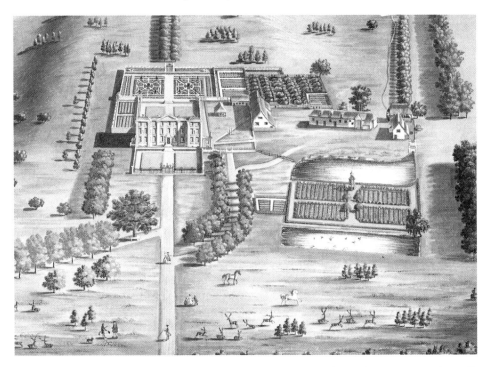

A bird's eye view of Bower Hall, Steeple Bumpstead, painted around 1755 (Essex County Council)

with their seniors in avenues and formal lines, all overlying the random trees of former wood-pasture.

From Bower Hall we return to developments at Audley End. Thomas Howard had barely finished his vast mansion and formal gardens than he was convicted of embezzlement and heavily fined. He no longer had the means required to support the estate he had created, and he left it encumbered by debt to his successors. Charles II took a liking to it, Newmarket being close, and the house became a royal palace, briefly, for William III struck a deal with the Howards by which it returned to their ownership. The gardens and park were now derelict, and in 1726 Daniel Defoe wrote 'I saw the ruins of the once largest and most magnificent pile in all this part of England, Audley End'.[10] By 1725 the buildings of the great forecourt had been partially demolished and other major reductions followed.

In 1762 the estate was inherited by Sir John Griffin Griffin, a successful career soldier, interested in the arts and familiar with new ideas, who was determined to restore his family seat to the renown in which it had once been held and threw his considerable energies into achieving it, taking a detailed interest in every aspect of the work. He lost no time in acquiring the western side of the valley to extend the park to the skyline, and similarly land to the north, where he secured the closure of two roads and the removal of a hamlet by private Act of Parliament. In 1763 he signed a contract with Lancelot 'Capability' Brown to design and carry out the remodelling of the park.

From the 1750s until his death in 1783, the invention and variety of the English school of landscape design were submerged beneath Brown's dominating personality and vast practice. The mood of patrons had changed, and bland, less exciting solutions were preferred to intricate, intellectual and experimental schemes such as Petre's Thorndon and Worksop. In 1756, Edmund Burke in his *Inquiry into the Origin of Our Ideas of the Sublime and the Beautiful*, had defined Beauty as characterised by delicacy of form and waving and serpentine forms. Brown avoided the Sublime, eschewing Pope's 'inexpressibly solemn and awful' or the precipitous cascades that had thrilled Addison in the Campagna,[11] while aiming to create a general and gentle serenity without sharp contrasts of topography and texture, employing serpentine paths and lakes, all according with Burke's definition of Beauty. Most importantly, he embraced the tradition of wood-pasture and the revived appreciation for this ancient landscape type, so suited to our climate, is a lasting debt to Brown.[12]

Brown could handle a large scale, sweeping landscape with ease; indeed, he was at his best. The rolling and gentle topography of the Cam valley was very appropriate to his style. His detailed plan for the great area of grassland to the west of the house, Howard's vast forecourt, survives.[13] The land was already level and the river dammed and canalized, and Brown proposed retaining it as a great sward of grass, bounded by a carriageway gently meandering through informal clumps of trees. The river was to be widened following a leisurely serpentine sweep. The work proceeded, but Griffin fell out with Brown and it appears that

Audley End House from the west

The Tea Bridge by Robert Adam in the Elysian Garden at Audley End

from this point the works continued under his own direction, although the result suggests that he followed lines that Brown may have put forward. The boundaries of the new, extended park were planted with tree belts and woodlands, and the further areas of grass studded with scattered trees; monuments marked focal points: temples, a great column and Robert Adam's elegant bridge over the Cam. Near to the house Griffin created the Elysian Garden, an intimate informal garden, with sweet-smelling flowers, magnolias and azalias, and architectural adornments, of which Adam's Tea Bridge and the former milldam converted into a rocky cascade survive.

An estate map of 1783 shows the scheme complete,[14] and it is pleasant to reflect that Sir John Griffin Griffin (now Lord Braybrooke), who died in 1797, would have had many years to enjoy his maturing landscape, embellished with the work of the finest architect of his time.

Audley End is of particular importance for two reasons. First, it has survived, and under the care of English Heritage now flourishes as a showpiece of an eighteenth century landscape which includes later developments, notably the recent

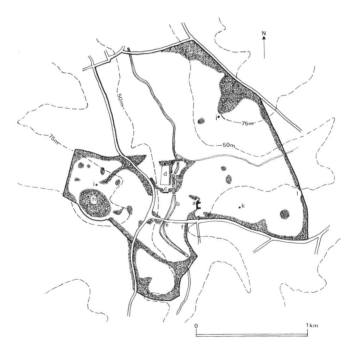

Audley End. Plan of the park from an estate map of 1783. KEY: (a) House; (b) The River Cam reshaped from a formal canal into a serpentine lake; (c) stables; (d) walled garden; (e) bridge designed by Robert Adam; (f) cottages removed and inhabitants rehoused; (g) Lion Gate; (h) Ring Hill, Iron Age hillfort; (i) Temple of Victory by Adam; (j) Lady Portsmouth's Column, 1774; (k) Temple of Concord, 1790; park gate and lodge at entrance from Saffron Walden

magnificent restoration of the parterre of c1830. Secondly, it embodies Brownian principles of landscape design, although Brown himself was sacked at a relatively early stage. The topography was ideal, gentle and yielding focal points for monuments. Perimeter belts enclose the Arcadia within, permitting an appropriate glance outside to a monument such as the lantern (now spire) of Saffron Walden church. The landscape of the ploughman and arable husbandry was banished. Yet despite an apparent scene of relaxed Claudian pasturalism, parks such as Audley End made an economic contribution to the estate. They provided grazing for the improved breeds of cattle and sheep, now replacing deer, which were themselves status symbols while conveying a sense of the harmony and comfort of a pastural life.[15] The woodlands furthest from the house were managed to bring an economic crop of estate timber. But above all, the Brownian park was cheap to maintain, as a comparison of the 8th Lord Petre's plan for Thorndon with that prepared for his son in 1778 after remodelling by Brown makes clear.[16]

The ninth Lord Petre was but a few months old when his father died so tragically young, and as we have seen, by 1762 the house was falling down, and the

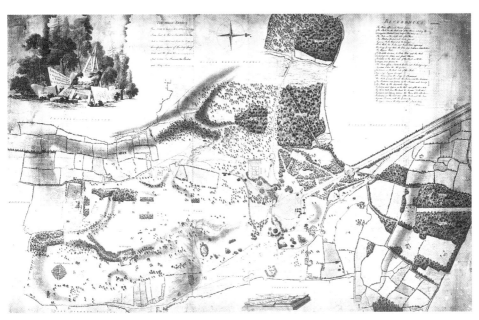

A Plan of Thorndon Park and Gardens, 1778 (ERO D/DP P30). Probably by J Spyers acting as surveyor and draughtsman for 'Capability' Brown. Compare with pp. 139 and 151. The Old Hall has been demolished and the new mansion built over a mile to the north by the ninth Lord Petre, at the head of his father's grand axis. The wood-pasture of Brown's style prevails and the mill pond/lake has been deformalised, but some 'platoons' survive from the earlier plan and the Octagon Plantation in the south-east corner, still a prominant feature of the Horndon Ridge. Childerditch Common, to the west of the new Hall, has been incorporated into the Great Park

nurseries overgrown amid a general scene of desolation. He resolved to make a fresh start, and in 1764 work began to the designs of James Paine on an enormous mansion over a mile to the north of the existing hall, at the head of his father's grand axis and flanked by his mounts. It must be said that the new house was a product of the architectural inflation of the time, by which the esteemed little manor houses of Palladio were often translated into the English scene after loga-rithmic enlargement.[17] New Thorndon Hall is redeemed by Leoni's elegant Corinthian portico, which was saved from the old hall and re-erected to grace the south elevation.[18] Although the designed landscape must have been ruinous, Brown would have found many established trees to use in his informal wood-pas-ture. Unfortunately, twentieth century fragmentation destroyed the overall unity, but substantial areas remain and are being managed with regard to their historic interest.

A landscape designer of particular importance for Essex is Richard Woods (?1716-93), an exact contemporary of Brown, who came to live at North Ockendon in 1768 and carried out many commissions in Essex. Woods was one of several gifted designers whose practices were not in the same league as Brown's, but were highly regarded, and rightly so, at the time. He was at his happiest and best when working on a small scale (40-100 acres) where he was extremely skillful in creat-ing harmony. His work at Wivenhoe has largely survived, to enhance Essex Uni-versity's campus, but it is at Hatfield Peverel Priory that his landscape style is best seen. From a plan of 1765, it has been lovingly restored by Adrian and Fiona Cow-ell, with its serpentine ponds and temple. Moreover, Fiona Cowell has published her extensive research on Woods which firmly places him in the pantheon of eigh-teenth century landscape designers.[19]

In 1788 the ubiquitous Repton set up to assume Brown's mantle. He was not a contractor and worked by selling designs by means of his 'red books' and publi-cations. He appears to have been associated with over 20 properties in Essex.

Returning to buildings in the landscape, another bland exercise in the Palladian style is Copped Hall, Epping, which replaced the Tudor mansion in the 1750s. It was gutted by fire in 1917 and has remained a shell, and interestingly, the geome-try of its chimney stacks exposed by the loss of the roof make it a far more origi-nal and unusual feature in the landscape than it probably was before. Visible from the M25, it is a most important landmark.

A building of real architectural distinction is John Johnson's Shire Hall in Chelmsford - hardly a building in the landscape, but so good that no book on Essex can ignore it. 'A thoroughly civilized public building, spurred probably by Adam's for Hertford a few years before and indeed considerably superior' was Pevsner's judgement. Johnson also designed the elegant bridge at the other end of the High Street, and worked on a number of country houses including Terling Place and Bradwell Lodge, a suitably quirky building for the effervescent Revd Henry Bate Dudley - journalist, duellist, playwright, agricultural improver and dedicated repressor of the desperate poor. From its gazebo, with its view of the

Copped Hall, Epping, in new guise as standard Palladian seat set in Brownian wood-pasture, (Watts, 1799). Compare with view on page 144.

North Sea, he could watch 'the moving picture of the whole commerce of London with the North'.[20]

The economic landscape

By the 1740s the cloth industry was in full decline and shrewd clothiers were investing in land. Around the middle years of the century, Essex farming entered a new and increasingly prosperous phase which peaked during the Napoleonic wars. Arable, in particular, expanded in response to the constantly rising demand from London for wheat, and barley for the capital's breweries. By 1800 London consumed half the total wheat crop from Essex. Experiment had become a matter of keen interest in the agricultural community, with the introduction of the Norfolk rotation, trials of alternative cropping to eliminate fallow years, and the improvement and development of implements: ploughs, drills and threshing machines. Experiments were also being made in the housing of livestock; turnips and clover enabled more cattle and sheep to be raised, and so more meat for the London market. The Epping area had become the centre for dairy farming.

All aspects of farming were described in detail by Arthur Young in 1807 in his *General View of Agriculture*. He applauded the innovation of 'hollow draining' on the heavy clays, a practice which spread rapidly after 1770, but had been developed earlier in the century and was regarded as an Essex invention. They were dug with a spade and filled with brushwood and straw. A parallel development came with the invention of the mole-plough by Thomas Knight, a Thaxted clockmaker. It was then improved in a version for John Vaizey of Halstead, which was drawn by fifteen to twenty horses.[21]

The incentives to increase production inevitably led to farming on a larger scale and the decline of small-scale farms. A consequence was that farm labourers became the largest single economic group in rural Essex, bringing disaffection and conflict when times became hard. Economics also encouraged 'engrossment' - the multiple occupation of several farms by one owner. The reaction of landowners, who had the power to dispose of the majority of the county's farms, was mixed. John Strutt, of Terling, limited the consolidation of farms on his estate, and an admirer wrote that 'he is possessed of a great number of farms and it is his pride to encourage the industrious by having as many tenants'.[22] However, most of his contemporaries preferred to promote large-scale farming, to encourage efficiency and hope that prosperous tenants would improve their farms, and in due course, pay higher rents. The more enlightened offered long renewable leases to encourage their tenants to invest.

The effect on the landscape, as always, depended entirely on whether the landowner was resident or absentee. Distant owners, such as Wadham College who owned an estate in Fryerning, encouraged their tenants to grub up small woods, enlarge fields and plough pasture.[23] The banks of the Isis and the Cherwell, after all, were not affected. Barely a wood or a green survived in the parish of Cressing where estates were small and the owners mostly lived elsewhere. As improvement developed into agrimania during the Napoleonic wars, it was on the estates of resident owners that a balance and long perspective was preserved. Woodlands and hedgerows with their timber were a long term investment, and also formed the habitats essential for the game birds and foxes that, as ever, played their part in preserving the amenities of the countryside.

In 1803 an encounter occurred in a Suffolk village that would have a far-reaching effect on the Essex landscape. Dr James Crowe found a female coerulean tree, a variant of the white willow and the ideal wood for making cricket bats, which has proved to be the ancestor of most setts today.[24] This beautiful and useful tree, harvested at fifteen to twenty years, graces the water-courses of many farms on the Till and is seen en masse in the Blackwater Valley, the world centre for its production.

During the years from 1750 to 1815, rural Essex moved from a mixed economy of farming and textiles to one entirely dependent on agriculture, which now directly dominated the villages. The towns, largely de-industrialized, drew their income almost entirely from their services to farmers, farming and the rural population. In 1814 agriculture was buoyant and seemed ready for further advance, but in 1815 a deep depression set in which was to cast a gloom over the next 35 years.[25]

Communications

As elsewhere across the country, the period saw the development of navigable waterways, paralleled by the improvement of the principal roads by turnpike trusts. How high shallow draught craft could reach on the county's rivers in earlier times is a matter of fascinating conjecture. But it seems unlikely that the Barnack stone used to face Hedingham Castle could have arrived other than by barge on the Colne.

The Lea had been improved as far as Ware by the late sixteenth century, and the Stort up to Bishops Stortford by 1769. It was intended to extend it to the Cam as part of a grand scheme to link the Thames to the Wash, but with the amenities of the house and park at Audley End in mind, Lord Braybrooke understandably and successfully blocked it.[26] The Stour Navigation to Sudbury opened early in the eighteenth century, but the Chelmer ran into determined opposition from the borough of Maldon and some flanking landowners. It had been proposed in the late seventeenth century but only opened in 1797, stretching from Springfield Basin to Heybridge Basin.

The availability of water transport acted as a magnet for the industries relating to agricultural expansion and the demands of the London market. The Stort Navigation was constructed partly for the benefit of the malt trade and large plants began to spring up along the major waterways. Greater cereal output led to a growing number of windmills, and to watermills of increased capacity, many completely rebuilt. Again, access by barge or proximity to a quay was a considerable commercial advantage.

An interesting survival is Beaumont Quay, built on a new cut off Hamford Water in the parish of Beaumont-cum-Moze in 1832. The area had a long history of landing places, and Roman and early medieval pottery have been found within 150 metres. The quay was built by the governors of Guy's Hospital who had bought the Beaumont Estate in the seventeenth century. By 1855 the site included 'House, Wharf, Warehouses, Yards, Coal and Lime sheds'[27] of which one building still stands, bearing a plaque which states that the stone for the quay came from old London Bridge. A circular brick limekiln, built around 1870, is a rare survival, and the site as a whole is a reminder of how vital waterborne transport was to the coastal economy. Beaumont Quay is a County Council guardianship site.

Brick was now in general use, and many farmhouses were given an up-to-date look by encasing in brick. Further down the social scale, weather-boarding was coming into use on domestic buildings. Often a cottage would present a smart white front to the road, plastered or boarded, while the side and back elevations were tarred boarding. This appears to be the period when purprestures on highway waste became a frequent feature, one solution to the land hunger of a growing population.

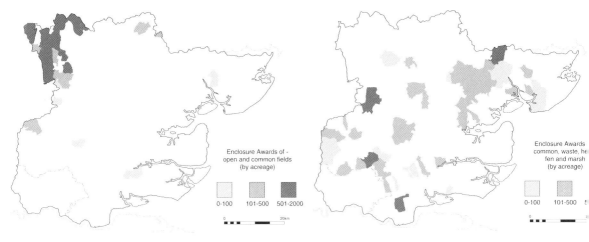

Enclosure Awards of common-fields   *Enclosure Awards of heaths, commons and greens*

Late enclosures

Between 1750 and 1850 huge tracts of the English landscape were replanned, a process which affected nearly 2½ million acres of common-fields and nearly 2 million of commons, heaths and 'wastes'. Common-fields, now seen as cumbersome and inefficient, were replaced by compact farms - a rational development already achieved over most of Essex in the preceding centuries. Commons and heathlands were regarded with scorn by agriculturalists and 'improvers', seen as archaic survivals that were not only inefficient but politically incorrect. The inhabitants, living at subsistence level, were independent, sometimes unruly and definitely 'untidy', and the fact that they represented an ancient and economically diverse way of life meant nothing to those with a moral (and financial) imperative to improve.[28] How far this may have applied in Essex is considered below.

Essex began late with only three, relatively small, enclosure awards before 1804. Messrs Griggs, reporting in 1794 to the Board of Agriculture and Internal Improvement, estimated that waste lands and forests, totalling a full 15,000 acres were capable of producing corn and 'after a certain time for necessary improvements could be made profitable to the community' by means of enclosure. The community in such reckonings took scant notice of the livelihoods of commoners. Griggs estimated 10,370 acres of forest and 14,237 of commons ripe for enclosure.[29]

The extreme north-west of Essex had remained exceptional to the rest of the county with large areas of arable in common-fields. This now changed rapidly, spurred by the phenomenal rise in corn prices caused by the Continental blockade. The fields of Great and Little Chesterford (2,582 acres) were enclosed in 1804; in 1805, Littlebury (2,000) and Hadstock (1,174), and in 1808, 1,147 in Chrishall. The momentum continued after peace in 1815, and despite the post-war depression in farming, huge enclosure awards followed in the Chishalls (1818), Wendens Ambo (1819), Arkesden (1819) and Wendon Lofts and Elmdon (1829). The last award was at Widdington in 1871.

The total area of common-fields enclosed in Essex between 1778 and 1871 by means of enclosure awards was 22,095 acres. Only one award, that for Langley in 1851, has a survey map of holdings as they were before enclosure, and it shows many areas of strips already consolidated in a landscape that had already evolved from one of huge open fields. On the evidence available it is not possible to say how far Langley was typical of this 'midland' corner of Essex.

Between 1770 and 1867 in Essex, 8,952 acres of heath, common, green and waste was enclosed by Act of Parliament, a low figure it seems when one considers the areas depicted on Chapman and André's Map of 1777. Griggs reckoned 3,000 acres in Little Braxted appropriate for enclosure, presumably Tiptree Heath, but only 703 acres in Great Braxted and Great Totham were subject to awards. Nevertheless, Tiptree Heath vanished.

The areas of common land had survived in particular areas for particular reasons. The largest tracts were the great heaths stretching northwards from Heybridge , encircling Colchester and reaching to the edge of the Stour Valley - the area earlier termed the Former Heathlands. Many commons still existed in the Wooded Hills. Scattered greens survived on the Till and on the Tendring Plain, both areas long enclosed for arable farming. Large fens with common grazing rights remained in south Essex at Orsett and Bulphan, but neither were subject to enclosure awards.

The map of 1777 shows the settlement beside the heaths as sparse and it may well be that enclosure was achieved over much of the land by agreement, satisfactory to the parties involved and without recourse to the process requiring an Act of Parliament. Only one award has been studied, that of Old Heath Common, Colchester, in 1818.[30] It appears that some cottagers were enjoying rights that they were not entitled to, which suggests that pressure on the land was low, and that here the small owner-occupier peasant farmer no longer existed. Apparently, a fracas did occur when the lord of the manor of Langford, who had enclosed the commons on his own manor, led the villagers to pull down fences on Tiptree Heath and drive their animals on to it.[31]

But overall, our knowledge of the Essex heathlands is meagre. We do not know how their landscapes appeared except by comparison with similar areas elsewhere, and their social history was never recorded. They have vanished utterly. Where commons survive elsewhere, they are now mostly areas of dense secondary woodland, as the grazing which maintained the traditional scene has long gone.

Grigg's recommendations had prevailed as far as commons and wastes were concerned, but the forests survived. Except Hainault, crown property, which was destroyed in 1851, causing a reaction that played a role in the demand by public opinion that the great surviving commons should have legal protection.

On the Till, some greens were enclosed but many survived. In 1300 it is likely they were densely fringed with tofts, dependent on an area of common grazing when all else was arable, valuable meads, emparked wood-pasture or embanked woodland. On the Walker maps, as we have seen, settlement had thinned and neighbours had added abandoned holdings to their own plots. This remained the pattern, and new opportunities for a piece of land were few - a purpresture if one was lucky, otherwise life as a landless labourer, service, or flight to the industrial centres. Times and circumstances would change. By the end of the nineteenth century, farm tenancies were available to anyone prepared to work in economic conditions very different from those of a century before.

John Constable and the Dedham Vale

If the heathlands of Essex have disappeared, forgotten and unrecorded, unlike those of Norfolk whose 'Dutch' appearance appealed to the painters of the Norwich School, the valley landscapes of the Stour inspired some of the best known and most loved paintings to have come from the palette of an Englishman.

The Dedham Vale, which Essex shares with Suffolk, is the length of the Stour Valley which stretches roughly from Nayland in the west to Cattawade in the east. Constable described it thus: 'The beauty of the surrounding scenery, the gentle declivities, the luxuriant meadow flats sprinkled with flocks and herds, and well cultivated uplands, the woods and rivers, the numerous scattered villages and churches, with farms and picturesque cottages, all impart to their particular spot an amenity and elegance hardly anywhere else to be found'.[32] It was prosperous country with good communications to the coast provided by the Stour Navigation, and in 1837 the Tithe Commissioners for East Bergholt observed that the water meadows were 'such as I have never before seen in Suffolk being of the richest quality and worth .... I should think, a full 60s per a.' In fact they were let for £2 per acre, double the rate for arable.[33]

John Constable (1776-1837) was born at East Bergholt, the son of a prosperous corn merchant who owned the milling business at Flatford Mill, a partnership in the mill at Dedham, river barges, two yards at Mistley and a corn ship.[34] Constable wrote of the impression the immediate landscape made on him as a child: '... the sound of water escaping from Mill dams, so do willows old rotten Banks, slimy posts, & brickwork. I love such things ... As long as I do paint I shall never cease to paint such places. They have always been my delight... I associate my 'careless boyhood' to all that lies on the banks of the Stour. They made me a painter (& I am grateful) that is I had often thought of pictures of them before I had ever touched a pencil'.

The family wealth gave him a measure of independence, to be his own man and go his own way. While he eventually achieved a measure of recognition, he was never embraced by the art establishment - he did not quite fit. His landscapes were real and familiar, not wild or remote, and when figures appear they are the workers who contributed to the agricultural prosperity from which the Constable family benefitted. They are not dressed in Arcadian robes and idealized, nor are they in the alternative convention that required that they be boorish or down-trodden.[35] Just as the inhabitants of commons and heaths appeared to 'improvers', to cognoscenti Constable's countrymen were politically incorrect. Interestingly, when his pictures were shown in Paris they caused much serious interest, Delacroix declaring that 'This man Constable has done me a power of good'.

While his work required that he live in London, it was to the Vale that he would return for the subjects and inspiration of most of his great canvasses. Time and again he would revisit a favourite viewpoint; Gun Hill, Langham, was a particular spot with its view of the tower of Dedham church, the sweep of the valley and the meanders of the Stour, painted in 1802, 1805, 1810, 1812 and 1828.[36] Willy Lott's house, lying just to the east of Flatford Mill, occurs in many sketches and paintings, culminating in the *Haywain* of 1821.[37] Perhaps the best known, and the subject of a myriad popular reproductions, is the *Cornfield* of 1826.[38] The mills, barges, locks, farms, cottages and the winding sunken lanes of the valley sides appear in a mass of drawings and sketches, sometimes worked up to form the finished works for exhibition in the Royal Academy.

Towards the end of his life he found, perhaps unexpectedly, that his connection with his home surroundings was noticed. He wrote to his engraver in 1832 'In the coach yesterday coming from Suffolk were two gentlemen and myself, all strangers to each other. In passing through the valley about Dedham, one of them remarked to me - on my saying it was beautiful - 'Yes Sir - this is *Constable's* country!' I then told him who I was lest he should spoil it'. And so it has remained.

It now seems remarkable how little change has occurred in many of the views he depicted, but it was very nearly otherwise. Fortunately, local pride and determination saw off some appalling proposals for development in the 1960s, and with the planning authorities converted to a similar view, the Vale was declared an Area of Outstanding Natural Beauty in 1968. The spread of arable farming at the expense of pasture on the valley floor ended with ESA[39] payments in 1988, and there is now more grassland than in Constable's day.[40]

CHAPTER TWELVE

From Victoria to World War Two

BY THE MID eighteenth century the population was passing the highest level postulated for 1300, and in 1801 stood at 227,682. By 1931 this had risen to 1,755,240 (including the county borough of Southend-on-Sea). In 1836 Acts of Parliament authorised the building of railway lines to Cambridge and Norwich. The line to Chelmsford opened in 1842, bringing great prosperity; the market became one of the busiest in Essex and the population grew by nearly a quarter between 1841 and 1861.[1] The London, Tilbury and Southend Railway was promoted in 1852, leading to the rapid growth of Southend (the South End of Prittlewell) which was already established as a watering place of fashion and reputation. The monumental Chapel Viaduct, 1,066 feet long with 32 arches, was constructed to carry the Stour Valley Line across the Colne, and the Chelmsford Viaduct is also no mean achievement although lacking the rural setting that so enhances the former.

Except where lost to urban development, in particular over Metropolitan Essex, the landscape changed relatively little over this period. In 1814 farmers looked back on the progress they had made, and confidently forward to further advance, but in 1815 a deep depression set in, casting a shadow for some 35 years. A recovery around 1850 was short lived, and from the mid 1870s there was a long period of depression. Faced with cheap imported grain and refrigerated meat, many farms went out of cultivation and their tenants and labourers swelled the numbers in Metropolitan Essex. Shoats and Canny Farms at Steeple (638 acres) was let for £760 a year in 1873, the tenant also paying a tithe of £140. In 1883, the rent was £460, and in 1886, it was £1.[2] It is, therefore, not surprising that apart from some minor tinkering, sometimes for game coverts, the landscape pattern changed little until the coming of World War Two.

With no money to be made from the ownership of land, and no end in sight to the depression, many owners sold up. The sale particulars make interesting reading for what they tell of farm and estate sizes, which must have changed little in the previous century. Three neighbouring estates in north-west Essex form a sample. Sampford Hall (1905) comprised 2,294 acres spread over the Sampfords, Great Bardfield and Thaxted, with eleven farms averaging 181 acres. The Hall, a Jacobean mansion, stood in grounds of 260 acres which had formerly been emparked; it was demolished and rebuilt in the 1930s. The Tindon End Estate (1905) had seven farms, averaging 119 acres, in the Sampfords and Radwinter totalling 965 acres. The house, remodelled in the Regency, has survived. Debden Hall (1903) covered 5,598 acres in Debden, Saffron Walden, Widdington, Wimbish, Thaxted and Broxted. Its 37 farms, which included four former manors, averaged 125 acres. The Hall, rebuilt by Henry Holland in 1796 and pulled down in 1936, stood in a park of 146 acres with waterfall, lake and bridge, possibly by Repton.[3]

It was the beginning of the end for these and many other estates. In the years following the Great War they disintegrated, and many farms were bought by their tenants at prices that had fallen to £10, £5 and even £3. 10s an acre. In many cases the tenants themselves were relative newcomers, for in the deepening depression many Essex farmers had given up and left the land. Landowners were desperate to find fresh tenants, for even if the rents were minimal, the land was kept from tumbling down to scrub. In 1884 the agent for the Petre estate at Thorndon Park advertised in Scotland and was rewarded with an influx of fresh tenants, mainly livestock farmers from Ayrshire, where it was said that there were twice as many farmers as there were farms for. By 1893 he had let fourteen farms to Scots, covering an area of 3,840 acres. Trains were hired which carried livestock, equipment, and the family with their furniture and moveables. Most of the migrants made a success, and instead of concentrating on cereals, turned to the husbandry they were familiar with: dairying, the sale of hay and potato-growing. Most importantly, the whole family worked on the farm - wives, daughters and sons - and the men worked longer hours than their labourers. The census of 1891 showed 58 Scottish farmers, concentrated broadly in the Ongar and Brentwood area, and on the Petre estate.

An important and interesting figure of the time was Primrose McConnell (1856-1931), author of *The Agricultural Notebook*, which he published in 1883, and constantly updated. The work has remained an important textbook; the nineteenth edition was published in 1995. He came to Essex in 1883 with his father, one of the first of the Scottish migrants to 'derelict Essex' and rented Ongar Park Farm, which he described as a 'dairy and mixed husbandry farm'. His reports in Scottish newspapers contributed considerably to the flow of migrants to a 'land of Goshan', and he recorded that one night in June 1885, sixteen Scotsmen slept at his farm, in readiness for an inspection of neighbouring holdings; all but one eventually took farms in the area. McConnell went on to purchase a farm near Southminster, and for the rest of his life remained a figure nationally respected as a writer and educator, for his wide knowledge, and for his shrewd and inventive approach.[4]

Migrations occurred simultaneously from other parts of the land to a county 'begging for tenants'. Between 1890 and 1914, mostly before 1900, Cornish families arrived on trains with their livestock and moveables and settled in west Essex, the area north of Ongar and Chelmsford, and south of Saffron Walden. Their family names are now a long established part of the farming scene - for example Trembath, Lukies, Rowe, Lanyon and Menhinick. I am told that there was an initial problem with their horses, who did not understand the Essex dialect. From Somerset came the Padfields, a familiar farming name, particularly in the Epping area, and many other farmers came from Lancashire. Briefly during the Great War, home farming flourished, to be confronted once more when peace returned with cheap imports and possibly the deepest depression of all. More doughty Scots came south to win a living from abandoned farms.

I am aware that this brief account of the farming families who migrated to Essex and kept its land in good heart is most inadequate, but information is lacking, and I would urge the families concerned to record their history. They are now Essex people, and the efforts of those who first arrived to face conditions of dereliction and hardship is a proud story that should not be lost by default.

During the years 1923 to 1929 only fifteen per cent of flour was home-grown, compared to 30 per cent during the Great War. In 1932, Sir Edward Ruggles-Brise, MP for Maldon, persuaded Parliament to pass the Wheat Act which coupled a Quota Scheme on imports with a guaranteed price on the home crop. It has been estimated that the Act saved 500 farms in the arable counties - East Anglia and Essex - and it is not surprising that Sir Edward became known as 'the Farmer's Friend'.[5]

A by-product of agricultural depression and cheap land was plotland. In many parts of England and on the fringes of Essex towns and villages, bungalows sprung up, sometimes well-built for retirement but often holiday shacks. Speculators bought land at Pitsea and Laindon from 1900 onwards and advertised plots as weekend retreats for Eastenders, served by the Fenchurch Street Line. It was a cynical exercise, boosted by champagne parties on special trains to exploit people's natural desire for a small plot of land to call their own. No services of water or drainage were supplied. In the inter-war period the influx increased with people seeking weekend retreats from overcrowding, smoke and noise. Some plots developed in a spirit of popular culture, but others remained derelict and there were no maintained roads or public services.

This area was subsequently redeveloped as Basildon New Town, a place of character due perhaps to its interesting terrain and the presence of a committed and talented architects' department. This may explain its contrast to the architectural morass of Harlow. But here we are concerned with landscape, not townscape, and of the brief phenomenon of plotland, an area was fortunately preserved at Dunton by the Basildon Development Corporation, which can be visited and its history explored.

During the 1930s, L Dudley Stamp organized his remarkable Land Utilisation Survey of Britain, with the Essex Volume by N V Scarfe published in 1942.[6] Scarfe goes into considerable detail - Essex is divided into fifteen land use regions - but he does not let the volume of figures and information mar a fascinating and very readable account of Essex on the eve of World War Two. It is interesting to compare overall figures of land use in 1939 with those for 1875, when the depression had begun but farmers looked back hopefully to the prosperous years from 1853 to 1862 which resembled the golden years of the late eighteenth century:

	1875	1939
Total arable	643,526 acres	386,870 acres
Permanent grass	179,374	302,803
Orchards	1,057	8,441

In general terms, north Essex was arable and south Essex grassland. Except for arable on Foulness and the western limits of the Dengie flats, the marshes were grazed by sheep; indeed, sheep farming was almost the only occupation there.

The Mid-Essex Zone varied, with a concentration of dairying around Ongar, fruit growing from Danbury to Tiptree, and fruit and market gardening on the former heaths to the north of Colchester and on the Tendring plain. The best soil in Essex lay in the Rodings and Easters, and their neighbouring parishes. 'All the soil is heavy, three-horse land, and is exceptionally fertile....It is a pleasure to see the well-trimmed hedges and clear ditches, the clean (ie weedless) deep tilth and the tidy farmyards of this area. It is a land of few trees and of low hedges lined with masses of primroses in spring; a land of thatched and whitewashed cottages, flint churches, tiny hamlets, small villages and scattered farmsteads; a land of wheat, barley and potatoes'. It does not seem very different from the area today.

Scarfe's South Essex Grassland covered a huge area: from Epping Upland through the southern margins of the area we have earlier termed the Wooded Hills, to the South Essex Hills, the Dengie Hills and the Layer Plateau. 'Each section, differs .... (but) they are all heavily wooded with masses of hedgerow trees and wide sprawling hedges. The country is everywhere rolling or hilly. There is a general absence of arable land with a corresponding lack of corn vegetables or fruit (except at Hadleigh)'. He was clearly shocked by the Laindon plotlands: 'Into this poor bramble covered region has penetrated a vast array of tiny bungalows, corrugated-iron shanties with dreadful rutted mud roads, reminiscent of the backwoods. Mankind seems to have sought relief from the rush and roar of London in the wilderness of wild nature with a few poultry, goats, rabbits and perhaps cows'.

He also did not care for the landscape of the London Clay Trough, stretching from Bulphan through Wickford to Latchingdon, although he was surprised to see at least a quarter of the land under cultivation. 'It is in no way an attractive area, being wet, foggy and muddy in winter, without woodland, heath or parkland. Elm trees are common, as are sprawling bramble hedges and weedy pastures.' But within a short time of Scarfe's survey, and well before its publication, the 'weedy pastures' would be made as productive as the farming technology of the time would allow.

In the summer of 1940 Britain was under siege and faced with the threat of invasion. Essex was considered to be in the front line, since a successful German landing on the East coast would have provided a short route to both London and the industrial Midlands. A defensive system was required that was capable of halting, or at least delaying, a German advance until the few heavy weapons which were available could be brought up to the danger areas. The solution, built with incredible speed, was a series of 'stop-lines' - parallel lines of defence using, where possible, natural barriers such as rivers, woods and marshes, supported by pillboxes and anti-tank obstacles. Four of these lines ran through Essex: the coastal 'Outer Crust', the Colchester Stop-Line, the GHQ Line and the Outer London Defence Ring.[7]

Much of the coast was seen as almost self-protecting due to the mudflats and sandbanks, but pillboxes followed the seawalls, and ditches were cut and scaffolding erected on the marshes to prevent gliders landing.[8] The major rivers were each protected by a minefield laid across its mouth which was controlled by a high tower, one of which survives to the east of Burnham, overlooking the estuary of the River Crouch.

The General Headquarters (GHQ) Line was the principal and most powerful of the country's defensive lines, stretching from Yorkshire to the Wash, then on to the Thames estuary, and from London to Bristol. It enters Essex at Great Chesterford and follows the Cam, Debden Water and the Chelmer south to Chelmsford. From there, lacking a natural waterway to act as a barrier, a massive ditch was dug which zig-zagged south to Canvey Island, backed by pillboxes which can be seen on both sides of the A130, which runs parallel to the GHQ Line between Chelmsford and the Rettendon Turnpike roundabout .[9]

Hundreds of pillboxes have survived, even when they form an obstruction to farm machines as beside the A130. When peace came, tradition relates, owners were compensated with a sum to pay for demolition, but fortunately the money was usually spent on other things. Now lichen-crusted and sometimes merged in scrub, these World War Two defences have become venerable monuments that form a part of the landscape's visible history.

By contrast, the wartime airfields have mostly left permanent scars, great holes in the landscape fabric. Before the war, in the RAF 'expansion period', the domestic, technical and administrative buildings were designed and landscaped to a very high standard, as can still be seen at Debden.[10] This was impossible in wartime when speedy construction was required. The arrival of the Americans in 1942 prompted a huge programme of construction, and Essex, along with Suffolk and Norfolk, saw massive development. The standard layout was a triangle formed by three runways bounded by a perimeter track linking aircraft dispersal pans.[11] Within this area all cover was erased, and so most have remained - open, lonely places - but with fine plateau views. We were certainly grateful for them when they were in use, and the sites today have their aficionados.

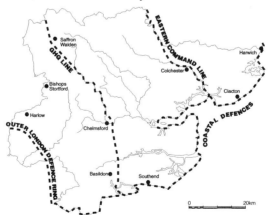

World War Two lines of defence (after Gilman and Nash, 1995)

CHAPTER THIRTEEN

The contemporary landscape

BY 1961 THE population of Essex had reached 2,288,058, of whom 1,184,442 lived in Metropolitan Essex which in 1965 became part of Greater London.[1] In 1991 the population stood at 1,528,577, almost a 40 per cent rise since 1961. The main areas of urban expansion to house this growth were the two new towns of Basildon and Harlow, and a massive expansion of Chelmsford and Colchester.

The main corridors of communication remain as they were in the days of the Romans: the A12 trunk road to Colchester and Ipswich, the M11 paralleling the Stort and Cam, and the A120 which awaits much-needed elevation to trunk road status. The landscape viewed from the M11 and M25 is a striking testimony to the success of Green Belt policies, and on any map showing the Home Counties it is notable how large tracts of Essex, close to London, remained undeveloped as the metropolis remorselessly expanded in all other directions. When Green Belt legislation came into effect, it acted to maintain an existing situation. Why these tracts should have survived until then is a question to which I have been unable to find a fully satisfactory answer, but a possibility is that the poor quality of the rail services and the squalor of Liverpool Street Station acted to deter would-be settlers from rural Essex. All has now changed with electrification and the transformation of Liverpool Street.

Farming and the landscape

In the early 1970s, it might have seemed surprizing that a fine and balanced farming landscape should have survived to grace the view from these motorways at the end of the century. At that time, efficient farming appeared set on a course that would prove incompatible with other demands on the landscape. Pundits were seriously suggesting that the future countryside would be a sea of arable, punctured by occasional nature reserves, and if we did not like the prospect, we should learn to do so - it was as inevitable as living in tower blocks.

To set this in context, the experience of the Second World War had shown the dependency of the population on the supply of imported food, and the vulnerability of the merchant navy to enemy submarines. In its aftermath it became government policy to modernise farming, maximise production from the land and guarantee prices. The effect was most marked in the corn-growing counties of eastern England where the farming scene hummed with investment and change in a manner reminiscent of the reign of George III, and further back, the manorial agribusiness of the thirteenth century. In Essex, mixed farming gave way to arable, meadows were ploughed up, copses vanished and fields were enlarged to meet the needs of mechanisation. At Cressing Temple, the fields of the former demesne returned to the acreages of 1300, and Walthambury also returned to earlier 'prairie farming'.

Farming change was encouraged with lavish grants, carried out with the haste and single-purpose vision that had marked the parliamentary enclosures of an

171

earlier time, and if the eradicating zealots of the Ministry of Agriculture, Fisheries and Food (MAFF) had had their way, much of Essex would now resemble fenland. Fortunately many farmers retained an element of conservative caution - their farmsteads were also their homes - and field sports were, for many, a part of rural life. Personal observation, confirmed by that of many others, records that those farmers who eliminated all cover had no concern for pheasants, partridges or foxes, nor interest in any other form of wildlife.

In the late 1960s a new and deadly strain of Dutch Elm disease entered the country from north America, carried on untreated logs. By the early 1970s, spreading from Tilbury, it had reduced the elm-dominant London Clays and Thames Terraces to a landscape of dead trees - an environmental disaster to those extensive areas. In the mixed hedges of the Till, groups of towering elms formed focal, well-loved local features, and they too became infected.

In 1972 Essex County Council considered a report, *Landscape in Decline?*, and called a conference of farmers and all interested parties to consider its implications. On the loss of tree cover, the report reasoned that 'The result is that already many parts of the county are becoming bleak and ugly in appearance. The countryside is losing its basic materials, trees and hedges, and gaining elements which detract from its landscape value.... (In the future) the principal features of the new open landscape will be poles, wires, pylons, crude prefabricated farm buildings, and the harsh edges of new buildings on the periphery of towns and villages'. Strong stuff, seen in retrospect, but a reasonable view of the future landscape at that time.

The report considered other issues: the ugly impact of developments on the countryside, the poor design of farm buildings and the crude impact of new roads and road improvements. The historic dimension had entered the scene, with the recognition of the antiquity of many hedgerows and of the value of many country lanes as comparable to that of the historic settlements they linked. The impacts of leisure and mobility were also addressed.

The success of the conference, evident in many positive results, was largely due to the commanding figure of Gerald Curtis, chairman of the County Planning Committee, who had served with distinction in the Indian Civil Service and on retirement had taken up farming, becoming a chairman of the Essex Farmers Union. He was listened to with respect, and secured the support of a substantial number of farmers and the Union itself. An immediate result was a well-funded tree planting programme (now the Landscape Conservation Programme) which has quietly added to the tree cover of Essex; a mark of its achievement being that its schemes have merged into the landscape and usually do not appear of recent origin. This is particularly true of the landscaping of many roads. In due course the planting came to be assisted by grants from the Forestry Authority for small woods and MAFF for hedgerow planting, and young trees are now very evident in the landscape, which was not the case in the 1970s.

While the planting of native species and the creation of new cover has played an important part, the appreciation and conservation of existing features has been the vital element in the balance achieved in many farming landscapes. This was due to the lead given by the Essex Farming and Wildlife Advisory Group (EFWAG), and to the example set at Bovingdon Hall, Bocking. John Tabor, a landowner and practical farmer, had seen the effect of new farming methods on the traditional landscape and felt concerned. As a result, Bovingdon Hall became the focus for experimental schemes to restore landscape cover, and when the Countryside Commission set up the Demonstration Farms Project, John Tabor happily agreed that his estate should represent the Boulder Clays of south-east England.[2]

The purpose of the project was to investigate and then demonstrate how conservation interests could be combined with commercial farming, and after very detailed studies by specialists, it was shown that the different demands and interests could be integrated into the management of the farm without significantly affecting its economic viability. Each year a series of demonstrations were hosted for parties of farmers, land agents, students and other groups involved with the countryside, to see positive management in action. They would see a wide range of conservation measures, examples among many being hedgerows managed as coppice with 'maidens' left to form future timber trees, a field amalgamation scheme in which all options were evaluated, and straw incorporation trials. The Countryside Commission acknowledged that Bovingdon Hall was much the most successful of the twelve farms involved in the project.

The Farming and Wildlife Advisory Group was formed in 1969 following a conference on a farm at Silsoe, Hertfordshire, where farmers and naturalists met to work out a compromise plan that allowed for both productivity and nature conservation. In subsequent exercises other interests became involved - sporting, forestry, archaeology, and landscape design and history. The first Essex exercise, held at Amberden Farm and Mole Hall near Widdington in 1975, was carefully researched and very well attended. This was followed by the establishment of an Essex branch of FWAG, which from 1984 has employed a full time adviser with remarkable results. Essentially EFWAG has been run by farmers, who are respected by other farmers, and this, together with the quality of the advice available, has given it credibility in the farming scene. In recent years, at the annual gathering when the five or so farms who have entered for the Farm Conservation Competition are described and illustrated in detail before the winner is announced, I find myself amazed at the high standards now attained on these farms.[3] Indeed, I am reliably informed that some excellent entries have initially been held back, as the farmers have been fearful of measuring badly against the others.

Looking back over the years since 1972, it is possible to reach some tentative conclusions. While the future of the landscape looked grim at that time, the bulk of farm improvement had been carried out and the pace of unsympathetic change was already slackening. *Landscape in Decline?* was valuable because it focused on what had been lost through removal of cover and elm disease, and if its predictions now seem a mite apocalyptic, it sounded a warning and achieved a positive response. The Essex landscape has subsequently improved overall in quality, and this is largely due to the example shown at Bovingdon Hall and to the ongoing work of Essex FWAG. There remain areas of arable desert, but these are far from the norm.

Two other factors contributed. First, the problem presented by crop residues as farming in Essex moved from a regime of mixed husbandry to one predominantly arable. Straw and stubble burning is fortunately now a memory, but the annual ordeal by fire suffered by the landscape was long defended by MAFF as an article of faith, denying the existence of a viable alternative. This official view persisted despite the evidence of farmers such as John Currie of Margaretting Hall, who demonstrated how his heavy London Clays had been improved over years by the shredding and ploughing in of his surplus straw. It must be recorded that impatient of government action, Essex County Council, in collaboration with the Essex Farmers Union, brought in a bylaw to enforce the voluntary (but often ignored) code of practice. In due course burning was phased out and most farmers felt a great sense of relief.

A second factor was a change in attitude by the rivers authorities. For long in Essex they had seen rivers in engineering terms, as agricultural drains to be straightened and canalized in a zone free of vegetation which might impede maintenance regimes. At a FWAG conference in 1982, a new manager of Essex rivers announced that in the wake of the Wildlife and Countryside Act 1981, new guidelines were to be issued which would encourage meanders and shoals, and riparian vegetation to consolidate and stabilize banks. It was momentous, and with the enlightened management that has followed, rivers as features of the landscape have markedly improved.

At around that time, farmers were coming under criticism for changes in the countryside. In the post-war decades, farm modernisation was welcomed for wartime privations remained a recent memory, and rationing only came to an end in 1954 when meat was de-rationed. Voices were not raised against hedgerow and habitat loss over those years. While the countryside remained taken for granted in the 1960s, concern surfaced nationally for the legacy of historic towns and buildings. People saw the crude redevelopment of their familiar town centres, the demolition of venerable buildings, and insensitive restorations. In particular, the 'Sack of Worcester' roused public opinion leading to the Civic Amenities Act 1967, which required local authorities to define Conservation Areas and employ specialist advisory staff.

In the 1980s concern moved from the built to the natural environment. Farmers who felt proud of the efficiency achieved and the massive rise in home food production, found themselves under attack for allegedly failing in their role as custodians of the countryside. This was at a time when farm profits were waning after the prosperous years of the 1970s. Individual farmers were attacked in the press, some rightly so, but others not, as in a disgraceful Essex case where a 'political' agenda was apparent. In fact, major changes in the Essex farming landscape had occurred much earlier, and unsympathetic developments were now taking place in other parts of the country, particularly in areas where livestock farming was traditional but were now moving into crop-growing, in response to the Common Agricultural Policy (CAP). Single-issue zealots and unaccountable self-appointed guardians of the environment were now a part of the scene, and remain so.

That was the down-side of a new popular interest in the countryside and its wildlife. The positive side was evident in the spectacular rise of county wildlife trusts, and a degree of acceptance by many Essex farmers that change had often been one-sided, and that the holistic approach advocated by FWAG and seen in practice at Bovingdon Hall had much to offer. This has been fostered by various schemes that encourage sympathetic management, foster environmental diversity, and compensate the farmer for the costs incurred in doing so. For example, at the time of writing, a new Arable Partnership scheme has been launched over a pilot area in East Anglia, which includes north Essex. It is designed to arrest the decline of key arable species, in particular farmland birds, and will be of benefit to all the elements that make up the landscape.[4] This must be the way forward, with support targeted to further environmental goals rather than the production of surpluses.[5]

Meanwhile, farm sizes have gradually risen. 350 acres is now small, 500 viable, and 500-1,000 the optimum area for an arable farm. The critical factor is the optimisation of capital investment in machinery. With this trend has come a rise in contract farming, partnerships and farm rentals, and a farmer can now contract much or all of the work on his land, while retaining personal control of what is done. Devaluation in the early 1990s boosted farm profits after the depressed 1980s, but now again all is in flux and faced with political pressures on a world scale, currency fluctuations and the uncertain nature of CAP reform, many farmers are apprehensive for the future.

Symbol for Essex Farming and Wildlife Advisory Group. Lino-cut by Sheila Robinson

New Housing at Church End, Stebbing (Higgins Plc; Melville Dunbar Associates, architects)

Buildings in the landscape

In the 1960s the rate of private housing development in Essex was the highest of any shire county, and Essex had grown more rapidly than any county in the south-east since the war. With a very few exceptions, developments had a dreary suburban uniformity, devoid of identity and sense of place, and were seriously eroding the quality of towns and villages. In response to this situation, and with the experience of raising standards of design for new buildings in Conservation Areas, Essex County Council published *A Design Guide For Residential Areas* in 1973, which looked at housing design from first principles, aiming to bring back quality into urban design with respect for regional and local character.[6] The *Guide* caused a sensation, nationally as well as in Essex where it was hated by complacent, lack-lustre architects and developers, but welcomed by able designers and flexible building firms.

Certainly the *Guide* raised standards, but they were variable in effect and it is no coincidence that the better schemes often came from adaptable small firms, and also from the willingness of the new district councils, as local planning authorities after 1974, to seek high standards. Its considerable success in urban areas, for which it was written, is not our concern here, but rather its effect on rural development. Here, Braintree District Council planners have consistently required and encouraged a high quality which is evident in many small schemes in villages, which merge happily into their surroundings and sometimes even enhance them.

But this has not always been the case elsewhere; in north-west Essex it appears that the 'executive home' is favoured - a euphemism for a building out of place and out of scale - and it can be disconcerting to see a cabin suddenly reincarnated as a pseudo-Jacobethan pile. In addition there is the baleful influence of all metropolitan fringes for urban incomers to prettify and, in doing so, to debase. Humble and unlistable purprestures emerge wishfully as Anne Hathaway's cottages with coachlamped porches, plastic leaded-lights and waggon-wheel gates. It may also be said that despite the care of some authorities for housing design, an industrial application that promises jobs appears to have an easy run in planning terms.

It is difficult to find buildings of recent years which are prominent in the landscape and also enhance it, but I would suggest the 'Temple of the Imagination' in Thorndon Park (south) on the ridge and visible for miles,[7] and the new water tower at Harlow beside the M11, a landmark structure which elegantly and geometrically displays the logic of its function.

For a real understanding of the logic of building in sensitive areas, one must look to the works of Raymond Erith, a rare and independent spirit who practised in Dedham until his death in 1973.[8]. This was at a time when architectural design was dominated by the Architectural Press, who promoted the Modern Movement as the only style 'for our times', and ignored or denounced those that would not conform. Erith would have none of it; like Constable, he was his own man and stuck with his classical principles, tempered by an appreciation of the traditional architecture of the Vale villages: 'Their builders understood perfectly that economy and comfort are both necessary to architecture.... It is this proper balance, and a conception of what is natural and right, that makes these old buildings seem so sensible and satisfying'.[9]

Although we have no urban development such as his terrace in Campden Hill, London W8, or his splendid Jack Straw's Castle, a tavern which graces Hampstead Heath, Erith's works are to be seen in Dedham and elsewhere in north Essex, always subtly enhancing their surroundings and setting a standard of design that evaded his contemporaries. They are buildings which delight, and each one repays study.

Conservation and recreation

In the 1930s legislation was enacted to enable local authorities to buy land for a green belt which would halt the spread of London and provide recreational areas in the countryside. From the late 1930s until the early '50s, Essex County Council pursued a steady programme of acquisition which reached a total of 4,500 acres; this included some fine parkland landscapes, and when the Countryside Act 1968 brought powers to establish country parks, Weald, Thorndon and Belhus, all near to London, were designated together with two in the Langdon Hills, and later, Cudmore Grove on Mersea Island. All contain ancient and interesting landscapes, and while amenity and recreation are of paramount concern, nature conservation, education, and an appreciation of archaeology and historic features all form a part of the management principles followed by the ranger service. In recent years ancient woodlands and former railway lines have been added to the recreational estate which now covers some 2,640 acres.

While the enjoyment of open country is the main concern of country parks and similar areas, management for nature conservation is necessarily the primary function on land acquired by the Essex Wildlife Trust. The rise of the Trust and its success, measured in membership numbers and acquisition of reserves, has been spectacular. Membership now stands at 15,280, the largest county trust in the country, and it holds 90 reserves which cover some 6,500 acres, and runs four centres. The Trust embodies and encourages the rise in popular interest in the countryside, and concern for its fauna and flora. It is outgoing in attitude, welcoming access to reserves and participation in their management.

A third force for conservation and access to the countryside is the comparative newcomer Thames Chase, a community forest launched by the Countryside and Forestry Commissions in June 1990.[10] It covers the rural margins of south-west Essex and east London (formerly Metropolitan Essex), a landscape smitten by elm disease, with a long history of mineral extraction and the usual problems of environmental stress on the urban fringe. The headquarters are now established at Broadfields Farm, Cranham, in a restored farmstead set in a landscape of new experimental woodlands, meadows and an orchard of Essex varieties of fruit. A second focus is the existing country park at Belhus Woods, a maturing landscape of lakes, groves and pastures on land reclaimed after mineral working, and now set to expand into and restore adjacent land. But this is only the beginning; the project has achieved much in eight years, and now looks set to fulfil its goals of environmental uplift - its vision of large blocks of woodland linked by greenways is becoming a reality. An exciting prospect.

Fine and useful arts

In this century, the Stour Valley was again the choice of a landscape painter of stature. John Nash (1893-1977), attracted away from his native Buckinghamshire by the arable scenery of the Essex/Suffolk border and the importance within it of the River Stour, lived at Wormingford, painting prolifically, from 1929 until his death. 'He himself became famous for what appears to be an indifference to any other art other than his own, and this was not because of pride, but because of the way in which he was entirely dominated by his vision of the landscape. Sickert used to warn artists off the Stour Valley, saying that it was a 'sucked orange' but John Nash painted it as though he had never heard of it being the most familiar river territory in English art.[11'] John Constable, Raymond Erith and John Nash; there must be something in the air of the valley, perhaps the genius loci, to foster such independent spirits.

In 1953, still in the grey post-war years - a time it seemed of never-ending austerity and mediocrity - several artists in Great Bardfield opened up their houses and studios to visitors. It was a magical moment that lifted the spirits and renewed confidence in the English contribution to the arts. Subsequently those

The Red House, East Bergholt (architect, Raymond Erith)

involved have become known as the Bardfield Painters. The leading figures at that time were Edward Bawden (1903-89) and John Aldridge (1905-83).[12]

Bawden was Essex born and bred, living in Great Bardfield most of his life. Eric Ravilious (1903-42), his fellow student at the Royal College of Art, came from the Sussex Downs to live in Bardfield, then Castle Hedingham and Shalford before his untimely death while serving as a War Artist. Both were brilliant artists and designers, depicting the Essex landscape with its churches and villages, alongside a prodigious output in the fine and applied arts: lithography, engraving, book illustration, murals, posters and wallpaper.

Coincidental with the arrival of these important artists in Bardfield came John Aldridge (1905-83), fundamentally a painter of landscape. He 'painted just because he liked to do so, following no fashion nor creating one. His love of land-scape was totally unaffected and gave new meaning to any scene most of us would take for granted'.[13] For this writer, John Aldridge more than any other understood the landscape of the Till, the quality of this curious and ancient corn-growing land, and the subtle beauties of its wayward irregularities.

This interesting and spontaneous group of artists had dispersed by the 1970s, but their work has been assembled in the Fry Art Gallery in Castle Street, Saffron

Walden, which contains a particularly good display of Aldridge's landscapes along with a broad spectrum of work by the other Bardfield artists.[14]

The term 'useful arts' is applied here to the work of plantsmen, horticulturalists and garden designers. Interest in historic gardens, formerly limited to a few, has grown phenomenally over recent years, and Essex now has an active Gardens Trust. The restoration of the Woods landscape at Hatfield Priory by Adrian and Fiona Cowell, and the re-creation of the parterre of c1830 at Audley End by English Heritage, both most impressive in their different ways, have been noted earlier. Four other gardens require a brief description, both for their high quality and because they form a part of the wider landscape fabric.

The Marks Hall Estate, near Coggeshall, was left to the nation by Thomas Phillips Price who died in 1932, but remained in the destructive hands of his widow until her death in 1966. A dreadful scene of dereliction then faced the trustees: the house and church demolished, the lakes choked and watergardens disintegrating, the great oaks of the park gone, and everywhere overgrown. First the farming estate had to be brought into order, and then work could begin on the gardens and lakes. Today it is a very different scene; the gentle valley of the Robins Brook is now young parkland, the cascades and watergarden through which it flows have been restored, the lakes dredged and their brick revetments repaired, and work is underway to create an arboretum which may one day be the Westonbirt of the eastern counties. Paths and rides link the gardens with the ancient lime woodlands of the estate beyond.[15]

The gardens of Easton Lodge are another example of rescue and restoration. The house was the seat of 'Daisy', Countess of Warwick, where she entertained the future Edward VII and the Marlborough House Set. In 1902 she commissioned Harold Peto (best known today for his Elysium on Garinish Island, West Cork) to design gardens appropriate for entertaining Edwardian society. But the great days of the house were over by the 1920s, and disasters followed Lady Warwick's death in 1938. The park, which dated back to 1302, was obliterated to make a wartime airfield, and in 1950 the main house was demolished and the gardens abandoned.

Frog Meadow, Dedham (architect, Raymond Erith; photo, Roy Farthing)

Brian and Diana Creasey, who live in Warwick House (the surviving west wing) embarked on the restoration of Peto's work in 1993, and have already achieved remarkable results. The work continues.

Saling Hall is a classic example of the early medieval siting of church and manor house an easy stroll apart. Its facade, cased in brick with Dutch gables, is dated to 1699, with its walled garden completed a year earlier. In the middle years of this century Lady Carlisle added a water garden and planted up eleven acres of adjoining land with Populus robusta, for which there was then a market for matches. Hugh and Judy Johnson came to the hall in 1971 and began to thin and underplant the poplar canopy with more interesting trees. Finding that there was no available book to give him general guidance on the families and species of trees, Hugh set out to write one, and the result is his classic *The International Book of Trees*. With a maturing arboretum, the watergarden and formal walled garden, Saling Hall is now an Essex garden of rare quality.

Glazenwood, Bradwell-juxta-Coggeshall, another 'layered' garden, lies surrounded by woodland on a flat plateau. It is well concealed, and a week before writing these words I barely knew of its existence. Samuel Curtis (1779-1860) arrived in 1821, creating an important arboretum and nursery, copious orchards of fruit trees, and a huge collection of roses. In more recent years, the garden was

John Aldridge, "Beslyn's pond, Great Bardfield", oil on canvas (Fry Public Art Gallery, Saffron Walden)

owned by the distinguished plantsmen Derek and Elizabeth Baers. More recently still, Peter Tyrie has developed the garden with a lake and turfed amphitheatre (from the spoil) on a scale, and of a quality, that is breath-taking. Geometric formality close to the house diffuses in the middle distance, and the whole then merges into the encircling woodlands.

Epilogue

Looking back over the last quarter of the twentieth century, there seems much to be proud of in the conservation of the landscape of Essex. There is more access for people to enjoy it, and many semi-natural areas are managed as reserves, but these lie in the context of a countryside of arable farming which provides the local areas of cover, important to the landscape and for nature conservation, and the linkages - the biological internet - which ties the whole together. Overall, the quality of the landscape has improved, and a sense of stewardship is evident over much of it - something which comes with the FWAG approach and not through legislation.

In 1972 it seemed possible that the Essex countryside could come to resemble a factory floor. Fortunately things turned out very differently, but this must never be forgotten, and neither should the hardship and dereliction of the farming depressions. In the arable counties, prosperity is a key ingredient of an integrated and harmonious landscape.

Bibliography

AE   Buckley, DG (ed), *Archaeology in Essex to 1500*, CBA Research Report 34, 1980

AoE   Bedwin, O (ed), *The Archaeology of Essex - Proceedings of the Writtle Conference*, ECC, 1996

CBA   Council for British Archaeology

CA   *The Colchester Archaeologist*

EAA   East Anglian Archaeology

EAH   *Essex Archaeology and History*, Transactions of the Essex Society for Archaeology and History

ECC, AS Essex County Council, Archaeology Section

ERO   Essex Record Office

ESMR Essex Sites and Monuments Record

PGA   Proceedings of the Geologists' Association

RCHME Royal Commission on Historical Monuments (England) - An Inventory of the Historical Monuments in Essex, 1916

TEAS   Transactions of the Essex Archaeological Society

VCH   Victoria County History (Essex)

Aberg, F A ed 1978 *Medieval Moated Sites*, CBA Res Rep No 17

Alexander, J A 1979 'Ambresbury Banks, an Iron Age camp in Epping Forest, Essex', EAH, 10

Andrews, D D ed 1993 *Cressing Temple: A Templar and Hospitaller Manor in Essex* Essex County Council, Planning

Andrews, D and Ryan, P 1998 'The sixteenth and seventeenth centuries: manors, mansions, parks and fields', in Green, forthcoming

Archer, L 1985 *Raymond Erith, Architect*, The Cygnet Press

Atkinson, M and Preston, S 1995 *Elms Farm Project, Heybridge - Site Narrative*, ECC, AS

Baker, C A, Moxey, PA and Oxford, PM 1978 'Woodland Continuity and Change in Epping Forest' in *Field Studies* 4, 645-669

Barlow, F 1995 *The Feudal Kingdom of England 1042-1216*, Longman

Barlow, F 1997 *Thomas Becket*, Phoenix Giant

Bassett, S R 1982 *Saffron Walden to AD 1300*, Chelmsford Archaeological Trust and CBA

Bassett, S R 1997 'Continuity and fission in the Anglo-Saxon landscape: the origins of the Rodings (Essex)', in *Landscape History*, Vol 19

Bedwin, O 1991 'Asheldham Camp - an early Iron Age hill fort: excavations 1985', EAH, 22

Berry, J 1966 *Tales of the West of Ireland*, Colin Smythe

Blythe, N 1995 *John Nash at Wormingford*, privately printed

Brassley, P 1995 'A Pioneer in Everything': Primrose McConnell, 1856-1931', in the *Journal of the Royal Agricultural Society of England*, Autumn 1995

Bridgland, D R 1994 *Quaternary of the Thames*, Joint Nature Conservancy Committee, Chapman and Hall

Briggs, N 1989 *Georgian Essex*, ERO

Britnell, R H 1981 'Essex Markets Before 1350', EAH, 13

Britnell, R H 1983 'Agriculture in a Region of Ancient Enclosure, 1185-1500', in *Nottingham Medieval Studies*

Brooks, H and Bedwin, O 1989 *Archaeology at the Airport: The Stansted Archaeological Project 1985-89*, ECC

Brooks, H and Havis, R 1991 *Fieldwalking and Excavations at Stansted Airport - Third Interim Report*, ECC, AS

Brown, A F J 1969 *Essex at Work 1700-1815*, Tindal Press, Chelmsford

Brown, A F J 1996 *Prosperity and Poverty: Rural Essex, 1700-1815*, ERO Chelmsford

Brown, N 1996 'The Archaeology of Essex, c1,500-500 BC', in AoE

Brown, N 1997 'A landscape of two halves: The Neolithic of Chelmer Valley/Blackwater Estuary, Essex', in Topping, P ed *Neolithic Landscapes. Neolithic Studies Group Seminar Papers 2*, Oxbow Monograph 86

Buchanon, R H 1973 'Field Systems of Ireland' in *Studies of Field Systems in the British Isles*, Cambridge University Press

Buckley, D G and Hedges, J D 1987 *The Bronze Age and Saxon Settlements at Springfield Lyons, Essex. An Interim Report*, ECC, AS

Buxton, E N 1884 *Epping Forest*, Edward Stanford, London

Caesar, C J 1982 *The Conquest of Gaul*, Handford, S A trans, Penguin Classics

Came, P J and Corrigan, P M 1966 *Danbury Common: A Study in the Evolution and Changing Function of a Landscape Feature*, thesis in ERO

Chambers, D 1991 'Painting with Living Pencils', in *Garden History*, Vol 19, No 1

Christy, M 1923 'The Excavation of Foundations on the Castle-keep at Pleshey', TEAS, NS Vol XVI, 190-204

Cook, O 1988 *The North West Essex Collection - An Introduction*, The Fry Art Gallery Society

Corke, D 1984 *The Nature of Essex*, Barracuda, Buckingham

Cormack, M 1986 *Constable*, Phaedon

Cowell, F 1986 and 1987 'Richard Woods (?1716-93): A Preliminary Account', in *Garden History*, Vol 14, No 2, Vol 15, Nos 1 and 2

Cowell, F 1998 'The designed landscape', in Green, forthcoming

Cromarty, D 1966 *The Fields of Saffron Walden in 1400*, ERO

Crummy, P, Hillam, J and Crossan, C 1982 'Mersea Island: the Anglo-Saxon Causeway', EAH 14

Crummy, P 1997 *City of Victory*, Colchester Archaeological Trust

Darby, H C 1971 *The Domesday Geography of Eastern England*, Cambridge University Press

Darby, H C 1977 *Domesday England*, Cambridge U P

Davis, R H C 1966 'The Norman Conquest' in *History* Vol 51

Davis, R H C 1976 *The Normans and their Myth*, Thames and Hudson

Deacon, M 1984 *Great Chesterford: A Common Field Parish in Essex*, M Deacon, Saffron Walden

Defoe, D 1991 *A Tour through the Whole Island of Great Britain* (1724-26), (ed) Furbank, P N and Owens, W R, Yale U P

Denney, P 1996 'The enclosure of Old Heath common 1811-1818; EAH 27

Drury, P J 1978 *Excavations at Little Waltham*, Chelmsford Excavation Cttee Rep No 1 and CBA Res Rep No 26

Drury, P J and Rodwell, W 1980 'Settlement in the later Iron Age and Roman periods', in AE

Drury, P J, Rodwell, W J and Wickenden, N P 1981 'Finds from the Probable Site of a Roman Villa at Dawes Heath, Thundersley, Essex', EAH 13

ECC, AS 1993 *Origins of Rayleigh*, Essex County Council and Rochford District Council

Edwards, A C 1978 *A History of Essex*, Phillimore

Edwards, A C and Newton, K C 1984 *The Walkers of Hanningfield: Surveyors and Mapmakers Extraordinary*, Buckland Publications Ltd

Ellison, R A, Knox, R W O'B, Jolley, D W and King, C1994 'A revision of the lithostratigraphical classification of the early Palaeogene strata of the London Basin and East Anglia', PGA Vol 105, Part 3

Emmison, F G 1976 *Elizabethan Life: Home, Work and Land*, Chelmsford, ECC

Faith, R 1996 'The topography and social structure of a small soke in the middle ages: The Sokens, Essex', EAH 27

Finberg, H P R (ed) 1972 *The Agrarian History of England and Wales 1042-1350* Vol II, Cambridge U P

Fisher, W R *The Forest of Essex*

Fletcher, R 1997 *The Conversion of Europe: From Paganism to Christianity 371-1386 AD*, Harper Collins

Francis, E B 1913 'Rayleigh Castle: New Facts in its History and Recent Explorations on its Site', TEAS, NS Vol XII, 147-85

Germany, M 1995 *Great Holts Farm, Boreham, Essex. Assessment Report Stage II*, ECC, AS

Gilman, P and Nash, F 1995 *Fortress Essex*, ECC, AS

Gimson, W A 1958 *Great Braxted 1086-1957*, ERO

Glasscock, R E 'England circa 1334', in Darby, H C ed *A new historical geography of England before 1600*

Going, C J 1996 'The Roman countryside', in AoE

Going, C J 1997 'Roman IV, The Countryside', in Glazenbrook, J ed *Research and Archaeology: a Framework for the Eastern Counties, I. resource assessment*, EAA occ paper No 3

Grant, M 1956 *Tacitus on Imperial Rome*, Penguin Classics

Green, S forthcoming *The Essex Landscape: in Search of its History*, ECC

Grieve, H 1959 *The Great Tide: The Story of the Great Flood Disaster in Essex*, Essex County Council

Hallam, H E 1972 'New Settlement', in Finberg, HPR 1972

Harrison, W 1994 (ed) Edelen, G *The Description of England*, Folger Shakespeare Library

Hartley, D 1931 (ed) *Thomas Tusser - His Good Points of Husbandry, 1557 Floruit*, Country Life Ltd

Harvey, J 1972 *The Medieval Architect*, Wayland Pub. London

Harvey, S 19 'Domesday England', in Finberg, 1972

Hawkes, C F C and Crummy, P 1995 *Colchester Archaeological Report 11: Camulodunum 2*, Colchester Archaeological Trust Ltd

Hedges, J 1978 'Essex moats', in Aberg, FA 1978

Hewett, C A 1982 *Church Carpentry: A study based on Essex examples*, Phillimore

Higham, N J 1990 'Settlement, land use and Domesday ploughlands', in *Landscape History*, Vol 12

Higham, N 1992 *Rome, Britain and the Anglo-Saxons*, Seaby, London

Higham, N J 1994 *The English Conquest: Gildas and Britain in the fifth century*, Manchester U P

Hunter, J M 1985 *Land into Landscape*, George Godwin

Hunter, J M 1993a 'The age of hedgerows on a Bocking estate', EAH, 24

Hunter, J M 1993b 'King John's hunting lodge at Writtle', EAH, 24

Hunter, J M 1993c 'The Historic Landscape of Cressing Temple and its Environs' in Andrews, D D 1993

Hunter, J M 1994a 'Medieval and Tudor Parks of the Middle Chelmer Valley', EAH, 25

Hunter, J M 1994b 'Littley Park, Great Waltham - historical survey', EAH, 25

Hunter, J M 1995 'Settlement and farming patterns on the mid-Essex boulder clays', EAH, 26

Hunter, J M 1997 'The age of Cressing field boundaries', EAH, 28

Johnson, H 1973 *The International Book of Trees*, Mitchell Beazley

Liddell, W 1987 'The Bounds of the Forest of Essex', in Neale, K (ed) *An Essex Tribute*, Leopards Head Press

Liddell, B and S 1996 *Imagined Land: Essex in Poetry and Prose*, ERO

Longworth, I and Cherry, J *Archaeology in Britain since 1945*, Brit Mus Publications

McCann, J 197 *Agrarian change and the cloth industry in Essex 1350-1500*, Thesis in ERO

Mallory, J P and McNeill, T E 1991 *The Archaeology of Ulster from Colonization to Plantation*, Inst of Irish Studies, Queen's Univ of Belfast

Mason, A S 1996 'A Measure of Essex Cartography', in Neale, K (ed)

Mattingly, H 1948 *Tacitus on Britain and Germany*, Penguin Books

Medlycott, M 1996 'A medieval farm and its landscape: excavations at Stebbingford Farm, Felsted 1993', EAH 27

Miller, E and Hatcher, J 1978 *Medieval England - Rural Society and Economic Change 1086-1348*, Longman

Miller, E and Hatcher, J 1995 *Medieval England -Towns, Commerce and Crafts*, Longman

Morant, P 1768 *The History and Antiquities of the County of Essex*,

Murphy, P 1996 'Environmental archaeology in Essex', AoE

Murphy, P and Brown, N 'The Archaeology of the Essex Coastal Landscape', in Green, forthcoming

Neale, K 1977 *Essex in History*, Phillimore

Neale, K 1996 'Saffron Walden: Crocuses and Crokers', in Neale, K (ed) *Essex 'full of profitable things'*, Leopards Head Press

Newton, K C 1960 *Thaxted in the Fourteenth Century*, ERO Publications No. 33

Newton, K C 1970 *The Manor of Writtle: the development of a royal manor in Essex c1086 - c1500*, Phillimore

Bibliography

Pevsner, N 1954 *The Buildings of England - Essex*, Penguin Books

Platt, C 1978 *Medieval England: A Social History and Archaeology from the Conquest to 1600 AD*, Routledge

Poos, L R 1991 *A rural society after the Black Death: Essex 1350-1525*, Cambridge Studies in Population, Economy and Society in Past Time 18, C U P

Powell, E R 1953 'The making of Essex Parishes' in *Essex Journal*, LXII (Jan and April 1953)

Powell, W R 1990 *Essex in Domesday Book*, ERO

Rackham, O 1976 *Trees and Woodland in the British Landscape*, J M Dent, London

Rackham, O 1978 'Archaeology and Land-use History', in Corke, D (ed) *Epping Forest: the Natural Aspect?*, Essex Field Club

Rackham, O 1980a *Ancient Woodland: its history, vegetation and uses in England*, E Arnold

Rackham, O 1980b 'The medieval landscape of Essex', in AE

Rackham, O 1989 *The Last Forest*, J M Dent, London

Rahtz, P 1969 *Excavations at King John's Hunting Lodge, Writtle, Essex, 1955-57*, London: Society for Medieval Archaeology Monograph Series no 3

Reaney, P H 1935 *The Place-Names of Essex*, Cambridge U P

Rippon, S 1991 'Early Planned Landscapes in South-East Essex', EAH, 22

Robinson, E and Worssam, B 1989 'The geology of some Middlesex churches' in PGA, 100(4) 595-603

Rodger, N A M 1997 *The Safeguard of the Sea - A Naval History of Great Britain*, Harper Collins

Rodwell, W 1978 'Rivenhall and the emergence of first-century villas in northern Essex', in Todd, M (ed) *Studies in the Romano-British Villa*, Leicester U P

Rodwell, W J and Rodwell, K A 1986 *Rivenhall: Investigations of a Villa, Church and Village, 1950-1977*, CBA Res Rep 55

Rodwell, W J *The origins and early development of Witham, Essex: a study in settlement and fortification, Prehistoric to Medieval*, Oxbow Monograph no 26

Ruggles-Brise, E A 1931 'The Wheat Quota', in *Journal of the Farmers Club*, Part 3 - April 1931

Rumble, A (ed) 1983 *Domesday Book 32 - Essex*, Phillimore

Russell, J C 1948 *British Medieval Population*, Albuquerque

Ryan, P M 1994 A History of Marks Hall, The Thomas Phillips Price Trust
Ryan, P 1993 'The history of Cressing Temple from the documentary sources' in Andrews, D D 1993

Salter, A E 1914 'Sarsen, basalt and other boulders in Essex', in *The Essex Naturalist*, Vol 17

Scarfe, N V 1942 *Part 82 - Essex*, in Stamp, LD (ed) *The Land of Britain - The Report of the Land Utilisation Survey of Great Britain*, Geographical Publications Ltd, London

Scarfe, N 1968, Essex - *A Shell Guide*, Faber and Faber

Schofield, R S 1965 'The geographical distribution of wealth in England, 1334-1649', *Economic History Review*, Dec 1965

Sealey, P R 1995 'New light on the salt industry and Red Hills of prehistoric Essex' in EAH 26

Sealey, P R 1996 'The Iron Age of Essex' in AoE

Sealey, P R 1997 *The Boudican Revolt against Rome*, Shire Archaeology

Sherlock, R L 1960 *London and Thames Valley*, Inst of Geological Sciences, HMSO

Smith, J R 1970 *Foulness*, ERO

Stenning, D F 1993 'The Barley Barn, the Wheat Barn, and the early development of barns in south-east England', in Andrews, DD 1993

Stenning, D F 1996 'Standing Timber-framed Buildings', in AoE

Sutherill, M 1995 *The Gardens of Audley End*, English Heritage

Thacker, C 1994 *The Genius of Historic Gardens in Britain and Ireland*, Weidenfeld and Nicolson

Thorpe, S 1996 *Military Airfields in Essex during World War Two*, ECC, AS

Tittensor, A M and Tittensor, R M 1986 *The rabbit warren at West Dean near Chichester*, Arundel: Tittensor

Tuchman, B W 1978 *A Distant Mirror - The calamitous fourteenth century*, M Papermac

Turner, B R G 1982 *Ivy Chimneys, Witham: An Interim Report*, ECC, AS

Turner, K M 1993 *Landscape Change in 'Constable's Country'*, thesis, Birkbeck College, Univ of London

Tyler, S 1996 'Early Saxon Essex AD c 400-700', in AoE

Victoria County History of Essex, Vols i-ix

Wallis, S and Waughman, M 1998 *Archaeology and the Landscape in the Lower Blackwater Valley*, EAA Rep No 82

Ward, J C 1983 *The Lay Subsidy of 1327*, ERO

Watts, W 1799 *The Seats of the Nobility & Gentry in a Collection of the Most Interesting and Picturesque Views*, London

Whiteman, C A 1992 'The palaeography and correlation of pre-Anglian-Glaciation terraces of the River Thames in Essex and the London Basin', PGA Vol 103, Part 1

Wickenden, N P 1996 'The Roman Towns of Essex', in AoE

Wilkinson, T J and Murphy, P L 1995 *Archaeology of the Essex Coast, Vol 1: The Hullbridge Survey*, EAA Report No 71

Williamson, T 1986 'The Development of Settlement in North West Essex' in EAH 17

Williamson, T 1988 'Explaining Regional Landscapes: Woodland and Champion in Southern and Eastern England', *Landscape History*, 10

Williamson, T 1995 *Polite Landscapes: Gardens and Society in Eighteenth-Century England*, Allan Sutton Publishing Ltd

Winmill, J M 1970 *Land and Buildings of Henham*, Henham Conservation Soc and Henham PC

Wright, T 1835 *The History and Topography of the County of Essex*

Wymer, J J and Brown, N R 1995 *Excavations at North Shoebury: settlement and economy in south-east Essex 1500 BC - 1500 AD*, EAA Rep No 75

Wymer, J J 1996 'The Palaeolithic Period in Essex', AoE

Notes

CHAPTER 1. Geology and landform

1 Sherlock 1960, 25
2 Ibid, 28
3 Ellison et al 1994, 191
4 Ibid, 194
5 Sherlock 1960, 34
6 Bridgland 1994, 280
7 Whiteman 1992, 41
8 'If Middle Pleistocene is accepted as commencing with the Brunhes-Matuyama palaeolmagnetic boundary, then the Oxygen Isotope curve from deep sea cores indicates that there have been eighteen cold phases and nineteen warm ones since then to now.' John Wymer, pers com 30.5.1996
9 Wymer 1996, 5
10 Bridgland 1994, 356
11 Rackham 1976, 40
12 Murphy 1996, 168
13 Ibid, 176
14 Salter 1914
15 Robinson and Worssam 1989, 603

CHAPTER 2. The Regions and subregions of Essex

1 Harrison ed Edelen 1994, 217
2 Rackham 1976, 17
3 Murphy and Brown 1998, (3)
4 Wilkinson and Murphy 1992, 50
5 Murphy and Brown 1998, (4)
6 Ibid, (6)
7 Ibid, (7)
8 Ibid, (8)
9 Smith 1970, 25
10 Grieve 1959, 12
11 McCann 1980, 12
12 Smith 1970, 26
13 Grieve 1959, 33
14 Ibid, 34
15 Quoted in Murphy and Brown 1998, (9)
16 Grieve 1959, 31
17 Ibid, 37
18 Sabine Baring-Gould (1834-1924): *Mehala: A Story of the Salt Marshes*, 1880
19 Rackham 1986, 1

20 Drury, Rodwell and Wickenden 1981, 66
21 Rippon 1991. Stephen Rippon's analysis and conclusions on the field systems of the South Essex Plain are the fullest and most convincing. He considers other explanations that have been put forward in his paper.
22 Rippon 1996, 125
23 Morant I 1768, 484
24 Faith 1996, 204
25 Came and Corrigan 1966, 57
26 Subsequent acquisitions have increased Forest land to some 10,000 acres (4,045 ha)
27 Baker, Moxey and Oxford 1978, 664
28 Oliver Rackham, pers com 1973
29 VCH Vol IV 20
30 Confirmed by the Forestry Commission, Westonbirt Arboretum, 14.01.92
31 Medlycott 1996, 159
32 Hunter 1993a, 114
33 Brooks and Havis 1991, 17
34 Rackham 1976, 163
35 ERO Q/RDc 41
36 Deacon 1984, xiv
37 Ibid, 22
38 Williamson 1986, 123
39 Ibid, 125

CHAPTER 3. Emerging landscapes

1 Strachan 1998, 2 & 3
2 John Hedges was appointed in 1972, and succeeded by David Buckley in 1983. For an account of the unit up to 1993, see Buckley 1996, 207-218
3 Generally with the Centre for East Anglian Studies, University of East Anglia
4 Core funding has come from the County Council and English Heritage (earlier the Department of the Environment), and various sponsors and developers for specific projects. Since the issuing of PPG 16 in 1990 the principle has been accepted that the developer must fund archaeological work required by the granting of a planning permission.
5 See AE and AoE in Bibliography. For the regional framework see Glazenbrook 1997
6 Wilkinson and Murphy 1995
7 Rodwell 199
8 Wilkinson and Murphy 1995, 87
9 Holgate 1996, 16 and Strachan 1998, 10
10 Strachan 1998, 13
11 I am much endebted to Nigel Brown for his guidance on the Neolithic and Bronze Age, in particular for his analysis and interpretation of the complex archaeological evidence and monuments of the lower Chelmer valley and the Blackwater estuary (see Brown 1997).

12 Strachan 1998, 8 and 11

13 Brown 1996, 27

14 Hunter 1993, 31

15 Strachan 1998, 19

16 For an interim report on the excavations, see Buckley and Hedges, 1987. Also see Strachan 1998, 20

17 Brown 1996, 30

18 Strachan 1998, 25-31

19 Caesar 1982, 111

20 Ibid, 114

21 Alexander 1979

22 In Latin: *Oppidum*. Archaeologists use the term for fortified settlements rather than hillforts. Caesar did not distinguish between the two. The terminology is confusing.

23 Bedwin 1991

24 Drury 1978

25 Crummy 1997, 21

26 Sealey 1996, 51

27 This is a reasonable hypothesis, which could be tested against palaeobotanic evidence if a suitable site is found.

28 Crummy 1997, 14

29 Hawkes and Crummy 1995 , 178

30 Crummy 1997, 27

31 Sealey 1996, 60

32 Caesar 1982, 79-80

33 Rodger 1997, 63'

34 Loom weights, indicative of a woollen industry, have been found on coastal sites and at the head of estuaries. Sealey 1996, 63

35 Philip Morant (1700-1770), historian of Essex, is best remembered for his *History and Antiquities of the County of Essex* (1760-68), always the first port of call for historical research in Essex. Morant firmly identified Camulodunum as Colchester. Previously there had been other candidates; William Camden (1607) had favoured Maldon, other antiquarians had suggested Saffron Walden and Castle Camps.

36 Wright 1835, Vol I, 353

37 *City of Victory*, Colchester Archaeological Trust, 1997

CHAPTER 4. Roman Essex

1 'Commander' - the traditional salute of conquering generals by armies in the field under the Republic

2 Hawkes and Crummy 1995 , 178. The site of the encampment has been largely covered by urban development, but a length of the Triple Dykes is preserved as a Scheduled Monument.

3 Grant 1956, 318

4 The abuse of proconsular power was exposed by Cicero in his prosecution of Verres, governor of Sicily. The event had a long term repercussion as it led, by its example, to Edmund Burke's decision to initiate the prosecution of Warren Hastings for the plundering activities of the East India Company.

5 Paul Sealey's *The Boudican Revolt against Rome* is recommended as an account of the rising, its causes and aftermath, supported by the latest archaeological information.

6 Crummy 1997, 79

7 Mattingly 1948, 72

8 Coins and pottery which could not date earlier than c AD 55 lay under the centre of the rampart

9 Crummy 1997, 107. The area of the portico, temple and theatre, some 163 acres, are now protected within an Archaeological Park.

10 Crummy 1997, 107

11 Going 1996, 97

12 Drury and Rodwell 1980, 70

13 Wickenden 1996, 76

14 Sealey 1996, 60

15 Atkinson and Preston 1995

16 The reader is referred to Peter Froste's reconstructions in *City of Victory*

17 Rodwell 1978, 11

18 Rodwell and Rodwell 1986, xii

19 Rodwell 1978, 15

20 Following a recent boundary adjustment, the Hills now lie in Cambridgeshire and are in the guardianship of the County Council.

21 Brooks and Bedwin 1989, 12-15

22 Strachan 1998, 37 and 39

23 The study of rural settlement in this period is seen as a priority by archaeologists in the region. See Going 1997, 38

24 Williamson 1986

25 Wymer and Brown 1995, 160

26 Wallis and Waughman 1998, 225

27 Germany 1995, 8. Also Strachan 1998, 22

28 Wickenden 1996, 86

29 Turner 1982

30 Sealey 1995, 65

31 Ibid, 76

32 Strachan 1998, 38 and 39

33 Grant 1979, 336

34 Going 1996, 104

35 Crummy 1997, 123

36 Going 1996, 104

CHAPTER 5. The Saxon Kingdom

1 Higham 1992. Chapter one: 'Hengest and the historians - an introduction', sets out a history of the historians of the period.
2 Ibid, 231
3 Higham 1994, 172
4 Fletcher 1997, 167
5 Tyler 1996, 111
6 Wallis and Waughman 1998, 227
7 Williamson 1986, 127
8 See above
9 Bassett 1997, 36
10 Crummy 1982, 77
11 Wilkinson and Murphy 1995, 195 and fig 119
12 Murphy and Brown forthcoming
13 Tyler 1996, 112
14 Buckley and Hedges 1987, 38

CHAPTER 6. Audit and Stocktaking: the late Saxon landscape

1 Rumble 1983, intro
2 Davis 1966, 286
3 Rumble 1983, intro
4 Ibid
5 Darby 1977, 90. Miller and Hatcher, however, suggest a figure between 1.25m and 2.5m with the probability that it would lie in the upper part of the band.
6 Hallam 1978, 48
7 It may be of interest to note that the census of 1991 recorded a population of 52,843 for Maldon district and 65,432 for Uttlesford, the two smallest districts. The population of the county was 1,528,577.
8 The Shorter Oxford Dictionary defines the acre as a measure of land, originally as much as a yoke of oxen could plough in a day; later limited by statute to a piece 40 poles long by four broad (=4840 sq.yds) or its equivalent.
9 'While the hideage figures are useful in estimating the relative areas of manors it must not be assumed that the DB hide was equivalent to 120 statute acres, nor the DB acre to a statute acre. Even in estimating relative areas the hideage figures must be used with caution, for there is evidence that the hide on royal manors was much larger than elsewhere, presumably giving a lower assessment and therefore less tax burden'. WR Powell, pers. com
10 Darby 1971, 220-221
11 Miller and Hatcher 1978, 13
12 The relationship of ploughland to ploughteams and acreages has generated a considerable literature over the past hundred years. For a summary see Higham 1990
13 In particular 'June' in the Très Riches Heures of the Duc de Berry

14 A good surviving fen can be seen in Hatfield Forest
15 Darby 1971, 240
16 Davis 1966, 279
17 As described by William Camden in Britannia, (1607) and Miller and Hatcher 1995, 15
18 Darby 1971, 243
19 Wilkinson and Murphy 1995, 208
20 Longworth and Cherry 1986, 148. Other early mills have been found and in some cases excavated in Britain and Ireland. A reconstruction based on an early ninth century site in Co Cork may be seen in the Irish National Heritage Park, Wexford.
21 Powell 1990, 5
22 Rackham 1980b, 106
23 Rackham 1976, 6
24 Rackham 1989, 35
25 Powell 1990, 31
26 Miller and Hatcher 1978, 5
27 In particular Meindert Hobbema and Jacob van Ruisdael
28 Going 1996, 97

CHAPTER 7. The Conqueror's dispensation

 1 Reaney 1935, xxx
 2 Ibid, xxxi-xxxiii
 3 Orderic Vitalis, Bk iv, ch 4
 4 Davis 1966
 5 A reconstruction in the Irish National Heritage Park
 6 Francis 1913. Suain's name has various spellings; I have followed that used by Round in VCH 1
 7 RCHME Vol 1, 70
 8 VCH 1, 346
 9 *Origins of Rayleigh*, ECC, AS
10 'The Castle that Eudo built', CA No 7, 1993/4
11 Eudo came from Rie near Bayeux and held at least 64 manors in the eastern counties. He served William and his sons as dapifer (steward), and governed Colchester for some 50 years until his death in 1120. He founded St John's Abbey, the leper hospital and possibly the Moot Hall.
12 The possibility that Eudo originally intended the castle to reach an even greater height is discussed in 10 above
13 Hunter 1994a, 116
14 Christy 1923
15 RCHME Vol 1, 51
16 Rackham 1989, 58
17 Miller and Hatcher 1978, 35
18 Barlow 1997, 273

19 Barlow 1995, 227
20 Hallam 1972, 164-5
21 Ryan 1995, 11 and 23
22 Miller and Hatcher 1978, 35
23 For a much fuller discussion of these events see Liddell 1987, 109-113
24 For a description of the administration of forest land in Essex see Rackham 1989, 49-62

CHAPTER 8. The High Middle Ages

 1 Harvey 1972, 59
 2 Britnell 1981. The figures apply to the pre-1965 county
 3 Bassett 1982, 25
 4 Dunmow Lane, now a grass road
 5 Hunter 1994a, 116
 6 ERO D/DTu 203
 7 ERO D/DTu 254A
 8 Miller and Hatcher 1978, 38
 9 Newton 1970, 34
10 Hunter 1995, 141
11 Ryan 1993, 11
12 Hunter 1993c, 31
13 Britnell 1983, 52
14 Hunter 1997,
15 Williamson 1988, 8 and 11
16 Mallory and McNeill 1991, 220-4
17 Buchanon 1973, 584 and Berry 1966, 52
18 Morant 1768, I, 141
19 Rackham 1980a, 191
20 The reader is referred to the two consecutive papers by Ray Powell on 'The making of Essex Parishes' (Powell, 1953). These deal fully with the origins and early history of the parochial system, and list churches and chapels existing before 1300, and between 1300 and 1540. The former also notes whether the church or chapel is known to have existed in the eleventh and twelfth centuries, and the latter notes the existence of chantries and guilds.
21 Powell 1953, 9
22 Davis
23 Pevsner 1954, 9
24 Pevsner 1954, 77
25 Hewett 1982, 62
26 Newton 1970
27 Rahtz 1 9
28 Newton 1970, 9

29 Hunter 1993b
30 ERO D/DP M546
31 Platt 1978, 45
32 Miller and Hatcher 1978, 242
33 ERO D/CT 109
34 Hunter 1993c, 34
35 Stenning 1993, 62 and 68
36 Hunter 1993c, 31
37 Tittensor and Tittensor 1986
38 Newton 1970, 9
39 Miller and Hatcher 1978, 245
40 Platt 1978, 195
41 Newton 1970, 25-6
42 Rackham 1976, 124
43 ERO D/DSm. Rackham 1976, frontispiece and 143
44 Chalkney is termed an Access Woodland. This was to avoid the term Country Park, which it was feared might bring more visitors than the wood could accommodate without damage. Garnet's Wood (Barnston) is also an Access Woodland.
45 Rackham 1989, 44
46 Newton 1970, 11 and 43-4
47 Lodge Farm would appear to date pre 1350
48 Rackham 1989, 43
49 The visitor centre has an exhibition on the history of the park and the area around, and Weald makes a good starting point for someone seeking the landscape history of Essex.
50 Rackham 1989, 75
51 Ibid, 12 and 92
52 Cottage plots with space for garden, licensed by the manor with responsibility for maintenance of adjacent road
53 Newton 1960, 10, 12 and 13
54 Ibid, 46
55 Poos 1991
56 Medlycott 1996
57 Brooks and Bedwin 1989, 19
58 Dorothy Cromarty's (née Monteith) *The Fields of Saffron Walden in 1400* 1966, is based on material from her earlier thesis *Saffron Walden and its environs: a study in the development of a landscape,* which extends the study to the twentieth century.
59 Subinfeudation often involved the grant of land to knights who then paid fees in lieu of service, and became sub-lords with their own courts.
60 Platt 1978, 111
61 Aberg 1978
62 Stenning 1996, 137
63 Hedges 1978, 68

CHAPTER 9. The later Middle Ages

1 Platt 1978, 95
2 Tuchman 1978, 24
3 Platt 1978, 111
4 Jim Bolton, the Morant Lecture, 1997
5 Newton 1970, 78-81
6 Ward 1983
7 Jennifer Ward, pers com 2.3.97
8 Newton 1960, 31
9 Newton 1970, 69
10 Glasscock 1973, 136-142. Suffolk was £14.1, Cambridgeshire £18.1, Hertfordshire £14.8 and Kent £17.1
11 Schofield 1965, 483-510
12 McCann 1980 , 18
13 McCann 1980 , 16. I am much indebted to John McCann's dissertation *Agrarian change and the cloth industry in Essex 1350-1500.*
14 Ibid, 17
15 Brown 1996, 12
16 Origins of Rayleigh, 5
17 Christy 1923
18 Most of the Months, which depict the castles, were the work of the Limbourg brothers c1416
19 Andrews and Ryan in Green, forthcoming
20 Ibid
21 Pevsner 1954, 26
22 'An Inquiry into the Foundation of the Parish Church of Thaxted in Essex', 1761 (revised 1764), ERO D/DU 856
23 Andrews and Ryan in Green, forthcoming
24 Edwards and Newton 1984, plates XIV, XXIV, XXX
25 For an account of other cartographers working in Essex, see Mason 1996
26 Hartley 1931, 99
27 Morant I, 213
28 Edwards and Newton 1984, plates XVII and XXVI
29 Hunter 1994a, 116
30 ERO D/DAc 96 and 101
31 ERO T/M 504/1
32 ERO T/M 529
33 ERO T/M 514
34 ERO D/DM P18
35 This information is based on research by R and A Tittensor who most kindly lent me a copy of their report, *Wealden Shaws: A Landscape Setting for Bayleaf Farmhouse,* 1986

36 I am grateful to Emma Hay who drew these interesting woods to my attention while researching woodlands belonging to the County Council.

37 Let Pat 30 Henry VIII

38 Hunter 1993a, fig 1

39 Harrison 1994, 348-56

40 In writing this brief account, I am indebted to Kenneth Neale who has brought together the many references and papers on the subject, sifting fact from fiction, in *Saffron Walden: 'Crocuses and Crokers'*, (Neale 1996, 225-244)

CHAPTER 10. Tudor and Stuart Essex

1 Pevsner 1954, 291

 2 Winmill 1970. The location of the medieval manor house is almost certainly the moated site across the field from the church.

 3 ERO D/Dz 19. Hunter 1994a, 116

 4 ERO

 5 Edwards and Newton 1984, 83 and plate X. The figures and examples cited here are drawn from Edwards and Newton's analysis of Walker maps and study of surviving buildings.

 6 Harrison 1994, 200

 7 Emmison 1976, 264

 8 Edwards and Newton 1984, plates XIV, XIX, XXVIII, XXXII and XXXIV

 9 A map of 1618 survives, surveyed by Thomas Pope, ERO T/M 30

10 Sutherill 1995, 20

11 Ibid, 23

12 Edwards 1978, plate 20

13 Newton 1960, map II

14 ERO D/DHw P5

15 Andrews et al 1994

CHAPTER 11. Georgian landscapes

1 Brown 1969, 95

 2 See Cowell 1998; Williamson 1995, 48-76; Hunter 1985, 89-110

 3 Petre 1998

 4 Hunter 1985, 99

 5 Chambers 1991, 60

 6 Petre 1998

 7 Chambers 1991, 68

 8 Cowell 1998,

 9 Property of Essex County Council

10 Defoe 1991, 39

11 Hunter 1985, 114

12 Ibid. Williamson 1995, 94

13 Sutherill 1995, 28
14 ERO D/DQy 8
15 Williamson 1995, 121
16 ERO D/DP P30
17 Hunter 1985, 101
18 Thondon Hall was gutted by fire in 1878, and long remained a sad shell. Happily, it has now been renovated with conversion to flats and its future as a monumental land mark is assured.
19 Cowell 1986 and 1987
20 Brown 1996, 105-7
21 Briggs 1989, 6
22 Brown 1996, 31
23 Ibid, 24
24 Ibid, 42
25 Turner 1993, 4.7.1.1
26 Edwards 1978, 87
27 Pattison 1996, 4
28 The best description I have read of the issues involved is in Patrick O'Brian's novel, *The Yellow Admiral.*
29 Griggs 1794, 9, 144 (table) and 165
30 Denney 1996, 244
31 Brown 1996, 173
32 Written in 1830 to accompany a series of engravings.
33 Turner 1993, 4.2
34 Cormack 1986, 12
35 Ibid, 16
36 Ibid, plates 32, 42, 55, 71 and 176
37 Ibid, plate 125
38 Ibid, plate 169
39 Environmentally Sensitive Area
40 Turner 1993, 4.2

CHAPTER 12. From Victoria to World War Two

1 Edwards 1978, 89
2 Ibid, 96
3 Smallholdings of less than 30 acres have been omitted from the averages. I am most grateful to Bruce Munro for the estate particulars.
4 For a general account of Primrose McConnell, see Brassley 1995
5 I am indebted to Sir John Ruggles-Brise for the information on his father, and for lending me 'The Wheat Quota', the paper in which Sir Edward set out the workings which became law with the passing of the Wheat Act 1932, (Ruggles-Brise 1931)
6 Scarfe 1942. The survey of Essex was made in the period 1931-1936

7 Gilman and Nash 1995, 16
8 Strachan 1998, 87
9 Gilman and Nash 1995, 19
10 Thorpe 1996, 1. The quality and style was not maintained in subsequent building and, sadly, the elegant early houses now have plastic windows.
11 Strachan 1998, 85

CHAPTER 13. The contemporary landscape

1 The figures include Southend-on-Sea, until 1974 a county borough of independent status.
2 The project consisted of twelve commercially run farms in England and Wales selected from a variety of landscapes and farming systems as well as size and ownership.
3 The competition is sponsored by Rhone Poulenc.
4 The scheme aims at returning to more traditional cropping mosaics, and with the creation of features such as conservation headlands, beetle banks and wildlife strips could significantly improve habitats for wild and game birds, as well as a range of other species such as rare arable weeds.
5 Other schemes and projects include Environmentally Sensitive Areas, which cover the flood-plain in the Dedham Vale and areas of grassland in the coastal marshes; Countryside Stewardship, which supports a variety of projects concerned with management and improvement, and the Hedgerow Incentive Scheme.
6 Now revised and expanded as *The Essex Design Guide for Residential and Mixed Use Areas*, 1997
7 The project architect was Laurie Wood, under County Architect Alan Willis.
8 See Archer 1985
9 'How to Ruin the Constable Country', an article by Erith in the *Spectator* (8 Jan 1965). He played a leading part in the campaign in 1965 to save Dedham Vale from large-scale speculative development.
10 It is run as a partnership between the Commission and the local authorities, and works in consultation with farming, wildlife and local interest groups, and with the mineral companies of the area and the Woodland Trust. Forest Enterprise are coming to play an increasingly important role.
11 Blythe 1995
12 Other significant artists who settled during and immediately after World War Two in Great Bardfield were Michael Rothenstein, Kenneth Rowntree, Walter Hoyle, Bernard Cheese, Sheila Robinson and George Chapman. Many other artists were also working in north-west Essex at that time but not concerned primarily with landscape. Although the work of the Bardfield artists was so diverse, their talents were fostered by their friendship and proximity (Cook 1988, 14).
13 Cook 1988, 18
14 The Fry Gallery is open 2.45-5.30 on Saturdays, Sundays and bank holidays from Easter until the end of October.
15 The arboretum is open from Easter to October, and the woodland walks all year. The designs for the Arboretum were prepared by Michael and Beverley Lear.

Index

Index

Index

Index